John Morris

What the critics have said about THE SURVIVAL OF DOGMA:

"[This] is a tightly knit group of essays advancing toward a common goal: how to substitute a new theological vision for static conceptions and shallow understanding . . .

"The major contribution of this book is its success in showing that our perception of the Church's magisterium is all too often sloppy and historically naive. Somewhere in the Spirit's gift of teaching authority we must save room for the clear-headed prophet and the prudent theologian who are not simply agents of the hierarchial teaching authority. . . . Avery Dulles shows in this book as in his other writings that the American theological scene is finally coming into its own." *America*

"Dulles' theological viewpoints offer a profound challenge to men of faith, to ecclesiastical authorities, and perhaps especially to other theologians, to get down to the business of hammering out a theology for the present and the future in the forges of sober philosophical, cultural, and exegetical thought . . . Father Dulles brings a note of hope to the survival of dogma; when the church and its thinkers take his program seriously, that hope will be well on the way to realization." *Commonweal*

"This collection of essays is a welcome discussion of many of the issues the church faces in trying to clarify its notions of the magisterium . . . Though one might not always agree totally with the author's treatment of a given point, one needs always to listen respectfully to his solid reasoning." *National Catholic Reporter*

"Father Dulles shows a deep awareness of the new theology and he manages not only to summarize current liberal thinking, but also to digest, scrutinize, explain and *precis* it . . . He sympathizes with and accepts many of the insights which have inspired the movement of the Church toward the *rapprochement* with the contemporary world. At the same time, his careful approach to the vexing questions of faith . . . . ble of overcoming the . . . . nservatives who fear th . . . . dangerous direction." . . . *lic World*

John R. Morris, O.P.

The Survival
of Dogma

AVERY DULLES

IMAGE BOOKS
A Division of Doubleday & Company, Inc.
Garden City, New York
1973

Image Books edition 1973
by special arrangement with Doubleday & Company, Inc.
Image Books edition published February 1973

Nihil Obstat: Brian T. Joyce
          Censor Librorum

Imprimatur: ✠ Floyd L. Begin, S.T.D., Ph.D., J.C.D.
          Bishop of Oakland
          December 31, 1970

"Those societies which cannot combine reverence to their symbols with freedom of revision, must ultimately decay either from anarchy, or from the slow atrophy of a life stifled by useless shadows."

Alfred North Whitehead

CONTENTS

INTRODUCTION

Several years ago, in 1968, I published a collection of essays to which I gave the title *Revelation and the Quest for Unity*. Written in the decade from 1956 to 1966, these essays dealt with the process by which the major families of Christian believers, in the two decades since World War II, came to rediscover each other through debate and dialogue regarding the nature and transmission of revelation.

In the past few years, the theological climate has notably changed. New points of view, less easily identifiable with established patterns, have been clamoring for recognition. All the Christian Churches, and Roman Catholicism more than most others, have been faced by anxious questioning. The most fundamental theological principles and categories have been subjected to radical challenge, not simply from outsiders but also from persons standing within the mainstream of the tradition. Like many other theologians, I have been repeatedly asked to speak and write on the critical intellectual questions raised by these developments. The topics most frequently proposed to me have centered about three main foci: faith, teaching authority, and dogma. From articles and lectures on these subjects, composed between 1968 and 1970, I have compiled the chapters of this book.

In each of these areas serious crises have arisen. Reflecting on the questions being asked, I became convinced that committed Christians in our time are greatly hampered by their lack of a sufficient sense of history. Imagining that the particular forms of doctrine and ecclesiastical order now in use are as old as Christianity itself, they seem to think that ours is the first generation to be confronted by the demand for radical change. Unaware of the Church's repeated self-adaptation to novel cultural contexts, they find themselves unable to deal constructively with the present turmoil. They lack a suitable methodology for evaluating change.

In the three main sections of this book, dealing respectively with faith, teaching authority, and dogma, I attempt to show that these various dimensions of the Christian reality, instead of evolving peacefully from within according to predetermined categories, undergo a discontinuous "quantum leap" each time that the culture in which Christianity is embedded passes into a new phase. The past two millennia have witnessed a number of abrupt cultural shifts, comparable in kind, though possibly not in degree, with that which we are presently experiencing. It would be surprising, even alarming, if the Churches were not a part of this radical transmutation. Quite evidently, the Christian self-understanding and the structures of the Christian community must be overhauled in order to correspond with the presuppositions, concerns, thought-forms, patterns of life, communications systems, and technical possibilities offered by the contemporary world.

We hear a great deal these days about "dissolution." It is said that we are living in a post-Christian era or even that religion is dying out. Is Christianity indeed dissolving? To me it seems clear that the present crisis will involve the dismantling of many venerable institutions and the virtual disappearance of some of the forms under which Christianity has been familiar to us. I should not be surprised if most Christian communities were to experience a decline in membership and influence in the coming generation. But it is far from evident that Christianity will cease to have a saving word to speak to the new civilization now dawning, or that that word will be less needed than in the past. In many sections of the Church there are thrilling signs of a new spirit of hope and community now being born.

By and large, however, the pastors and faithful have not welcomed these new developments with enthusiasm. They regard the old as sacred and the new as necessarily profane. The innovators themselves, identifying the Church with the forms they are seeking to transcend, often feel like rebels and apostates. Much of the problem, in my opinion, stems from a shallow understanding of the main themes of this book—faith, teaching authority, and dogma. Many look upon faith as a mere matter of subscribing to statements made by other believers in the past, upon teaching authority as a *carte blanche* placed in the hands of church officials, and upon dogma as a rigidly defined proposition admitting no further discussion or examination. These static conceptions, firmly lodged in the minds of both traditionalists and radicals, obstruct the processes of orderly discussion and renewal. Too often the option is presented as a choice between servile conformism and defiant rebellion.

The central thesis of this book, as the author understands it, is that terms such as "faith," "authority," and "dogma"—to which one might add others, such as "revelation," "tradition," "doctrine," and "law"—have been too statically conceived. The non-historical thinking of the Enlightenment, reinforced by the reactionary clericalism of the nineteenth century, has given a negative and coercive connotation to terms which in themselves are positive and dynamic. It is a mere historical accident that faith today is so often conceived of as antithetical to reason, that authority is contrasted with personal insight, and that dogma is seen as an intellectual strait jacket. All these classical concepts can be revitalized if they are newly thought out against the background of a more flexible and processive world view. As Christianity seeks to articulate its meaning and message for the revolutionary world of tomorrow, it will experience anew its need for faith, authority, and dogma. Then these Christian realities may once again "come alive."

In this book I am not concerned with finding specific answers to particular questions, but rather with helping to establish an atmosphere in which such questions can be fruitfully approached. My aim is to achieve a general vision of the dialectical interpenetration between stability and change, fidelity and initiative, in the areas of faith, authority, and dogma. For this purpose I have sought to examine, in a general way, the relationship between Christian faith and its historical forms, between ecclesiastical authority and personal insight, between dogma and the demand for innovation. If these relationships were better understood, there would be more openness and less polarization in the Church. Pastors might be more sensitive to their responsibility to lead their people courageously into the future, and the faithful might be more ready to accept new and untried ways. True fidelity to the past includes a readiness to move forward, inspired by the example of our predecessors.

The various chapters of this book, having been composed for separate occasions, are independent units. In compiling the present volume, I have arranged the chapters in what I felt to be an acceptable order and have introduced some editorial links to facilitate continuous reading. While eliminating some repetitions, I have deliberately left a few overlappings in order to avoid destroying the internal unity and coherence of the individual chapters. The reader is therefore free to choose his own order, as his interest may incline him, without feeling that the later chapters presuppose familiarity with the content of those that precede.

AVERY DULLES, S.J.

I. FAITH AND INQUIRY

The Changing Forms of Faith

It is difficult for a contemporary Christian, living in close contact with the world about him, to accept Christianity with the same kind of faith that he himself or his parents would have possessed thirty or fifty years ago. What is not too clear, from the empirical evidence, is the nature of the present crisis. Is it that Christian faith is itself becoming more difficult to attain? Or is it simply that the cultural forms in which Christianity has become clothed have ceased to be appropriate today? We must inquire whether the present crisis of faith may not be due in part to the transition from older styles of expression to forms more suited to our time. If such is the true interpretation of the present crisis, we need not regret that it is occurring.

To be in a position to judge whether faith is being threatened in its essence or simply in its time-conditioned forms, we should at the outset ask ourselves what we mean by faith. Avoiding technical definitions, such as those found in manuals of Scholastic theology, I should like to propose a phenomenological concept. From this point of view, I shall maintain, faith may be viewed as a wholehearted acceptance of something that comes upon one with the strength of a revelation—something that proves capable of giving meaning and purpose to a man's total existence. Faith, so conceived, can be broken down into three main elements. First, it implies a firm conviction regarding what is supremely important—that which Maurice Blondel called "the one thing necessary" and which Paul Tillich called "the object of infinite concern." Secondly, faith implies dedication or commitment. The man of faith, to the extent that he really deserves to be so called, is prepared to make sacrifices for what he believes in— even to pay the ultimate price of life itself. Unless a man has something he is ready to die for, he is not fully a man of faith. Thirdly, faith gives a man access to something on which he can totally rely and hence provides a basic trust, confidence, and optimism. A person may be of the opinion that the world is falling apart and that the future of history is utterly bleak, but he can still be a man of faith if he is convinced that there is a benign power above the world and beyond history that can give salvation, if need be, by restoring the dead to life. Thus the three principal elements of faith, as I understand it, are conviction, commitment, and trust.

It is often asked whether an atheist can be a man of faith. Certainly some believers do not use the term "God" to designate the power in which they ultimately believe. But in the context of my own approach, I should like to give the name "God" to the reality on which a man pins his faith. The one who gives ultimate meaning to our life is our God; the one for whom we are prepared to sacrifice everything is our God; the one whose power we trust to save us even from the ultimate evil of death is our God. To reject God is to that extent to foreclose the very possibility of faith in the full sense of the term. Where faith exists without belief in a transcendent God, idolatry creeps in. The finite is treated as if it were infinite, the creature as if it were the creator.

The preceding observations about faith and about God are intended to be non-controversial. In my description of faith I do not imply that one ought, or ought not, to be a man of faith. If there is a God—an ultimate source of meaning, value, and hope—it would be appropriate to be a man of faith; but if there is no God, faith in the strong sense of the term is an illusion. From all I have said thus far, faith might be judged to be a sign of overconviction, overcommitment, overoptimism. Only the man of faith can affirm that it is not.

On the basis of this preliminary description of faith, let me set forth the central thesis of this chapter. I would hold that in different sociocultural situations, faith changes its form and that it must do so in order to retain its hold on man—that is, in order to remain faith at all. At different times the threats to meaning, commitment, and hope change their forms; men turn to new substitutes for God. Faith must present God under new aspects in order to show that he alone is the true principle of meaning, value, and hope and that it is superstitious to look elsewhere for that which ultimately satisfies the human mind, the human will, and the human heart.

The changing forms of faith, I shall maintain, are appropriate reflections of the changing human situation. If we are to understand the situation of faith today, and the pressures now at work on the man of faith, it will be helpful to consider, in a general way, how faith in the past has adapted to new situations. As John Dillenberger puts it, "our conditioned present needs the illumination of the light enshrined in the ages." In order to liberate ourselves from the time-conditioned features of faith as it has expressed itself in the recent past, Dillenberger adds, we must be aware of the dynamics of grace and history. We must "enter into all times and places in order to overcome history within history." So great are the cultural shifts, says Dillenberger, that "contradictory statements made in different cultural periods may in fact be closer to one another than the repetition of the same statements from different cultural periods."[1]

Within the Judaeo-Christian tradition I find it appropriate to distinguish seven forms of faith which have existed in the past and which, to some extent, still survive.[2] The faith of most Christians today is a residue or refraction of one or more of these past forms of faith, yet none of these seven forms survives as such with full vigor today. Hence it is normal for Christians in our time to feel a certain malaise. A new form of faith is demanded. On the other hand, we cannot simply dismiss the past forms. Such is the underlying continuity connecting the historic forms of faith that it seems clear that any new form will have to emerge from those which have previously existed. Every authentic reformation in Christianity thus far has taken the form of a "resourcement"—a rereading of ancient sources in the light of a new situation. Paradoxically, faith moves back in order to move forward; it never loses contact with its own previous history.

Using very broad strokes of the brush, and putting aside the scruples which would deter the professional historian, let me then proceed, with certain inevitable oversimplifications, to sketch the seven principal forms of faith which I have just mentioned. The first is what I call "Old Testament faith." Israel found itself a tiny people whose national existence was continually imperiled by the great powers to the north and to the south of her (as is once more the case today). The men of faith, however, preached that Israel had nothing to fear from these human powers because she had a powerful ally in heaven. Yahweh by his mighty arm had made Israel a people, his very own. He had bound himself by a solemn pact to help and protect her, to give her peace and prosperity, provided she kept her side of the bargain. Revelation, then, was primarily understood according to the paradigm of an alliance or covenant. Yahweh, the senior treaty partner, was conceived of as Israel's vindicator against all her enemies.

Faith, in this perspective, meant firm reliance on the Lord of the Covenant, adherence to him alone, fidelity to his law. The Old Testament view of faith is compactly summarized in a statement of Isaiah to King Ahaz which might be translated: "Unless you take your stand in God [i.e. have firm faith in God], you shall not be firm" (Is. 7:9).[3] Since God was utterly firm in standing by his promises, Israel could be assured of firmness in its national existence, provided it was firm in its faith. The opposite of faith, in the Old Testament view, was fickleness. The faithless man was one who put his trust in some human force, such as the chariots of the Egyptians, or in demons, or in other gods. The great sin against faith was idolatry, which the prophets equated with adultery, inasmuch as it involved a breach of Israel's monogamous covenant relationship with Yahweh.

Today most Christians do not commonly visualize their relationship to God in terms of a collective covenant between their nation and God, or even between mankind and God. The modern Western concept of the autonomy of nature has made it difficult to look upon secular history as something shaped by a free interpersonal relationship between God and his elect people. We have lost the naïve confidence that the ancient Israelites had in the mighty interventions of God's powerful arm protecting his chosen friends from calamities. While some Christians are convinced that national prosperity is normally a reward for virtue, their faith in Providence is vague, abstract, and colorless in comparison with the robust faith of the Old Testament prophets. Old Testament faith, in its original form, is scarcely available to us in our historical situation.

The New Testament offers a second form of faith, more familiar to most Christians. As in the Old Testament, faith is associated with salvation from death and misery. The most significant change is that God's covenant is no longer with a single nation, but is extended to the whole world. God wants all mankind to hear the good news about Christ and to enter through faith into a new community of love. Also in the New Testament, the concept of salvation differs from that commonly found in the Old Testament. The messianic blessings are no longer viewed in terms of peace and prosperity for the Israelite nation, but rather in terms of heavenly rewards for those who unite themselves with Jesus, whom God has raised from the dead. Faith is the act whereby a man accepts the kerygma and confidently confesses Jesus as his Savior. As a typical expression of New Testament faith we may quote the following: "If you confess with your lips that Jesus is Lord and believe in your heart that God raised him from the dead, you will be saved" (Rom. 10:9). The Christ event is the principal paradigm and reference point for the Christian life of faith.

The opposite of faith in the New Testament sense is not polytheism or even, in the usual sense, idolatry. Rather it is spiritual obtuseness which makes man deaf and unresponsive to the message. From the standpoint of the New Testament, the Jews themselves are unbelievers. To adhere to the Old Covenant when the fulfillment has come is regarded as a form of infidelity. Thus the New Testament quotes against the Jews the words of Isaiah 6:9–10: "Go and say to this people, 'hear and hear, but do not understand; see and see, but do not perceive.' Make the heart of this people fat, and their ears heavy, and shut their eyes, lest they see with their eyes, and hear with their ears, and understand with their hearts, and turn and be healed." The central importance of this text in the propaganda of the early Church is indicated by the fact that it is quoted, at least in part, in all four Gospels (Mt. 13:14–15; Mk. 4:12; Lk. 8:10; Jn. 12:40) as well as in the book of Acts (28:26–27) and Paul's letter to the Romans (11:8). The passage contains, so to speak, a description in reverse of what the New Testament understands by faith.

Modern kerygmatic theology has attempted to repristi-nate the New Testament form of faith, as just described. It seeks to proclaim the Christian message in the language of Paul and Acts, but it does not generally meet with an en-thusiastic response. As Gabriel Moran remarks, religion teachers who make this effort generally find their students "indifferent, uncomprehending, and uninterested in the whole thing."[4] Moran writes, "It is not that our students have never heard about Christian revelation; many are sick to death of hearing about it. The introduction of a new artificial stage in which one pretends that none of this has happened or that one can start all over is not likely to help."[5]

In the patristic period the gospel had somewhat lost its character as a piece of good news to be loudly proclaimed by heralds just arriving on the scene. The Church now found itself in competition with the pagan mystery reli-gions and with philosophical sects which purported to offer salvation from mortality and worldly calamities by inner purification and by spiritual enlightenment leading to un-ion with the divine. This natural mysticism was unaccepta-ble to Christians, who looked upon salvation as the gift of a free and personal God.

St. Augustine of Hippo, perhaps the most eminent theo-logian of the patristic era, is generally receptive to the Plotinian program of an escape from the flesh and from mortality through saving gnosis. But he holds that man, enchained by sin, cannot rise to this contemplative union by his own forces. One must humbly accept the foolishness of the Incarnation, in which God abases himself to cure man's pride. Faith therefore means an inner enlighten-ment that is gained, in the first place, through simple ac-ceptance of the fleshly form of revelation through history and through the Bible. As an epitome of this notion of faith we might take the watchword of Augustine (a quota-tion from Isaiah 7:9, in the Septuagint translation): "Un-less you believe you shall not understand." What had been for the ancient Israelite a prerequisite for standing has become for the contemplative Augustine a prerequisite for *under*standing.

The opposite of faith in its patristic form is the pride of philosophical mysticism or Stoic asceticism, which seeks to rise to the divine by turning away from the flesh. Gnos-ticism and Pelagianism, with their reliance, respectively, on human intellection and human volition, are the chief heresies of this period.

The Augustinian idea of faith inspired the monasticism of the Latin West and gave rise to a deep, mystical piety that nourished itself on the spiritual senses of the Bible. Until the thirteenth century "faith seeking understanding" remained the watchword of theology and contemplative prayer. For most men today, however, this option does not seem fully viable. We no longer spontaneously accept the philosophical dualism on which it is based. Unlike the Greeks we do not take for granted a higher world that is purely spiritual and changeless. We regard it as irresponsible to flee from the things of time in order to devote ourselves to the eternal. Augustinianism rests on the supposition that salvation consists in an escape from the flux of matter, in a Plotinian "flight of the alone to the Alone." The modern Christian normally sees it as his duty to labor within the world and thereby to contribute to the realization of the final Kingdom of God.

In medieval Scholasticism, faith underwent yet another epochal change. Christianity then had to face the challenge of Averroistic Aristotelianism, which claimed to construct a self-sufficing wisdom through demonstrative philosophical argumentation. Averroism came into collision with certain biblical and traditional doctrines, such as the creation of the world, personal immortality, and resurrection. In opposition to the scientific wisdom of naturalistic philosophy, St. Thomas Aquinas, more than any other single thinker, formulated the Christian alternative. Faith, in his system, took on the form of "sacred doctrine," that is, a body of truths too sublime for philosophy, but accepted by the simple believer on the authority of the revealing God.

Just as Augustine had accepted the goals of Plotinus, but had denied their attainability without submission to Christian revelation, so Aquinas accepted the Aristotelian ideal of science, but denied its attainability without faith. Faith for the Scholastic tradition became a superscience, a divinely given supplement to philosophy. The opposite of faith, on this view, was an autonomous human science which did not look to revelation for guidance. Represented by Averroes in the Middle Ages, this spirit of independence was to flower in the Renaissance thanks to historians such as Lorenzo Valla, philosophers such as Giordano Bruno, and scientists such as Galileo Galilei.

The Scholastic concept of faith has shown extraordinary durability. It dominated the pronouncements of Vatican Council I (1869–70) and was spelled out in greater detail by Leo XIII in his encyclical *Aeterni Patris* (1879). A generation ago it inspired the "Christian philosophy" of Étienne Gilson and Jacques Maritain. Yet the declining popularity of this view of faith raises the question, at least, whether it too is not becoming obsolete. Was it not basically a defense reaction against a triumphant rationalism that has seen its day? When science or philosophy claims to be able to solve all the riddles of life, Christianity feels warranted, perhaps, in presenting itself as a superscience or a superphilosophy. But in so doing it loses something of its native vigor. Once the Christian message is depicted as a philosophy, the believer becomes too much engaged in theoretical abstractions; he is distracted from works of charity and from the concrete imperatives of salvation. Forgetful of Christ, he looks in the wrong direction for the foundations of his faith.

The Scholastic view of the sciences and of philosophy as ancillary to theology leads likewise to severe interdisciplinary problems. Contemporary man, with the struggles against Galileo and Charles Darwin still fresh in his memory, is not inclined to turn to the Bible to solve theoretical questions, whether in science, in history, or in philosophy. He is not likely to be impressed by the cosmology of Genesis or by the metaphysics of Exodus. He does not rest his philosophy on the fact that Yahweh, according to the Septuagint, said of himself: "I am who am" (Ex. 3:14). The Thomistic notion of faith as a divinely revealed science has fallen upon hard times.

Toward the beginning of the sixteenth century there were sharp reactions against the overintellectualization of faith in the Scholastic tradition. With the general breakdown of medieval culture, the elaborate systems of the schoolmen no longer carried conviction. Martin Luther, in particular, desired to recover the simplicity of a personal relationship to Christ founded upon the Bible alone. "Such faith," wrote Luther, "which throws itself upon God, whether in life or in death, alone makes a Christian man."[6] Faith, as seen by the Reformers, is a confident trust in God's saving mercy. The opposite of faith, in their view, is reliance upon "good works"—a term which in Luther's vocabulary often signifies reliance on the ecclesiastical machinery of justification rather than on the merits of Christ and the power of the gospel.

During the past four centuries the Lutheran form of Christian faith has had enormous influence in all the Churches issuing from the Reformation. It still remains vital, for example, in the conservative evangelicism of rural America. But in present-day civilization it is not easy to keep alive the religious concerns which gave rise to evangelicism. Few of our contemporaries are so oppressed by the sense of guilt and depravity that they feel the imminent threat of eternal damnation. A contemporary urban American, when he drives down the freeway in an air-conditioned car and comes across a roadside placard JE-SUS SAVES, can scarcely escape a mild feeling of embarrassment. The simplicity of evangelical piety has become quaintly archaic and seems, in the eyes of many, socially irresponsible.

The Catholic Church, in its response to Luther, insisted more vehemently than ever upon the ecclesiastical means of grace. For the Counter Reformation Church, faith was equated with orthodoxy, and by "orthodoxy" was meant an explicit or implicit adherence to all the teachings of the official magisterium. Interestingly enough, Protestantism developed its own orthodoxy, almost as ecclesiocentric as that of Roman Catholicism. In each confessional body, faith was viewed as an enthusiastic acceptance of everything one's own church stood for. It was a form of intellectual loyalty to the institution. In many Catholic catechisms, from the time of Trent until almost the present day, faith is described as the virtue by which we believe whatever the Church teaches as divinely revealed. The enemy of faith, especially for Catholics, was private judgment. The opposite of faith, in the age of confessionalism, was skepticism or indifference with regard to official doctrine. Polemicists, both Protestant and Catholic, joined forces against the infidelity of the Enlightenment.

The Protestant-Catholic debates about the nature of justification, the structures of the Church, and the sacramental system were carried on energetically for several centuries. Each side could claim a roster of distinguished controversialists. But toward the middle of the twentieth century the polemics began to grow stale. As Dietrich Bonhoeffer put it: "Antiquated controversies, especially those between the different sects; the Lutheran versus Reformed, and to some extent the Roman Catholic versus Protestant, are now unreal. They may at any time be revived with passion, but they no longer carry conviction. There is no proof of this but we must simply take it that it is so. All we can prove is that the faith of the Bible and of Christianity does not stand or fall by these issues."[7] As Bonhoeffer went on to say, "to entrench ourselves persistently behind the 'faith of the Church'" is a way of evading the honest question as to what we ourselves really believe.[8] To hold that the content of faith is the Church's business, not that of the individual believer, is to shuffle off the responsibility of one's faith onto an impersonal institution and thus to risk falling into insincerity.

In the early twentieth century a new threat to man's humanity arose with modern science and technology, which tended to call into question the ultimate importance of man. The exploration of what Blaise Pascal had precociously identified as the two "infinites"—the infinitely small known to atomic physics and the infinitely vast known to astronomy—evoked a feeling of horror and emptiness, an anxious suspicion that life might, after all, be a meaningless accident in a mindless cosmos. Nihilistic existentialism rescued man's dignity by the desperate expedient of either heroically embracing the absurd or else defiantly rebelling against the universe. Christian faith, cast into an existential mode, took the form of an affirmation of ultimate meaning or value where none was apparent. By a leap of faith, the believer embraced the absolute paradox of the Incarnation or the Cross. Relying on categories forged by Sören Kierkegaard, existential theologians such as the early Karl Barth, Rudolf Bultmann, and Paul Tillich popularized the notion of faith as an ineffable encounter with absolute mystery, a meaning beyond meaning. Martin Heidegger, Jean Paul Sartre, and Albert Camus, as secular counterparts of the new style of believer, became the principal dialogue partners of Christian theologians in the 1940s.

But existential theology, to all appearances, is itself being left behind. No sooner had it established itself than it was forced to face the charges of irrationalism and irrelevance. Bonhoeffer ridiculed the efforts of Tillich and others to drive men into existential despair by focusing all attention on boundary experiences.[9] Harvey Cox in *The Secular City* agreed: "There is a certain validity to the Marxist assertion that existentialism is a 'symptom of bourgeois decadence,' since its categories of *Angst* and vertigo seem increasingly irrelevant to the ethos of the new epoch."[10] The existential view of faith, though it still makes a certain impact, has been losing influence because it is too individualistic, too pessimistic in its estimate of the world, too dependent on rarefied experiences that are accessible only to highly sensitive persons on relatively rare occasions. Many today are inclined to seek faith, as Bonhoeffer did, not at the borders of life but in its midst.

At this point we must face the following question: What form of faith can be considered appropriate for the man of our day? It is obvious that there is no one modern man. Even in Western Europe and the United States there are many different types of persons whose religious faith will inevitably reflect something of their individual temperament and social conditioning. One cannot impose a single pattern on the Mississippi sharecropper, the London businessman, the Sicilian peasant, and the German university professor. But younger persons who are heavily involved in the forms of life that are characteristically new in the twentieth century seem to experience the crisis of faith in similar ways. As noted at the opening of this chapter, they seem to be incapable of sincerely believing in the same way that their parents or grandparents did.

To call for a new form of faith adapted to the times might seem like a form of disloyalty to the past. It might be interpreted as a program to dilute the word of God in order to make it acceptable to the "itching ears" of a perverse generation. But a refusal to change may, in a different way, dilute the faith by diminishing the intelligibility and relevance of the gospel. Ecclesiastical conservatism may be a sign of timidity, of bigotry, of arrogance, of narrowmindedness. In the words of Karl Rahner:

Faith can fail to achieve the form demanded of it, and the believer may lack sufficient courage to change himself and accept new forms; instead he clings to forms which were once valuable but are now ineffective and meaningless; he will not abandon the condemned mentality of a dying era but sees it as the only climate suited to faith; he banishes from his mind all that belongs to the mentality of a new age. Faith such as this is threatened more surely than if it were exposed to the dangers of a change of form; its witness is unconvincing and ineffectual. For this reason it is of vital importance to become aware of the forms of faith demanded of us today, here and now. If we refuse to do this in theory and in practice, then—and this runs counter to the whole nature of Christian faith—we are living a form of faith which will involve faith itself in its destruction, in so far as men contribute to the rise or the decline of Christian witness.[11]

Very frequently, it seems, faith is made an unnecessary burden because it is mistakenly tied to the thought-forms and styles of an earlier age. Too many Protestants have absolutized the mentality of Luther or John Calvin; too many Catholics want to perpetuate faith-forms suited to the intellectualism of the medieval university or to the curialism of the age that accepted the divine right of kings. The feudal and absolutist forms of ecclesiastical life are not a part of the gospel, nor are the forms of faith that correspond to these types of Church polity.

More positively, we may say that if faith is to do its job it must answer the deepest hopes, aspirations, fears, and anxieties of the contemporary world. In the past, Christianity has been able to enter into dialogue with each successive age. By an excessive attachment to the glories of its past, the Church could prevent faith from having a vital impact in the world today. To identify faith with a wooden conformity to ancient formulas and practices might be an evasion of present responsibility. As Herbert Richardson has noted, an irrelevant form of faith is really a form of infidelity, for it fails to meet the challenges presented to faith at the present moment.[12] It fails to combat the demonic forces actually at work in the world. Perhaps it even connives with these forces by giving a good conscience to those who compromise with evil.

To discern the type of faith that is presently needed, one would have to achieve some general view of the characteristics of our time and assess the hopes and fears to which these give rise. To me it would appear that we have moved from the era of science, dominant since the seventeenth century, into an era of technology. What has caught the imagination of our contemporaries is not man's ability to amass new information or formulate new laws, but rather his ability to transform both his environment and himself. We live in an age of vastly increased control, leading to the planned economy, the planned society, family planning, eugenics. Man's interest and attention are riveted not on the past, nor on the present, nor on the eternal, but on the future—a future that, to all appearances, depends, for weal or woe, upon the use that man makes of his new-found power.

This prospect for the future awakens, on the part of some, delirious hopes. Our modern Prometheus has the feeling of holding in his own hands the fire formerly reserved to the gods.[13] He proclaims that God is dead, that he can now do for himself all that God was formerly relied upon to do for him. He controls his own environment, his own future history, his own biological make-up, and even, through psychedelic manipulations, his own religious experience. Is not man a veritable God unto himself?

And yet there is fear and anxiety. Man, alas, is far from being a God in wisdom or in virtue. None of us really trusts the new providence of professional bureaucracy. We resent being enslaved by colossal organizations that seem to be driven by a limitless need to expand. We resent being manipulated in mind and body by the forces of "human engineering." We cannot really put out of our minds the fear of a gigantic holocaust brought about by human miscalculation. We are all too conscious of how man is squandering the resources of the earth and poisoning his own environment.

What characteristics can be prescribed for faith as it adapts itself to this era of technology? I shall limit myself to three, though the list could obviously be extended. Faith must be transcendent, it must be fraternal, and it must be hopeful. These three attributes can be brought into a rough correlation with the three aspects of faith as meaning, as commitment, and as trust.

First, then, faith must be transcendent. In its quest for ultimate meaning, the human spirit cries out for liberation from proximate and ambiguous goals. If there is nothing absolutely good, nothing ultimately worth while, there is no possibility of faith. Faith today must be able to make contact with the transcendent, or it is nothing. Men no longer look to faith for curious bits of information about how the world began, about how the angelic hierarchies are ordered, or about the ultimate logical consequences of every dogmatic statement. They go to faith, in the last analysis, to answer one question, the all-encompassing question that man inevitably is to himself. Faith must be able to discern an ultimate significance in human life as it unfolds in relationship to the unconditioned source of meaning and of value.

Secondly, faith must be fraternal. It must be capable of building and sustaining genuine community among men. Modern society, as it is organized, thrusts men into numerous functional groupings. Men become categorized as Americans or Russians, as property owners or workers, as manufacturers or consumers; and often enough they feel as little community with their supposed colleagues as with their competitors. Society becomes torn by senseless conflicts between men who do not hate each other, but accidentally find themselves thrust into opposite camps in the collective struggle of rival organizations for primacy and power. Faith, if it can do anything, should be able to deliver men from the absurdity of "ritual ideological conflict," as Richardson has called it.[14] It should take the form of a "commitment of man to oppose the separation of man from man."[15] Cutting across all the barriers that divide men from their brothers, faith should provide a basis for community in mutual respect and love.

Thirdly, a contemporary form of faith must be shot through with hope. It must not be backward-looking and anxiously conservative, but fully open to the breath-taking possibilities that technology has opened up before our eyes. It must take seriously what is new and different, rather than constantly harp on the sameness of the future and the past. Faith will be dismissed by the most energetic and progressive members of society unless it is able to hold forth a vision of the future as exhilarating as the dreams of scientific humanism or utopian socialism. Anchored in God, it must give men courage to face the unknown and to overcome their gnawing anxieties about what the future may portend.

It may not be easy for the Church to rise to the challenge of the times. As the Second Vatican Council (1962–65) noted more than once, the Church is always in danger of concealing rather than revealing the authentic features of Christ.[16] While in theory the Church should mediate the transcendence of God, it could, by absolutizing itself and its authority, become a barrier. It could appear as just one more of the many institutions that enslave the spirit and thwart man's aspiration to the divine. Secondly, the Church could easily take on the characteristics of a particular religious faction, thus dividing its members from the rest of the human family and erecting one more wall of involuntary hostility. Thirdly, the Church, by insisting too much on the binding nature of its own past affirmations, could prevent man from courageously opening themselves to God's future which lies before them. The ambiguity of the Church, as both a help and a hindrance to faith, is acutely felt by men of our day.

The general lack of confidence in the ability of the churches to meet the present crisis has led some to surmise that the influence of Christianity is drawing to a close. But the type of faith demanded for our times is, as I see it, that which the Christian Church is uniquely fitted to provide. From its inception Christianity has been, among all faiths, the most transcendent, the most fraternal, and the most future-oriented. To actuate these qualities once again, Christianity has only to return to its own true genius and to become what, in principle, it has always been.

Christianity is a transcendent faith, because it affirms that man, in the depths of his being, is in contact with God. It affirms that God, to whom the human spirit reaches out in darkness, has lovingly chosen to make himself immediately accessible to every human person. God has drawn unutterably close to mankind in the Incarnation, and through the grace of Christ he comes to each individual. He stands at the door and knocks. He is not far from any one of us, "for in him we live and move and have our being" (Acts 17:28).

Secondly, Christianity is a fraternal faith. It affirms that in Christ all men are brothers, each of them called to union with God, each of them redeemed by the blood of God incarnate. Committed to serving Christ in the least of his brothers, the believing Christian is oriented to loving union even with strangers. As Paul so many times asserted, Christianity is able to surmount every human barrier and to overcome the otherwise insuperable hostility of classes, nations, and ideological factions. "[In Christ] there is neither Jew nor Greek, there is neither slave nor free, there is neither male nor female; for you are all one in Christ Jesus" (Gal. 3:28).

Finally, Christianity is par excellence the religion of the future. Its primary theme was initially, in the preaching of Jesus, and still remains, in the most recent theology, the coming Kingdom of God. Christianity enlists men voluntarily in the task of preparing the earth, insofar as human effort can, to be transformed by the Spirit of God and at the same time liberates them from the debilitating anxiety that the human enterprise will ultimately fail. For the future Kingdom does not depend in the last analysis on man, but on the free promises of God—God who has struck a new and everlasting covenant with man in Jesus Christ. The Resurrection of Jesus, the center of Christian hope, guarantees to us that the perversity of man will never be able to nullify the gift of God.

There is no cause, therefore, for the discouragement and bewilderment of so many Christians. There is no need to engage in a frantic search for new formulas and slogans. In order to prove itself credible, meaningful, and relevant to the men of our age, Christianity has only to be its genuine self. Transcendent meaning, fraternal commitment, and unconquerable hope—these are the very makings of Christianity. To be fully modern, Christianity needs but to overcome its own distortions and to be more evidently what it by nature is: a trustful and wholehearted commitment to the transcendent God as he has made himself infinitely close to us in the Incarnation, as he lovingly identifies himself with the least of our human brothers, and as he progressively leads mankind to the blessed future which he has promised in his Son.

Authority and Insight in the Assent of Faith

Greek philosophy distinguished between opinion, as mere affirmation without cogent evidence, and scientific knowledge, in which the individual could himself perceive the necessary grounds for the truth of his own affirmation. Scientific knowledge (*epistēmē*), as Plato and Aristotle understood the term, surpassed mere opinion because it was able to render an account of itself. Christian theologians, seeking to situate faith in relationship to this scheme, were not satisfied to call it either opinion or scientific knowledge. According to Aquinas, faith shares with opinion the quality of not being grounded on demonstrative evidence and with *epistēmē* (*scientia*) the quality of being a firm and unwavering assent. It owes its certitude to the authority of the revealing God.[1]

The difficulty with this approach, of course, is that we do not have evidential knowledge of the testimony of God himself. Theologians have commonly appealed to human witnesses as guarantors of the invisible authority of God. This appeal was already used by Augustine, who in his work *Of True Religion* holds that the historical facts at the basis of Christian faith cannot be known except as vouched for by the biblical writers.[2] The grounding of Christian faith on authoritative historical testimony became, in the seventeenth century, the chief point of contrast between faith and science. The contrast, as then conceived, is admirably formulated by Pascal:

If it is desired to know who was the first king of the French; at what point geographers place the first merid-

ian; what words were commonly used in a dead language, or anything else of this sort, what other means
than books can give us what we want? And who could
possibly add anything to what they tell us, since we wish
only to know what they contain?

Authority alone can enlighten us in these matters.
But such authority has its principal force in theology,
because there it is inseparable from truth, and truth is
unobtainable in any other way. Thus, to give complete
certitude concerning matters most incomprehensible to
reason, it is sufficient to show that they are found in the
sacred books; and to demonstrate the uncertainty of
things which seem quite evident, it is enough to point
out that they are not contained in Scripture. For the
principles of theology are above both nature and reason. Since the mind of man is too feeble to attain them
by its own efforts, it cannot achieve such lofty understanding unless it is borne by an almighty and supernatural force.

But in matters which lie within the scope of the
senses and of reason, the situation is far different. Here
authority is useless; reason alone is in a position to know
them. The two types of knowledge have their separate
prerogatives. In the former area authority had all the
advantage; here reason reigns in its turn.[3]

On this theory, theology is in effect reduced to history;
that is, to the writings of human witnesses who were in a
position to record God's revelations. History, in turn, is
treated as a discipline in which criticism can hold no
place; one simply has to accept the statements of the witnesses or else resign oneself to ignorance. Thus religious
knowledge is made abjectly dependent on authority, and
authority is depicted in extrinsic terms.

We live in an age when, for better or for worse, extrinsic
authority is mistrusted; and if theology can do nothing but
reason from authority, theology will be dismissed as a
sterile pursuit. The sources of the modern distrust of authority are many, and would include considerations such
as these:

—Authority is felt to be a threat to vitality. What is
proper to life is immanent action—i.e., action that begins
spontaneously from within the subject and leads to self-
fulfillment. Authority—in the sense explained above—acts

upon a man from outside, and he is largely passive with respect to it.

—Authority seems to be pitted against freedom. The more finality is claimed for authority, the less room is left for free choice and creativity. A man is at least morally constrained to accept what is presented to him, rather than to follow his own judgment.

—Authority is suspected of being inimical to truth. In any society the ruling authorities are tempted to suppress inquiry or criticism in order to protect their own position and to avoid any questioning of their own competence. Contemporary man has grounds for supposing that where there is a lack of free inquiry, criticism, and debate, truth is likely to be suppressed. One of Charles Davis' principal charges against the Roman Catholic Church is what he calls its concern for authority at the expense of truth.[4]

—In our contemporary democratic society, authority runs against the grain because it erects a privileged class which is held to have primary access to the sources of wisdom. In Christianity the ordinary believer is in danger of being reduced to the status of a second-class citizen in comparison with the authorized interpreters of the tradition or of Scripture.

—When the decisive authority is that of witnesses from the past, there arises the further difficulty that true progress seems to be impossible. Modern man is rarely content to do what could equally well have been done, and was perhaps better done, by his ancestors. He does not feel that his own experiences and reflections should be dismissed as insignificant.

These difficulties against authority in religion and in faith may prove nothing more than the pride and insubordination of modern man. But before we rebuke the times in which we live, we should look closely to see whether there is a true incompatibility between Christianity and the modern *Zeitgeist*. If we turn to the New Testament, we can find many indications that Christianity was originally heralded as a way of gaining fullness of life, freedom, truth, human equality, and progress. According to John 10:10, Jesus came in order that we might have life, and have it more abundantly. Repeatedly in the New Testament, truth and freedom are stressed as central Christian values (e.g., Jn. 8:32; Gal. 5:1). The Bible, too, makes much of the immediate relationship between each indi-

vidual believer and the Holy Spirit (e.g., Jn. 6:45; 1 Jn.
2:27) and hence permits no total subjection of one man
to another. Further, the New Testament intimates the
possibility of future progress within the Christian community. For example, it promises that the Holy Spirit will
lead Christians into all truth and will teach things that
the disciples were not in a position to hear from the lips
of Jesus (Jn. 16:12–13). Thus the Christian sources themselves suggest inadequacy of presenting Christian faith as
a passive submission to what human authorities hand
down to us from the past.

Pascal's statement that the principles of faith lie beyond the limits of both nature and reason is scarcely applicable to Christianity as it existed in New Testament
times. Even those mysteries which modern theology usually places altogether beyond the scope of reason—such as
the Incarnation and the Trinity—were learned by reflection on the data of experience. If the early community
accepted Jesus as Messiah and Lord, this was not so much
because he explicitly claimed these titles for himself (very
likely he did not) as because his entire ministry and career
—as apprehended by the disciples—could not be accounted
for on any other supposition. So, too, the doctrine of the
Holy Spirit, the third person of the Trinity, was gradually
built up in the light of the experiences of the early community, including the extraordinary charisms that came
upon the Church after Pentecost. The early preaching of
the apostles did not take the form of heralding a strange
set of historical facts, but rather that of a commentary on
well-known public events—such as miraculous healings,
glossolalia, persecutions, conversions, etc. Faith and reason
supported one another to the extent that they did not
actually coincide. Faith aimed to give a positive intelligibility to facts that clamored for explanation.

Since apostolic times, no doubt, Christian faith has inevitably had to rely in great part upon testimonies transmitted from the past. Resting upon the appearance of
God's mercy in Jesus Christ, faith would be impoverished
if it cut itself off from its historical sources and sought to
feed upon present experience alone. As in science and
culture generally, so in religion man progresses by being
able to stand on the shoulders of his predecessors, rather
than having to begin always anew.

Christian faith, however, is not a blind authoritarianism in which one simply substitutes another's thinking for one's own. As Augustine constantly insisted, faith in some sense validates itself by yielding an understanding that eludes the unbeliever. In *The Usefulness of Belief* Augustine recounts how he himself, misled by the promises of the Manichaeans, sought in vain to achieve wisdom without faith and was thereby brought to the verge of skepticism. At length, however, he resolved to "follow the way of Catholic discipline" "until either I discovered the truth I was seeking or was persuaded that nothing was to be got from seeking."[5] In his later works Augustine returns time and again to the idea that faith is an initial step toward an understanding that begins on earth and is to be consummated in the eternal vision.[6]

The Augustinian-Anselmian formula of "faith seeking understanding," in my opinion, has many advantages over modern two-level theories, which would depict faith as the acceptance of a body of truths simply beyond the scope of reason. These theories, which owe something to Thomas Aquinas, were carried to inordinate lengths in some modern authoritarian systems of theology, resulting in what Blondel identified as an extrinsicist and alienated view of revelation.

As a result of radical changes taking place in the self-understanding of both science and theology, the traditional opposition between scientific reason and theology, as conceived, for example, by Pascal, is rapidly breaking down. For one thing, science is no longer thought to rest upon self-evident principles, or to proceed by stringent demonstration, or to seek only universal, necessary, and immutable truths. It deals readily with particular facts, with the process of change, and with probabilities. It extends not only to the mathematical and physical realms, but also to human affairs, including psychology, sociology, and religion.

In particular, the opposition between science and history, so fundamental to Pascal, has evanesced. No self-respecting historian considers himself abjectly dependent on what his sources state. He appraises the sources in view of the opportunity the authors might have had to verify the alleged facts, the likelihood of confusion, bias, fraud, etc. Then he reconstructs the events with due allowance for distortions that may have crept into the record. Since the nineteenth century a critical approach to the Christian sources, including the Scriptures, has been accepted by most churches, and this acceptance has drastically altered the relationship between faith and reason.

Further, as Bernard Lonergan has noted, theology has ceased to be the kind of deductive science that it was thought to be in the age of high Scholasticism: "It has become an empirical science in the sense that Scripture and Tradition now supply not premises, but data. The data has to be viewed in its historical perspective. It has to be interpreted in the light of contemporary techniques and procedures."[7] The modern theologian is not content to quote statements from Scripture or from the documents of tradition. He feels obliged to evaluate these, taking account of the historical stresses and strains that may have influenced the statements in question and asking to what extent the statements would have to be reformulated in order to be suitable expressions of Christian faith in the circumstances of our day.

As a result of the changes that have taken place, I believe that it is no longer useful to set up a contrast between faith on the one hand and science on the other. As a kind of thesis I should like to propose that there is a basic similarity of structure in man's progress toward knowledge in the scientific and religious spheres. In every human discipline both authority and personal insight play a role—though the types of authority and insight, and their respective proportions, vary according to the nature of the subject matter in each particular case.

To clarify the thesis just proposed it will be helpful to distinguish between two aspects of knowledge in any field —whether secular or religious. The first is learning, the acquisition of what has already been achieved by others; the second, discovery by which we mean a more original conquest of the mind. In each of these two areas faith has a place, but the concept of faith is somewhat different.

In the learning process, it is always necessary to rely heavily on the authority of predecessors. Michael Polanyi points out how essential is this reliance even in the secular sciences:

> The assimilation of great systems of articulate lore by novices of various grades is made possible by a previous act of affiliation, by which the novice accepts the ap-

prenticeship to a community which cultivates this lore, appreciates its values, and strives to act by its standards. This affiliation begins with the fact that a child submits to education within a community, and it is confirmed throughout life to the extent to which the adult continues to place exceptional confidence in the intellectual leaders of the same community.[8]

What Polanyi here says of the scientific community is applicable a fortiori to a community of religious faith. If an individual wishes to expose himself to the full impact of the highest religious insights that have been attained in a given tradition, he must affiliate with the group, accept apprenticeship within the community, and place his trust in its religious leaders. If I wish to understand yoga I must live under the tutelage of a yogi; if I wish to understand Christianity I must join the Christian community and gradually become initiated into its mysteries. The meaning of religious rites and doctrines simply cannot be understood by an outsider, a mere spectator. Only if I am willing to contemplate life through the eyes of believers can I discover whether the vision of faith is helpful and acceptable to me. This quasi-experimental kind of commitment appears to correspond with what Augustine advocated in his celebrated formula, "Unless you believe, you shall not understand."

It may be objected, of course, that submission to education within a group—with all the confidence in the group that this implies—will limit the individual's possibilities of making an original contribution. Of course, there is such a thing as a mechanical and passive submission to authority that never passes on to the stage of active appropriation and understanding. But normally speaking, education aims to put a man in a position in which he achieves insights that would otherwise lie beyond his capacity. In this sense it enhances rather than restricts the originality of the individual.

In all human traditions, the transmission of knowledge and skills involves a constant process of revision. This is evident even in the field of language. As words are used in new contexts, the previous usage is continually being modified. So, too, when we agree with someone else's opinion we almost inevitably modify his thought, no matter how slightly. My assent cannot be a perfect carbon copy of yours. And conversely, there is no such thing as total dissent. The sharpest disagreement includes a partial submission to an existing consensus. Even the most radical revolutionary appeals to certain principles accepted within the society he is trying to revolutionize.

This dialectic of continuity and innovation, which is at work in all human acceptance of authority, plays an important part in the history of religion. Great disciples have never been content to repeat verbatim the lessons of their masters, but rather to go forward in their footsteps. As we know from history, the major innovators in Christianity have always been men deeply steeped in their religious tradition—men who drew from the tradition the weapons by which they fought against the existing forms of church life. This is evident in the case of Roman Catholic reformers such as Bernard of Clairvaux, Francis of Assisi, and Ignatius Loyola, as well as among Protestants such as Luther, Calvin, and Kierkegaard.

The Christian tradition makes room for creative criticism of itself, for it teaches that human sinfulness, as well as the grace of the Holy Spirit, is at work in the entire history of the Church. Sinfulness, of course, is at work in the religious revolutionary too: he must seriously ask himself whether he has been sufficiently attentive to what the tradition might have to say to him. Paradoxically, it is only a thorough immersion in the Christian tradition that puts one in a position to bring an authentically Christian criticism to bear against it.

The learning process, therefore, both in religion and in other disciplines, involves at least a provisional and to some extent critical submission to authority. In Christianity the submission can never be absolute because a man can never transfer to anyone else the responsibility for his own religious faith. That must be a matter between himself and God. Nobody's faith can be an exact replica of someone else's; the act of faith is necessarily our own. And yet it cannot be so completely our own that it does not grow out of, and partially reaffirm, the faith of the community.

According to Thomas Aquinas, the authority of the teaching Church is merely pedagogic; it is a preliminary that brings us into a situation in which the truth of God itself illumines our minds:

There are three things which lead us to the faith of Christ: natural reason, the testimony of the Law and the Prophets, the preaching of the Apostles and others. But when a man has thus been led as it were by the hand to the Faith, then he can say that he believes for none of the preceding motives; not because of natural reason, nor because of the witness of the Law, nor because of the preaching of men, but only because of the Truth itself. . . . It is from the light that God infuses that faith derives its certitude.[9]

In more modern terminology we might say that faith really comes into its own when we no longer believe precisely because of the apologetical arguments that extrinsically point to Christ and the Church as organs of revelation, nor because the Bible or the Church tells us that we ought to believe as we do, but because we personally derive effective guidance and illumination from what Christianity teaches. Throughout all our religious lives we have to keep striving to appropriate the Christian tradition—to make it real and effective for ourselves—and as we do so, we shall find that we are able to express it in new formulas that are authentically our own. In Tillichian terminology we might say that the authority of revelation ceases to be "heteronomous" and becomes "theonomous."[10]

Thus our discussion of the learning process has ineluctably led into our second question—that of personal discovery. By "discovery" I here mean a mental illumination that makes things fall into place. Discovery brings with it a certain firmness of conviction, sometimes so overpowering that we feel it to be irreversible. If personal faith involves discovery, we should ask ourselves at this point what is the place of reason in discovery.

As we shall see more fully in Chapter 3, discovery is normally the achievement of reason operating not by fixed rules or syllogisms, but by personal assessment of concrete situations in the light of what John Henry Newman calls "antecedent probabilities." While verbal argument is sometimes useful for outlining the main steps of an inference after it has been made, language is too crude an instrument for the initial discovery, which Newman attributes to a faculty he calls the "illative sense." This sense, as Newman explains it, is a spontaneous power of inference, not dependent upon formal rules. In a sentence that some linguistic analysts of our century would do well to ponder, he wrote: ". . . the mind itself is more versatile and vigorous than any of its works, of which language is one, and it is only under its penetrating and subtle action that the margin disappears, which I have described as intervening between verbal argumentation and conclusions in the concrete. It determines what science cannot determine, the limit of converging probabilities and the reasons sufficient for proof."[11]

In an important article, "Faith and Reason,"[12] Polanyi proposes as the best paradigm for religious discovery the kind of informal inference that is at work when we recognize comprehensive entities in the objects of our experience. When we come to see a person as a person, rather than as a mere blob of color, we actively synthesize a multitude of details that cannot be exhaustively enumerated. A similar mysterious process is at work when we get meanings out of the words on a printed page or when a doctor makes a diagnosis. There is no way of specifying in the abstract when there are enough symptoms to warrant a judgment that a victim has epilepsy. Only the skilled physician can say, by applying his acquired skill in discernment to a particular concrete case.

Theologians in the past have generally paid far too little heed to the individual logic of discovery, as outlined by authors such as Newman and Polanyi. It is my conviction that greater attention to this aspect of epistemology could be of immense importance for many questions in apologetics, such as the nature of salvation history, the value of miracles and prophecy, the value of the life of Christ or the saints as signs of faith, the Church as a sign of credibility, and the like. In all of these cases we have to do with patterns of intelligibility that point to a divinely given meaning. There is no way of strictly proving that the meaning is really there. Either one recognizes it or one does not. As we contemplate the scene, there seem to be moments when the pieces fall into a pattern. It is as though the meaning were given to us; we perceive it as a gift, a grace. And yet we cannot say that reason is not at work. The illative sense reasons in its own way.

The process of religious discovery resembles the recognition of a familiar face, the judgment that someone is making a sign to me, or the diagnosis of a disease. The main difference between these illustrations and the case of religious conviction is that a religious inquirer is concerned with the ultimate meaning of the whole universe, including his own personal existence. To determine the presence of such a meaning, one has to rely on clues that permit the divine ground, so to speak, to shine through certain specific events. In a moment of grace we apprehend the infinite, the absolute, the incomprehensible.

If religious meaning, in the moment of recognition, bursts upon one unpredictably, it would seem to follow that faith would not be prerequired in the search. But the contrary must be said. According to Polanyi, the way to find a hidden meaning, even in non-religious areas of knowledge, is to focus not on the details but on the meaning itself, which, although as yet concealed, is believed to be present. In major scientific discoveries, he contends, the investigator is always sustained by a confidence that what he is looking for is really there to be found. "Our heuristic cravings," writes Polanyi, "imply the existence of answers, and only by concentrating on the anticipated solution can we successfully line up the data."[13] When the solution does come, it commands assent because accredited in advance by our confidence that it would be there. Thus the process of discovery turns out to be simply another instance of the general rule: "Unless you believe, you shall not understand."

As Polanyi observes, the heuristic process, even in the physical and mathematical sciences, is sustained by passion. Hence the discovery, when it occurs, evokes the kind of heuristic delight expressed prototypically in the "Heureka!" of Archimedes.

The great theologians have always been conscious of the role played by the affections in religious inquiry. The older Scholastics, including Aquinas, used to speak in this connection of a knowledge by connaturality or sympathy.[14] The more a man is akin to God by love or desire, the more sensitive will he be to the signs of God's presence. What is a sign to one person may not be a sign to another, because active receptivity is necessary to enable one to read the meaning of personal signs. To the lover the smallest gestures of the beloved are charged with significance that strangers cannot discern. Hence the need for moral purification and purity of heart for a "real assent" to the divine.

To ask whether reason can demonstrate the existence

of God or the credibility of the Christian religion is therefore to put an ambiguous question, to which no simple answer can be given. If the words "reason" and "demonstration" are used in the sense of rigorous deduction from principles self-evident to every man, the answer must be "no." For the proofs to impart true conviction there must be an antecedent openness and concern that can, in some wide sense of the word, be called "faith." The explicit act of faith is a further determination of a primordial or implicit faith, which guides the process of inquiry and serves as a heuristic basis for the interpretation of the signs.

If these contentions are valid, it must be concluded that in the realm of religious knowledge, and indeed in all knowledge, reason necessarily proceeds on the basis of what may in some wide sense be called "faith." The faith in question—faith antecedent to reason—may be taken on two levels, never adequately distinct. In the first place there is a personal orientation born of an implicit supposition that there is a total meaningfulness to life and the universe. This anticipation of a transcendent or religious meaning directs one's personal process of inquiry and enables one, at times, to discern the divine, thanks to the signs that have been given.

On the second level, that of "authority," faith means a trusting acceptance of the tradition of the community to which one adheres. This confidence may be either weakened or confirmed by personal reflection. If one finds tradition to be a useful guide in making sense of what is known from other sources, one becomes increasingly committed to it. But in reaffirming the tradition we always develop and modify it. Tradition cannot be simply a static collection of answers handed down from the past.

Reason in this framework means the process of verifying whether the anticipations set up by faith are or are not an adequate guide for the interpretation of other data. Reason may lead away from faith, but it may also strengthen and develop it. The movement of reason can, and often does, bring faith from an implicit and provisional stage to one that is explicit, personally ratified, and mature.

When faith becomes luminous and leads to understanding, does it cease to be faith? Is the authority that led to faith now cast aside in favor of personal apprehension?

This is the common view of rationalists, but it is not, I think, a valid position. The mainstream of Christian thought has consistently opposed such rationalizing tendencies. The encounter with transcendence that constitutes the basis of religious conviction never occurs without the mediation of some created agency—the humanity of Christ, the Church, the Scriptures, the sacraments, or whatever. Thus even when one appropriates the Christian faith with the fullness of personal conviction, one remains dependent on external signs to present and commend the content of faith. An element of authority remains.

The authority may be significantly appropriated and internalized, so that one could not relinquish it without forsaking something of one's own, but still it remains to some extent other than oneself. Although pure "theonomy," as Tillich describes it, is always an ideal to which we tend, it is never perfectly realized under the conditions of this life. A measure of "heteronomy" remains. Thus, while insisting that the religious authorities ought not to be viewed in sheerly extrinsicist terms, we acknowledge that man's situation in this life must always remain that of one seeking the fullness of understanding. No matter how advanced he may be, the Christian may rightly be admonished: "Unless you believe, you shall not understand."

Faith and understanding, therefore, enter into a dialectical unity. Understanding and believing are not identical, but it is when I believe that I best understand, and it is when I understand that I believe most fully, as I should. The Christian is convinced that the beliefs of his own tradition are capable of leading to the fullest and highest understanding available to man.

Faith, Reason, and the Logic of Discovery

The question whether faith is reasonable has a good claim to being one of the perennial issues of Christian theology. In one form or another, this question has confronted theologians of every epoch. Distinguished thinkers, such as Étienne Gilson,[1] H. Richard Niebuhr,[2] and Herbert Richardson,[3] have attempted to construct typologies of the faith-reason relationship. Without reviewing their findings in detail, one may distinguish three main positions. One school so stresses the opposition as to conclude that one must either accept faith at the expense of reason —the fideist view—or renounce faith in order to follow the demands of reason—the rationalist view. Theologians of a second type, impressed by the harmony of faith and reason, assert that the two support one another or even that they are two different routes to the same goal. A third school would situate faith and reason in two different spheres and would consequently deny the possibility of any genuine conflict or mutual confirmation. This school would say that faith gives one type of truth, reason another, and that there can be no overlapping, provided only that each remains in its proper sphere.

To achieve any adequate grasp of the problem, one must take into account the various meanings that the terms "faith" and "reason" have had in different epochs of history. In our first chapter we have already seen some of the meanings attributed to the term "faith." There have been corresponding variations in the term "reason," which has sometimes been used to designate intuitive knowledge (as in the Platonic tradition), sometimes deductive knowledge (the primary meaning in Aristotelianism), sometimes induction from measurable phenomena (as in modern positivism), and sometimes a sound interpretation of a mass of phenomena that admit of no logical systematization. Some Christian theologians have limited the term "reason" to what man could learn without grace or revelation, or even to what lies within the grasp of fallen and unredeemed nature. Obviously the relationships of faith and reason will be differently visualized according to the varying definitions attached to the two terms of the comparison.

In Old Testament times the problem of faith versus reason can scarcely be said to have existed. It was taken for granted that the process by which man comes to know God is simply the reverse side of the process by which God manifests himself to man. To know God as he has revealed himself in nature and history, by word and deed, was thought to be simultaneously an act of reason and of faith. While some of the prophets polemicized against the false wisdom of the diviners (cf. Is. 47:10; Jer. 8:9, etc.), the sapiential literature exalts wisdom as the gift of God (Wis. 7:7, 8:21, etc.). It was recognized, of course, that God might do astonishing things that would upset man's previous expectations, but to accept God's word was not regarded as anything irrational. Faith was not viewed as being intellectually anomalous.

In the New Testament the problem of faith and reason becomes acute when the tidings of the gospel are proclaimed in the atmosphere of Greek intellectualism. Paul in 1 Corinthians, chapters 1 and 2, points out that while there is a false human wisdom which rejects Christ, to accept Christ is nevertheless in conformity with a higher divine wisdom. In the Captivity Epistles (Col. 1, 2; Eph. 1), Paul particularly stresses the value of a wisdom based upon faith and enlivened by the Holy Spirit.

In patristic times and in the Middle Ages reason was generally identified with the body of knowledge that man could achieve without benefit of supernatural revelation. Faith, on the other hand, was looked upon as a docile acceptance of God's testimony. Reason was equated, for practical purposes, with the achievements of Greek logic and philosophy; faith, with the corpus of Christian doctrine derived from the Scriptures. Faith and reason, so conceived, were the twin elements out of which the great theological systems of Augustine, Aquinas, and others were forged. Augustine preferred to think of reason, or understanding, in Platonic and intuitive terms; Aquinas, in terms of syllogistic logic according to the Aristotelian model. For Augustine understanding was the fruit of faith cultivating itself; for Aquinas, reason was rather the presupposition and the instrument of faith. For both of them, reason and faith harmoniously interlocked.

The modern period, which may be dated from the Renaissance, set great store by the security of autonomous reason, operating by means of exact inference from evident data. The climate, from the sixteenth to the nineteenth century, was dominated by a rationalism which viewed faith as an inferior form of knowledge. With various degrees of orthodoxy or heterodoxy, such rationalism is found in Baruch Spinoza, John Locke, Immanuel Kant, and G. W. F. Hegel. Faith was increasingly relegated to the sphere of the imaginative, the emotional, the esthetic, the ethical.

In opposition to the philosophical rationalism of the times, Vatican Council I reasserted the essential position of Aquinas—that faith is objective knowledge compatible with, but superior to, human reason. The stark affirmations of that Council are rightly understood only if one understands reason as an autonomous power, inalienably implanted in human nature as such, rather than as a responsive and interpretative power, variously exercised under the historical conditions of actual life. Vatican I was reacting to the threat posed by a triumphant reason that claimed the power to master the whole of reality, including the most secret things of God. Because this kind of militant rationalism scarcely exists in our time, the declarations of Vatican I on faith and reason no longer speak appropriately to our situation.

Since Vatican Council I the clashes between faith and reason have occurred less on the terrain of philosophy than on that of science. In the mid-nineteenth century the great geological and anthropological discoveries associated with the names of Charles Lyell and Charles Darwin called into question the literal understanding of Genesis, which many Christians took to be a matter of faith. Then, in the closing years of the century, ancient history and archaeology raised acute problems concerning the historicity of the Bible, thus provoking a contest between faith and historical reason. Some non-believing historians argued that scientific history refuted the faith, while Christian apologists replied that disinterested historiography confirmed the Bible. In our own time, historians and apologists have learned to make many necessary distinctions concerning the presuppositions, method, and scope of history in its various uses. Rudolf Bultmann still maintains that scientific reason has nothing to do with faith, but most of his disciples feel that it is theologically necessary and methodologically possible to apply historical method to the problem of Jesus. Another German Lutheran, Wolfhart Pannenberg, goes so far as to contend that objective historical reason, without any supernatural light, can securely establish the fact of Christian revelation.

While I do not fully accept Pannenberg's restriction of the term "faith" to a purely fiducial act, following upon a prior knowledge of revelation, I find great value in his efforts, against the Barthians and Bultmannians, to assert the basic harmony between revelation and reason. He is careful to state that the "reason" which can establish the fact of revelation is not autonomous or syllogistic reason, but rather interpretative or historical reason, operating in a climate of revelation under the healing influence of the Holy Spirit.[4]

Perhaps the most useful analysis of the relationship between faith and reason, for our time, remains that of Newman in his *Oxford University Sermons*. He points out that while the term "reason" is frequently used in senses in which it can be opposed to faith, there is a sense in which faith itself can be said to be an act of reason. If by reason one means simply the mind's power of proceeding from things that are perceived to things not perceived, faith itself, as the "evidence of things not seen," may be classified as an act of reason. It is an informal type of inference from the data of experience interpreted by the help of antecedent presumptions and expectations aroused in the religious inquirer through the supernatural workings of grace. I see no compelling argument why the discernment of revelation, by a person so assisted, should not be called an act of reason.

In order to avoid misunderstanding, it is helpful at this point to distinguish, as Newman did, between formal and informal (including "spontaneous") inference. Formal inference operates by a set of carefully articulated rules; informal inference by a kind of spontaneous or natural logic, better adapted to many of the real situations of life, in which the evidences are too complex to be methodically analyzed.

As Newman pointed out in his *Grammar of Assent*, formal inference rarely leads to new or startling insights. "The great discoverers of principles," he wrote, "do not reason. . . . It is the second-rate men, though most useful in their place, who prove, reconcile, finish, explain."[5] In his investigation of the logic of discovery, Newman piled up instance after instance of what Locke had called the "surplusage of belief over proof."[6] Original thinkers, according to Newman, often find it difficult to explain how they arrived at their conclusions. This is scarcely surprising, for all of us, I dare say, in quite ordinary matters, have experienced embarrassment in seeking to defend or justify certitudes that we feel to be entirely warranted. As Newman said, very few people can articulate the grounds for their conviction that Great Britain is an island. If we were to limit out convictions to things we can prove by rigorous logic from indubitable premises, we should sink to a subhuman level of existence.

In fields such as art and literature, politics and history, our beliefs rest upon an accumulation of evidence that defies distinct enumeration. Good judgment rests upon an incredibly complex process of synthesis and evaluation, of which we can give no full account, but which is not on that score suspect. If implicit reliance on unanalyzed assumptions is to be called "faith," we shall have to say that practical living is a constant exercise of faith. We take it for granted that our senses and our memory are not deceiving us, although it is logically possible that they might be doing so. So too, the whole fabric of our interpersonal relations in society rests upon a network of fiducial relations to other men. When it becomes impossible for a man to trust in the honesty and good faith of his associates, society is on the way to breaking down.

Applying these general principles to the field of religion, we may say that religious insight is rarely, if ever, the product of strict formal inference. It is ordinarily achieved somewhat in the way in which great discoveries are made in other disciplines—that is, through a long and passionate search for a hidden meaning, followed by a sudden and overpowering experience of discernment or disclosure. These disclosures then become socially influential. The recipients of such privileged experiences are caught up with enthusiasm and try to articulate what it has been given to them to see. By their "prophetic" testimony they enable others to share something of the joy and conviction that are theirs. In this way a social situation is produced in which the soil is prepared for deeper and more specific disclosure experiences, as occurred in that great phylum of revelatory encounters recorded in the Bible.

Tradition is to be held in honor as a means by which the religious insight of a privileged period can be made available to posterity. But at the price of becoming stale and insipid, tradition must continually stimulate new religious encounters, leading to new insights and new symbols. When tradition becomes too rigid—as may easily occur when it is too highly esteemed—it often loses its vitality. We seem to be living in a moment of history that calls for an intense revitalization of the Christian symbols, lest they lose their power and credibility. The younger generation, especially, complains that the inherited symbols no longer speak to it.

Some representatives of the tradition, witnessing the present crisis, wish to bolster the power of the religious symbols by appeals to authority. But even if successfully imposed, such a passive submission to authority could scarcely result in a vital and contemporary faith. A living faith must be free and spontaneous in character: it cannot be the fruit of dutiful obedience alone. Nor is it particularly helpful to produce logical arguments for believing the testimony of the Bible and the Church. For a genuinely religious adherence to the Christian message, a rediscovery of its revelatory value must be made.

To illustrate what I mean, I should like to distinguish between "proofs" for the existence of God and what Henri de Lubac, in the title of his fine book, refers to as "the discovery of God."[7] The proofs, as they are often presented, purport to deliver God as the necessary conclusion to a set of premises that do not presuppose any knowledge of God. Such a process I believe to be invalid: for if God were completely unknown there would be no way in which a valid concept of him could be constructed. From Augustine to Karl Rahner theologians of stature have repeatedly affirmed that if we did not somehow know God in our experience we could not even raise the question of God. Before we begin to search for God, we already apprehend him obscurely and implicitly in the restlessness of our own hearts, in which his grace is operative. Our active knowledge of God, as the one for whom we are looking, is preconceptual but real. It is a kind of inchoate faith and serves to direct reason in its quest. When we do find in Christ—or elsewhere—the appearance of God our Savior, we spontaneously feel that we are recognizing what we already knew in an obscure anticipatory way.

In the concrete order, man's search for God is always something more than a search for a faceless infinite. The metaphysical question of God arises rather late in the history of any individual or civilization, and when it does arise it is but a pallid reflection of a previously religious search for God. This search is prompted by man's concrete historical experience. Men find themselves in a universe that seems to them in some respects astonishingly friendly and benign, and yet somehow also curiously out of joint. We consequently feel that life is not what it should be, that the world is unduly cruel and unjust, that we ourselves are sinful and alienated, that death is hateful but inevitable. But in spite of all this, we do not cease to hope. We aspire unceasingly to a better order: we feel that the world, and even we ourselves, are not beyond possibility of redemption. These vague sentiments, or others like them, prompt man to look for a redeemer from beyond the world, for a God who manifests his mercy and love and who bestows the blessed companionship for which man looks in vain within the world. If God were to call man into union with himself, all would be well.

Quite obviously these needs and aspirations do not strictly prove that there is a God nor that he will redeem man. They may, however, create a legitimate expectation of the possibility of divine redemption. At the very least, they pose the question of God in a meaningful way. They prompt us to ask whether Augustine was not right in declaring that God made us for himself and that our hearts cannot find rest until they rest in him. Our acceptance of Augustine's interpretation of the human situation will depend upon whether we find that God has given convincing signs in history of his presence and salvific will. Our interpretation of the historical signs, conversely, depends on the questions and expectations with which we approach the signs themselves.

Among the reasons which have been traditionally claimed as proofs of revelation, miracles, in one form or another, have long held a place of honor. The miracles of Jesus—including his Resurrection—modern miracles such as Lourdes, and the so-called "moral miracle" of the Church occupy innumerable pages in the manuals of apologetics. Many of these treatises, however, fail to advert sufficiently to the difference between the logic of syllogistic argument and the logic of discovery or recognition. The miracles are treated not as religious signs, but as evidence capable of convincing even the non-religious observer. The manuals abound in vain efforts to prove that the miracle stories could not possibly be fictitious, that the happenings in question could not have been worked by unknown physical forces or by demons or unknown spiritual beings, etc. All these demonstrative efforts raise more doubts than they settle.

If the argument from miracles has any validity today—and I would feel that it does have a certain validity—it must be completely recast. The idea of miracle as an exception to the laws of nature, so basic to the "evidential" approach, is no longer serviceable. Instead we must substitute the idea of the miracle as a sign which speaks to the religiously disposed inquirer, one in earnest search for clues to the presence of God. Divine signs, like the meaningful gestures of men, can sometimes be recognized, but their reality as signs cannot be, in any geometrical or cogent fashion, proved.

The best illustration of the difference between proof and sign might be the way in which we interpret human gestures, such as a smile, a handshake, or the like. There is no way of strictly proving that the apparent meaning is really there. Either one discerns it or one does not. The friend knows how to interpret the gesture of his friend; the lover, that of the beloved. For the religious seeker, too, there may be events, persons, and situations in which the divine meaning of the universe is felt to be symbolically present, so that God is apprehended in them, expressing his being and his attitudes in a historically tangible way. In this way we may speak of Christ and of various events in the history of Israel and of the Church as divine signs.

Rather than attempt to generalize further about the process of religious inquiry I should like at this point to focus primarily on a particular question, which might be illustrative of others. How could it happen that a man would be moved to accept the saying of Jesus, "He who loses his life for my sake will find it"? This statement, while it is not the sum and substance of Christianity, is surely central to our faith. It is one of the few sayings of Jesus reported by all four of our Gospels (Mt. 16:25; Mk. 8:35; Lk. 9:24; Jn. 12:25). The idea of entering life through dying, of receiving through giving, runs like a golden thread through the entire New Testament. It confronts the prospective Christian with a challenge to adopt an entirely new point of view, to cease to judge by appearances, and to accept the challenge of an immense paradox. Our willingness to make the venture of being a Christian will in great part depend on whether we can believe that in renouncing ourselves for the sake of others, with full reliance on Christ, we shall come to our full stature as persons. Christ's call for total conversion—for a "transvaluation of all values"—is brilliantly compressed in this one brief sentence, and the entire New Testament might be regarded as an expansion of this basic principle. What, then, makes the principle credible?

Negatively, I might begin by saying that a man's acceptance of such an axiom in faith could not be based simply on extrinsic evidences. An older approach to apologetics would have argued that we have to accept such statements because Jesus was clothed with divine authority, an authority proved by miracles and the like. Without totally rejecting such extrinsic agrumentation, I should like to remark that of itself it does not result in a firm and personally appropriated faith. It produces a kind of conditional commitment, which is likely to be upset at any time by some new factor that might cast doubt on the validity of the argument. A firm conviction demands the perception of an affinity between reality as I experience it and the vision of reality set forth in the statement which I accept. Such an affinity can, I believe, be established with regard to a statement of faith such as, "He who loses his life for my sake shall find it." I can think of at least five lines of approach, each of which I shall briefly summarize.

1. *The Moral Pattern.* Very few people, if any, want to be completely unethical. Most feel a conscious need of some integrating ideal capable of giving a pattern to their lives. The gospel principle of selfless charity as a path to authentic fulfillment appeals to many as offering a definite style of life which corresponds to man's highest ethical insights. A man feels that he would be better than he is if he could live according to the Christian principle of "agapaic" love—if he could follow Jesus in his role as the "man for others." By embracing this ideal, man acquires a standard by which he can measure his success and failure, plan his future, determine his course of action.

The objection can of course be made that the Christian ethic is fundamentally selfish because it is ultimately directed to self-fulfillment, to finding one's life as a result of losing it. But to this it may be fairly answered that the Christian is asked to serve his neighbor out of love and not for the sake of any gain to himself. The Christian promise assures a man that in giving of himself—even in giving his "self"—he is not harming himself. This assurance corresponds to a hope or inclination deeply rooted in human nature. Long before Christ, Plato taught on purely philosophical grounds that it is incredible that a man really harms himself by doing his duty or that a man benefits himself from evading his duty.[8] Most people feel, I believe, that they would come closer to their full stature as human persons if they did have strong ethical ideas such as are embodied in the gospel precept. They are in quest of values which transcend private self-interest—values worth living for because they are also worth dying for. Because the gospel answers to this innate generosity of the human heart, it draws men who are generously inclined.

2. *Practical Benefits.* Society would stand to gain immensely if there were more people prepared to follow the evangelical ideal of emptying oneself out for the sake of others. Other ethical systems provide a basis for loving those who love us, or who can help us, or who are naturally attractive to us: but the gospel is distinctive in that it gives effective motives for extending one's charity to those who are naturally unattractive to us and who, perhaps for that very reason, are most in need of being loved. A man cannot be an effective healer of society unless he is capa-

ble of disinterested love. Such love, like the charity of Christ, is creative, redemptive, divinely therapeutic.

Not only is the gospel ethic beneficial to society, but it is also, paradoxically, a source of strength and balance to the individual who adopts this ideal. A purely acquisitive form of life fails to yield true happiness, but a life of self-less generosity provides deep satisfaction. Where no such ideal has been found, men feel a certain inward void in their existence, a sense of ultimate meaninglessness and futility, which can easily lead to anxiety and neurosis. As Viktor Frankl has said, "existential boredom" is a wide-spread phenomenon in the twentieth century. The frus-trated will to meaning often leads to a recrudescence of primitive forms of the will to power, the will to money, and the will to pleasure. "The sexual libido becomes ram-pant in the existential vacuum."[9]

3. *Discipleship.* People are not satisfied to find abstract principles that seem to them unexceptionable. They keep looking for men who inspire them by having embraced such principles and lived them out in the concrete. An ap-pealing feature in Jesus' program of love is that it brings one into a relation of discipleship with a leader of extraor-dinary, even unique, holding power. This personal union with a leader and lord who can be admired and followed has always been viewed as an essential attribute of Chris-tian faith. The believer feels himself to be bound to Jesus by the ties of mutual love.

I am the good shepherd, and I know my own and my own know me. (Jn. 10:14)

If any one serves me he must follow me; and where I am, there shall my servant be also. (Jn. 12:26)

You are my friends if you do what I command you. No longer do I call you servants, for the servant does not know what his master is doing; but I have called you friends, for all that I have heard from my Father I have made known to you. You did not choose me, but I chose you, and appointed you that you should go and bear fruit . . . (Jn. 14:14–16)

To object that this personal dimension is merely emo-tional, is, I think, to separate man's faculties in an unrealistic way. In the decision of faith, intellect and will interpenetrate. The fact that the gospel ethic has been concretely lived out by at least one man, and that he invites us to follow him in personal friendship, gives serious intellectual reasons for confidence in the ideal itself. A true ideal must make men better. Jesus himself, according to the common consent of men, stood far above the norm of humanity: and those who truly respond to his invitation to follow him in service become, to that extent, more admirable and lovable as persons.

(In speaking here of the personal goodness of Jesus I am not, of course, saying that he was just "a very good man." Everything he is reported as saying about himself makes it impossible for any true disciple to take that view of him. By his words and actions he claims to stand in the place of God; he teaches that our eternal salvation depends on our attitude toward him and that he is, in an altogether special sense, the Son of the eternal Father. Discipleship therefore involves accepting in some sense the divinity of Jesus. At the moment, however, I am concentrating on the formal concept of discipleship, not on the question who Jesus really was.)

4. *Community*. All men experience the desire for community. They feel alone and need the support of other like-minded persons who will give them inspiration, counsel, sympathy, and support. Most of the social groupings in which we live have a professional or sociological basis, but fail to draw us together in our spiritual ideals. The family, the club, etc., provide an atmosphere of friendship and relaxation, but do not usually establish the same type of relationship for which one turns to a community founded upon faith. To become a Christian is to enter such a community—one founded on the sharing of the highest moral and spiritual ideals. In the Church the ideal of selfless sanctity is constantly held aloft, and through word and sacrament the members are gathered in a worshiping community with their crucified and risen Lord.

If this is more a description of what the Church ought to be than of what it actually is at all times and in all places, at least it may be said to represent what the Church feels called to be; and every member is invited to help make it such. The world needs an open community of this kind—one that recognizes no social or racial or geographical barriers, but that binds men together in terms of their common dedication to an ideal that transcends them all. The fact that such a community exists, at least imperfectly, in the Church is reasonably regarded as a recommendation for Christianity.

5. *Resurrection*. The evangelical statement, "He who loses his life for my sake will save it," is a promise that we might be inclined to believe for all the reasons just given. But the consideration that seems to have been crucial for the faith of the primitive community is the fulfillment of that promise in a visible way in the Resurrection of Jesus. In his earthly life Jesus was overcome by the human hatreds and antagonisms he was trying to heal; he was crushed by the factionalism of parties and the rivalry of nations. Faithful to his mission of service, he sacrificed his earthly life, but God raised him up to a new life of glory. The apostles were convinced that this was not just a beautiful story but an actual fact, and their conviction gave them the strength to commit themselves unreservedly to the way that Jesus had taught and practiced.

The Resurrection, then, is not merely a marvel that extrinsically validates whatever message Jesus might have proclaimed. It is a historically tangible concretization of that life-through-death which formed the core of Jesus' teaching. Paul caught the true meaning of the Resurrection when he wrote to the converts at Philippi:

> Let each of you look not only to his own interests, but also to the interests of others. Have this mind among yourselves, which you have in Christ Jesus, who, though he was in the form of God, did not count equality with God a thing to be grasped, but emptied himself, taking the form of a servant, being born in the likeness of men. And being found in human form he humbled himself and became obedient unto death, even death on a cross. Therefore God has highly exalted him and bestowed upon him the name which is above every name . . . (Phil. 2:4–9).

The "form of Christ" which every Christian is asked to put on must be seen, therefore, not statically but dynamically. It is a passage from an initial state of dignity, through self-humiliation for the sake of others, to final exaltation. It is a realization in actual life of the promise of the gospel that he who humbles himself will be exalted. And it is the pattern of the life to which every Christian commits himself by his acceptance of the gospel.

These reflections on a possible approach to Christianity are offered only for the sake of providing an example in which it may be possible to study the relationship between faith and reason. Undoubtedly some converts to Christianity have come by entirely different ways, while others who have studied approaches such as I have here outlined would find them completely unconvincing. I offer this outline, however, to indicate an approach which would be persuasive, I think, to many, including myself.

I do not of course deny that there are religions other than Christianity and that for each of them one could perhaps set forth rational approaches along the same lines as that which I have offered in speaking of the Christian ideal. In the last analysis, I believe, every authentic religious impulse draws a man closer to the kind of charity and courage that one finds embodied in the life of Christ; and thus I do not believe that there is any real conflict, or ultimate incompatibility, between the religions of sincere and generous men. They differ, rather, in the kind of experiences that they take as the material in which to discern and express man's authentic relationship to the divine.

Many Christians would probably feel that in my discussion of faith and reason I have put too much stress on the process of personal discovery and that I have underplayed the element of authority in faith. Invoking the Augustinian maxim, "Unless you believe, you shall not understand," some might argue that belief on the basis of authority comes first and that reason should enter only at a later stage. The role of reason, according to this view, would be simply to verify the credibility, and penetrate the meaning, of what has been already accepted by adherence to the tradition.

To this I would reply that, as Augustine himself recognized, the priorities between faith and reason are mutual. If reason is nourished by faith, faith is made possible by reason. "No one believes anything unless he has first thought that it is to be believed."[10] Before one can prudently lend credence to anyone else, one must have reasons for accepting him as an authority.[11] The most simple believers, in point of fact, have such reasons, though they do

not always spell them out. In the preceding pages I have
tried to indicate the type of reasoning which I suspect is
normally operative, in an existential and implicit way, in
practically any adherence to religious authority.

Christianity has a tremendously rich spiritual heritage,
built up over many centuries, and no one who is privileged to be raised a Christian should be hasty in dismissing this. His spontaneous inclination should be to accept
this tradition as his dwelling place unless he finds it to be
positively inadequate, and even then to try to remedy or
supplement it rather than to destroy or abandon it. My
remarks, then, are not intended to suggest that anyone
ought to suspend his allegiance to Christianity until he can
appropriate all its teachings as a matter of personal insight. But even while resting one's faith upon the authority
of tradition or ecclesiastical leaders, one would do well to
seek to make it progressively more a matter of personal
conviction.

An increasing number of Christians in our time are finding it hard to give full credit to the Christian tradition.
The reasons for this alienation are, in my opinion, chiefly
cultural and sociological. Modern, urban, secularized man
cannot experience God in the same way that his ancestors
did, and there is no reason why he should be forced to.
For the survival of Christianity as a major religion it is
important that new forms of creedal statement, new styles
of worship, and new ethical attitudes compatible with the
gospel should be encouraged. Contemporary man must
rediscover the Christian message in his own way: and when
this discovery is made, it will—I suspect—be as close to the
New Testament as were the styles of Christianity built
up in the Middle Ages or in early modern times. To facilitate this essential process of rediscovery, it is imperative
to gain a better grasp of the logic of man's normal approach to faith.

The standard apologetic has, I believe, been too rationalistic and jejune. It has relied too much on proof and
argument, as though faith could ever be the achievement
of technical reason. While insisting that the logic of faith
is not that of formal inference, I have sought to show that
faith has a logic of its own. Pascal recognized this when he
spoke of "reasons of the heart," Newman coined the term
"illative sense," and Polanyi writes of "tacit knowing." All

these terms illuminate what I have been calling here the "logic of discovery."

The logic of formal inference may have its uses for a man who wishes to see the connections between things he already believes, but it cannot lead to faith because it is incapable of engendering a new point of view. In syllogistic deduction, the categories of the conclusion must coincide those of the premises, and hence the conclusion cannot contain any real surprises.

In the logic of discovery, on the other hand, the inquirer proceeds with radical openness. He begins not with premises but with questions—questions that he accepts as real and urgent, even though he does not know exactly what they imply in terms of affirmation. These questions are religious if they touch on the ultimate meaning of man's life. A man is prepared to face the problem of God once he has asked, with passionate concern, whether moral obligation is binding in the face of death, whence comes the goodness, love, and generosity of the human heart, why the universe is at once so benign and yet so cruel, why the innocent suffer and the guilty go free. All these questions plainly exhibit the unintelligibility of the world as it appears on the surface. They put a man face to face with the issue of whether things finally have a hidden meaning or whether the universe is cold, indifferent, brutal, and absurd.

The logic of discovery, having begun with existential questions, passes on to the phase of contemplation. It gazes on the vast spectrum of human experience and seeks to determine whether there are high points in which the meaning of the whole is specially disclosed. In scanning the data a man looks not for proofs but for signs. He is like a stranger wandering in a forest who comes across markings on a rock. If the markings sufficiently resemble the letters of the alphabet, and if all the letters, taken together, make up intelligible words, he can securely judge, though he cannot prove to the hardened skeptic, that someone has been there and has expressed his mind. So it is possible for the religious inquirer to judge from certain sign-events that the true meaning of life and death has been disclosed.

For the Christian, the disclosure of the divine is not to be found in any precise answer. He has no solution to the problem of evil nor, for that matter, to the problem of good. He speaks of God, but he has no unambiguous experience of God and could not by any means attempt a definition of him. To the extent that he has an answer, the Christian points not to a statement but to a person. The meaning of life and of death is summed up for him in a person—Jesus the man of sorrows and Jesus the exalted one. In the identity-in-difference between these two stages in the life of Jesus, he finds the strength to live, and if necessary to die, in a meaningful and satisfying way, with courage and resolve. Jesus becomes for him the paradigm for the interpretation of man's total religious pilgrimage.

The logic of discovery, therefore, does not move merely from reason to faith or from faith to reason. It begins to a kind of inchoate faith by accepting the seriousness of ultimate questions. It ends in faith by accepting the value of an answer which, from a logical point of view, is no answer at all. The believer feels that he has encountered truth, and that truth, in the last analysis, is mystery. In union with God, as he appears in the form of Jesus, the Christian is convinced that he has come into contact with ultimate reality.

Unlike the logic of formal inference, the logic of discovery can lead to conversion. What discloses itself through religious signs is new and unexpected. It is not something that the mind can master, but something that masters the mind. The gospel proves its undying power by enabling men, generation after generation, to look upon the world, upon life, upon their own existence, with new eyes: to seek what previously they despised and to despise what previously they sought. So long as Christianity continues to win adherents of this sort, who live lives based on self-renunciation and service, it will continue to be a vital force in the world and will be equal to all the taxing problems of historical change.

Toward an Apologetics of Hope

The discussion of the rational approaches to faith in the preceding two chapters has already involved us in some consideration of apologetics. We have seen how a man with certain existential orientations might find in the death and Resurrection of Jesus the focus of meaning for his own life. In the present chapter I should like to attend more particularly to the dimension of hope in Christian apologetics.

Blaise Pascal, one of the most eminent apologists of all time, commented on man's ceaseless tendency to delve into his own past and future:

> We do not rest satisfied with the present. We anticipate the future as too slow in coming, as if in order to hasten its course; or we recall the past, to stop its too rapid flight. So imprudent are we that we wander in the times which are not ours, and do not think of the only one which belongs to us; and so idle are we that we dream of those times which are no more, and thoughtlessly overlook that which alone exists. . . . We scarcely ever think of the present; and if we think of it, it is only to take light from it to arrange the future. . . . The past and present are our means; the future alone is our end. So we never live, but we hope to live; and, as we are always preparing to be happy, it is inevitable that we should never be so.[1]

If this preoccupation with the future is inseparable from human nature, it has greatly intensified in our time, as the literary trends bear witness. A century ago it used to be common to write books about the origins of man and of civilization. Later it became fashionable to write about the recent past. Books included in their title the word "yesterday." Then it was thought necessary to write only about the contemporary; books did not sell unless they were entitled "today." But within the past few years even to write about the present is to invite boredom and disdain. Unless an author addresses himself to the future, he feels that he has no claim to be taken seriously. The dust jackets in our book stores therefore bear titles such as these: *The Future of Man, The Future of the Church, The Future of Religion, The Future of Belief,* even *The Future of God.* One can hardly suppress a sense of envy at the endowments of those who feel able to write so voluminously about things which have yet to come into being.

This increasing preoccupation with the future is no doubt a result of the progressive acceleration and radicalization of change. Until recently it seemed possible to look upon change as a superficial phenomenon that occurred only within a stable and immutable framework of nature. But modern science and technology have called into question, and to a great extent undermined, the apparent stability of nature itself. We know now that there are no immutable particles of matter; that the earth is in rapid and constant motion; and that there are no fixed stars above us. The days, the seasons, even the movements of the heavenly bodies are subject to interference and disruption. Man can even go to work on himself and drastically alter his own physical and mental constitution. Conscious of this, we have lost the secure feeling that what is basic and essential in reality is permanent.

It has generally been assumed, at least since the eighteenth century, that change means progress. With man's increasing mastery over himself and his environment, it began to appear that he could overcome most of the hostile forces that his ancestors had dreaded. Some God-is-dead theologians even proclaimed that God had become superfluous, now that man was in a position to do for himself the things which God had traditionally been supposed to do for him. But in the years since 1967, especially here in the United States, such optimism has all but vanished. The mounting social problems, the increase of crime and drug addiction, and the frustrations of the war in Vietnam are but symptoms of man's inability to carve out for himself the bright future of which he was but recently dreaming. Amid threats of thermonuclear disaster, violent revolution, world starvation, and environmental pollution, some are seriously questioning whether mankind can anticipate a tolerable existence on this planet—or any planet—for more than another generation or two. If the world has no future, is not all man's toil in vain? Might not a nuclear holocaust be the best escape from the impossible muddle in which man now finds himself?

For a ray of hope, some look to the religions. As Kant maintained in his *Critique of Pure Reason*, the question, "What may I hope for?" is the proper sphere of concern for religion.[2] And to this he added, in his *Critique of Practical Reason*, that the hope of happiness begins with religion only.[3] The current outburst of "theology of hope" literature reflects a serious effort on the part of Christian thinkers to meet the current wave of anxiety about what lies ahead.

The new theology of hope is not a mere fad, but the recovery of a basic theme that has not received its proper share of attention in classical theology. Judaeo-Christian faith, as set forth in the Bible, was always, most fundamentally, an acceptance of God's promise, and therefore it contained within itself an element of hope. According to the New Testament, to be a believer and to be a man of hope are practically synonymous. The heathen, for Paul, are "those who have no hope" (1 Th. 4:13). Abraham, in Paul's view, was the spiritual prototype of Christians inasmuch as he, "against hope, believed in hope" (Rom. 4:18). If Paul teaches—indeed as he does—that we are saved by faith (cf. Rom. 1:16–17, 3:28), he is equally ready to say that "in hope we have been saved" (Rom. 8:24). Faith itself, according to Hebrews 11:1, is "the assurance of things hoped for."

In terms of the recent emphasis on hope, the nature of theology is being redefined. For the traditional concept of theology as "faith seeking understanding" (*fides quaerens intellectum*), Jürgen Moltmann proposes to substitute the definition, "hope seeking understanding" (*spes quaerens intellectum*). A question must therefore be raised about apologetics. Traditionally it has been viewed as the effort to set forth in a systematic and convincing way the reasons that tell in favor of the truth of the Christian religion considered as a set of speculative statements about what God is and what God has done. Would it not be better today to think of apologetics as the discipline that seeks to exhibit the reasons for Christian hope? The centrality of hope to apologetics is indicated by the one text from the Bible that deals most explicitly with apologetics. 1 Peter 3:15 exhorts its readers: "Always be prepared to make a defense (*apologian*) to anyone who calls you to account for the hope that is in you." Without denying the necessity of an apologetics of faith, as traditionally understood, I should personally accept the desirability—and urgency—of an apologetics of hope.

The element of hope has not always been prominent in Christian apologetics. When Christian existence was conceived of primarily as an acceptance of eternal and necessary truths, apologetics concentrated primarily on showing that the Christian, rather than the pagan sage, was the true man of wisdom. In recent centuries, when revelation was viewed primarily in the categories of history, apologetics sought to show that men were obliged to accept the Christian message, since that message was so conspicuously accredited by prophecy and miracle. Only with the Modernists and Blondel do we begin to sense a new orientation. Reinterpreting religious truth in terms of the dynamism of the human spirit, they sought to show that Christianity leads to an enrichment and intensification of life. In this perspective apologetics became concerned with the capacity of Christianity to answer questions such as those asked by Blondel with passionate intensity at the beginning of his *L'Action* (1893): "Has human life or has it not a meaning, and has man a destiny?"[4] In his *Letter on Apologetics* (1896) Blondel points out that it is not sufficient to oblige a man to assent to religious truth as something imposed by extrinsic evidences. There must be something in the message of Christianity that meets man's inner aspirations and speaks to his anxieties and concerns. "Apologetics must tend not only to make us know and believe," writes Blondel in an article on Cardinal Victor Dechamps, "but . . . also and primarily to make us be and act more and better."[5] Thus the problem of credibility, for Blondel, could never be separated from the problems of human hope and destiny. With Blondel we are already on the way to an apologetics of hope, and in this respect he must be accounted the master of Pierre Teilhard de Chardin. Part of Teilhard's enormous influence is no doubt due to the fact that he, from his own specialized point of view, developed a full-fledged theology of hope. There is perhaps no other Christian thinker of whom this can be said.

Whatever one may hold about the nature of apologetics in general, it seems clear that an apologetics for our times must take seriously the problem of hope. It must answer the question, so insistently asked by many of our contemporaries, whether man's efforts are doomed to ultimate frustration or whether the things he does in time are laden with eternal consequences. Apologetical theology must take cognizance of the exorbitant hopes and fears which alternately raise man to the heights of optimism and plunge him into the depths of despondency. An apologetics of hope might be expected to establish two propositions: first, that it is fitting and proper for man always to hope and never to despair, and secondly, that Christianity sustains the type of hope that it is good for man to have. Of itself this argument does not prove that Christianity is true, but it provides strong reasons for taking the Christian message seriously.

At the outset it will be helpful to distinguish between hope and hopes—a distinction more easily made in French, which has the two words, *espérance* and *espoir*. By hope (in the sense of *espérance*) I mean a general attitude, a subjective stance of hopefulness. Such hopefulness is not tied to any determinate object, that is, to anything we can imagine within the sphere of worldly possibilities. No amount of money, health, friends, learning, or the like can ever so satisfy a man that he does not crave for something more. On the other hand, no amount of destitution or deprivation can ever annihilate man's hope. Man's hope, therefore, exceeds his hopes. As Gabriel Marcel puts it, "By a *nisus* which is peculiar to it, [hope] tends inevitably to transcend the particular objects to which it at first seems to be attached."[6]

There is an analogy here between hope and faith. Man's primordial attitude of faith, as an orientation to transcendent mystery, is incapable of being exhausted by any enumeration of truths in which we believe; faith itself is more than the beliefs by which it is articulated. So too, hope is neither essentially bound to, nor exhausted by, any of the determinate realities toward which our hopes are directed.

If one were to think of hope as essentially tied to particular objective realities, one could easily dismiss hope as fragile, if not illusory. Any one of the specifiable things for which we hope may fail to come to pass. Does this mean that our hope was excessive? Does disappointment teach us to hope less? Rather, disappointment might be described as an educative experience that weans our hope from illusory attachments and liberates it for the transcendent. When it is truly itself, hope can be detached from everything a man can specify to himself as its object.

The Heidelberg physician Herbert Plügge published in 1962 a number of psychological studies on incurably ill patients.[7] He found that, at the very point when the hope of a physical cure was abandoned, there very often arose not despair or bitterness but a vague and nameless kind of hope which he called "fundamental" or "authentic" hope. It was directed toward nothing that a person might expect to receive or "have," but rather, as Josef Pieper puts it, toward "what a person 'is,' with the selfness of the human being."[8] This inarticulate hope, transcending every kind of representation, is not destroyed by disappointments, but comes into its own through the loss of all illusions.

Despair, properly so called, is the abandonment of transcendent hope. When our particular hopes are disappointed, the possibility of despair confronts us. We are tempted to decide that there is no way out at all. But to assert this would be to anticipate our own destruction, to go to pieces under the threat of a sentence that has not yet been pronounced. The temptation to despair, by challenging the very existence of hope, enables it to rise to its full stature. "The truth is," writes Marcel, "that there can, strictly speaking, be no hope except where the temptation to despair exists. Hope is the act by which this temptation is actively and victoriously overcome."[9]

Is hope as a transcendent attitude justifiable? In contrast to many authors, who would seek to vindicate man's transcendent hope in terms of previously ascertainable grounds, Peter Berger argues from the fact of hope itself to the reality of the transcendent. The kind of hope we have been describing would be, in Berger's vocabulary, a "signal" of the transcendent. In his own words:

Man's "no" to death—be it in the frantic fear of his own annihilation, in moral courage at the death of a loved other, or in death-defying acts of courage and self-sacrifice—appears to be an intrinsic constituent of his being. There seems to be a death-refusing hope at the very core of our *humanitas*. While empirical reason indicates that this hope is an illusion, there is something in us that, however shamefacedly in an age of triumphant rationality, goes on saying "no!" and even says "no!" to the ever so plausible explanations of empirical reason.[10]

Since transcendent hope, by its very nature, goes against the appearances, one would look in vain for external evidences establishing its validity. By its nature it is "hope against hope." But man's spontaneous tendency to hope is itself an evidence, "the evidence of things unseen." Hope bears witness to its own divine origin when it feels secure enough to dispense with the conventional calculations of human prudence and to do without empirical support.

If there is any rational (or discursive) justification for this vague, implicit, transcendental hope, I should be inclined to seek it, somewhat as Kant did, in the realm of practical reason. Kant argued that without belief in God and in immortality—without acceptance of a God who knows us for what we are and who rewards our reverent fidelity—a man would not have the necessary motivation to submit, as he knows he ought to, to the demands of the moral law. Kant here substantiates, within the framework of his own systematic position, Plato's contention that it is impossible for the good man to be harmed by doing good, even though he must pay the price of life himself. Plato goes further than Kant in maintaining that the moral argument for a future life has speculative as well as practical validity. For if it were not speculatively true, we should have to admit that the universe is ultimately immoral and absurd. Besides, a hope that it is necessary for man to have in order to live well cannot be illusory and deceptive. Otherwise man would be simultaneously obliged to believe (on practical grounds) and to disbelieve (on speculative grounds). He would be in an absurd and contradictory situation.

The pragmatic argument for the legitimacy of hope can easily be substantiated by instances from a variety of situations. I have already referred to the medical studies of

Plügge on patients facing the prospect of imminent death from incurable diseases. Similar findings are offered by many studies of the behavior of prisoners in concentration camps during World War II. Viktor Frankl in his little classic, *Man's Search for Meaning*, speaks of the moral and physical degeneration of prisoners once they had lost their faith in the future. "Any attempt to restore man's inner strength in the camp [at Auschwitz] had first to succeed in showing him some future goal. . . . Woe to him who saw no more sense in his life, no aim, no purpose, and therefore no point in carrying on. He was soon lost."[11]

The ultimate meaningfulness of life, as Frankl has said in this and other works, cannot possibly depend on external and contingent factors. He speaks of the "purgatory" that he himself endured in the concentration camp after the loss of the manuscript of his first book:

> Later, when my own death seemed imminent, I asked myself what my life had been for. Nothing was left which would survive me. No child of my own. Not even a spiritual child such as the manuscript. But after wrestling with my despair for hours, shivering from typhus fever, I finally asked myself what sort of meaning could depend on whether a manuscript of mine was printed. I would not give a damn for it. But if there is a meaning, it is unconditional meaning, and neither suffering nor dying can detract from it.[12]

Frankl here comes close to repeating, in a far different theological framework, what Josef Pieper maintained in his 1951 lecture "The Hope of the Martyrs," namely, that there is no point in speaking seriously about hope unless there is hope for the martyr—that is, for one whose expectations within this world have been entirely erased.[13]

To verify the beneficial effects of a transcendent hope, we do not need to limit ourselves to boundary situations such as the death camps and religious martyrdom. Daily life puts heavy demands on men's generosity, patience, tolerance, courage, and perseverance. Transcendent hope, by placing man's true security beyond anything this world can give or take away, bestows a sovereign freedom of action. It protects a man from falling prey to a cynical nihilism that is at root bitter and rebellious. It helps to cure the weakness that undermines our best efforts. If we could really locate our hopes where the center of meaning of our lives is to be found—that is, in a transcendent fulfillment—we would not react so defensively when our position, reputation, or property is attacked. We would not become hostile, aggressive, devious, and dishonest. A transcendent hope, freeing us from pessimism and anxiety, would enable us to commit ourselves generously and enthusiastically to the tasks before us and if necessary to accept what, in the eyes of men, appears to be defeat.

Presupposing now that transcendent hope is justifiable, either intuitively by reason of its own attributes or discursively by reason of its beneficial effects, and that despair is never an appropriate human attitude, I should like now to turn to my second major point, to the effect that Christianity is to be esteemed as a provider of hope. The non-Christian, as we have seen, can possess very meaningful implicit (or nameless) hope. But Christianity, I shall maintain, is a uniquely powerful thematization of hope, and as such it focuses, directs, and fortifies the fragile, existential hope which we have thus far been considering.

In the remarks that follow I shall not attempt to compare Christianity with any other religion, though such comparison would be relevant to a complete apologetics. I shall simply compare the condition of the Christian with that of the man who lacks any articulate religious faith.

First of all, it must be recognized that the Christian doctrine of God and man gives powerful motives for hope. God, according to the Bible, is both loving and powerful. If he were loving but not powerful, our hope would not be secure, because he might prove incapable of accomplishing the good things he intends. If, on the other hand, God were powerful but not loving, men would still have no solid basis for hope. Instead they would have to stand in dread of God's arbitrary cruelty or of his just punishments. The God of the Bible, however, is both powerful and forgiving. His mercy is above all his works. Since God both rewards the virtuous and holds out hope of pardon to the wicked, belief in him brings with it a lively and consoling hope.

Christian anthropology, moreover, is able to account for man's irrepressible tendency to hope, of which we have been speaking, and to show the justification for this tendency. According to the New Testament, hope is instilled in us by the Holy Spirit who has been poured forth into our hearts and who gives testimony within us that we are sons of God and fellow heirs with Christ (Rom. 8:14–17). Being gifted already with the "first fruits of the Spirit" (*ibid.*, v. 23), we have already received some anticipation of the eternal blessings. This grace-experience provides the psychological basis for that capacity of "hope against hope" that is so highly praised by the biblical writers.

Theology therefore puts us in a position to account, in some degree, for the transcendent hope so admirably described by Marcel and Berger. Hope, like faith, is a grace. It is grounded not in anything that a man can point to or objectively verify, but in a deep preconceptual experience of the God who lovingly communicates himself in grace.

By accepting the Christian doctrine of God and man, we can solidify and thematize the implicit hope that arises, by a kind of instinct, within the human heart. The theological reasons give strength, security, clarity, and joy to a hope that would otherwise be troubled, threatened, and obscure. Revelation enables us to proclaim a hope of which we should otherwise only stammer.

If we take time to examine more closely the attributes of Christian hope, we shall be further struck by its capacity to bring out the best that is in man. Christianity offers man a hope that is invincible, comprehensive, realistic, and fruitful. Let me say a few words about each of these four attributes.

Christian hope is *invincible* because it is founded not on creatures but on God. We cannot entrust ourselves with total confidence to any created agency. The evolutionary process, not being God, might fall short of its goal. Our fellow men, even at best, are not completely reliable, and therefore we should not totally rely upon them. Of Jesus himself it is written that he did not entrust himself to those who believed in him, "for he himself knew what was in man" (Jn. 2:25).

A hope totally centered on God cannot collapse because it is built upon an unshakable foundation. "Heaven and earth will pass away, but my words will not pass away" (Mt. 24:35). Because it rests upon the one who alone can never prove false, our hope is well described in Hebrews 6:19 as a "sure and steadfast anchor of the soul." Expressing this sense of invincibility, Paul can conclude his great hymn to hope in Romans 8:38–39 with the triumphant cry: "I am sure that neither death, nor life, nor angels, nor principalities, nor things present, nor things to come, nor powers, nor height, nor depth, nor anything else in all creation will be able to separate us from the love of God in Christ Jesus our Lord."

The second characteristic of Christian hope is its *comprehensiveness*, its unlimited breadth. It is not simply an individual hope, a hope of each man for himself. A purely private hope might narrow man's outlook, making him selfish and inconsiderate. Theology, however, teaches that God's redemptive love, the basis of our hope, is extended to all men in Christ. There is not a single individual on earth—even the most obdurate sinner—for whom we may not and should not hope. We therefore hope not just for ourselves but for one another. We are brought together into a community of hope. "There is one body and one Spirit, just as you were called to the one hope that belongs to your call" (Eph. 4:4). The corporate dimension of our hope is expressed in various biblical images, such as that of the "Kingdom of God." In the final Kingdom our common hope will be fulfilled in such a way that we will be sharers in one another's joy.

To speak of the Kingdom of God in terms of human solidarity is still too narrow. In its full meaning, hope embraces even the inanimate world. Paul, in Romans 8:19–22, tells us that the whole of creation "waits with eager longing for the revealing of the sons of God"; all creation is "groaning in travail together" until such time as it will be "set free from its bondage to decay." Man's hope, therefore, extends to the material world about him. With the apocalyptic writers of the Old and New Testaments, we can eagerly anticipate "a new heaven and a new earth" (Is. 65:17, 66:22; 2 Pet. 3:13; Apoc. 21:1). In these days of ecological consciousness it is well to reflect on the cosmic dimensions of our Christian hope.

Thirdly, Christian hope is *realistic*. It can look at the world with sober realism and is not obliged to take refuge in illusions. The Christian has no need to shrink in fear from the prospect of poverty, disgrace, captivity, physical pain, apparent failure, even death. None of these eventualities dejects him because he has been taught that to share in Christ's sufferings is the normal way to prepare oneself to share in his glory. He does not feel compelled to look upon man's future, in some pollyannish way, as an endless progress. He soberly recognizes that no utopia will ever be constructed through human planning.

The Christian has little enthusiasm for what Ernst Bloch holds forth as the ideal of a "messianic kingdom of God—without God."[14] Such a dream bears all the marks of an illusion concocted by an alienated mind. Like a mirage, it recedes further and further into the distance as we march toward it. And even if attainable it would not satisfy the deepest cravings of the human spirit. If man could be so domesticated that he ceased to yearn for the transcendent, he would have forfeited his greatest claim to dignity. In reply to Friedrich Nietzsche, Père de Lubac acutely observed: " 'Nothing but the earth' is the cruellest of all illusions."[15]

Lastly, Christian hope is *fruitful*. Rightly understood, it is not a sterile aspiration for eternity that divests the things of time of all interest and importance. The believer knows well that his own redemption and that of his fellow men will not be accomplished without human co-operation. Like the Incarnate Christ, the Christian is turned in compassion toward the earth and its children. Only by seeking to realize on earth some anticipation of the Kingdom of God can we hope to have a part in the final Kingdom in eternity. Christian hope therefore impels us to follow Christ in his life of obedience and service. In view of the biblical teaching, "as a man sows, so shall he reap," we dare not be idle.

It is often objected that because Christian hope is concentrated on what happens beyond historical time, it deprives man's activity on earth of any real significance. This charge, at its most extreme, includes the accusation that religion is the "opium of the people" and that it seeks to quiet men's legitimate aspirations by promising them "pie in the sky." This charge is difficult to answer because Christians are not totally agreed as to the relationship between man's toil on earth and the final consummation of history. Some world-renouncing eschatologists profess a basically Neoplatonic contempt for the world and concentrate almost exclusively on the blessings of the life to come. Other socially involved Christians stress the importance of human activity almost to the point of seeming to hold that man has a commission to build the Kingdom of God here on earth.

A balanced view, in my opinion, would avoid both these extremes. God does not dispose of man without regard for what man makes of himself. But the completed Kingdom, according to the Christian sources, is not something that man can achieve by his own planning and resourcefulness. Just as the Resurrection of Jesus presupposes that Jesus lived and died in total fidelity to God, so the final transfiguration of the cosmos presupposes that men have labored and suffered in selfless love. In this sense, man's fidelity to the moral demands of the gospel is a precondition for the full realization of the Kingdom. It is not necessary, however, that man's efforts should always be attended by what the world can recognize as success. It is quite possible that Christ's faithful followers, like their master, may have to suffer rejection and humiliation. This they can willingly accept because their hope is transcendent.

The most celebrated contemporary apologist of Christian hope, Teilhard de Chardin, seems to express a more terrestrial hope. At one point he suggests as the hypothesis most congenial to his system that the final maturation of mankind will consist in a gradual recession of evil. "Disease and hunger," he writes, "will be conquered by science and we will no longer need to fear them in any acute form. And, conquered by the sense of the earth and human sense, hatred and internecine struggles will have disappeared in the ever-warmer radiance of Omega. Some sort of unanimity will reign over the entire mass of the noösphere. The final convergence will take place in *peace*."[16] This, however, is only one of several possibilities envisaged by Teilhard. In various texts he admits darker eventualities as also likely: on the material plane, the exhaustion of the physical resources of the planet, and, on the human plane, a profound schism leading to a paroxysm of evil, an ecstasy of discord, a strike in the noösphere.[17]

Authentic Christian hope, I submit, is not tied to any particular speculation about the manner in which history will close. We should not imitate those sects that seem to specialize in esoteric interpretations of apocalyptic texts so as to excite the imaginations and emotions of the faithful. The Bible, having no intention of supplying detailed predictions, is content to speak in figurative or hyperbolic language about the events of the end-time. The trustful believer, secure in the faith that God is Lord of history, is content to leave to him not only the times and the moments, but also the circumstances of the Parousia.

The only point I should wish to underscore, in the present context, is that man's activity is not futile. Every thought and word as well as every deed makes an eternal difference. The time and characteristics of the final Kingdom will depend, to some extent, upon man's fidelity to his mission. In a certain sense, man has a hope because he has a mission. Because God has committed a task to man, man can be sure that God will be with those who faithfully perform their mission and that he will crown their efforts in the end.

Before concluding I should like to say a word about the special urgency of Christian hope today. On this point, too, Teilhard de Chardin can be our guide. He was essentially correct, I believe, in his analysis of the historical juncture in which we find ourselves. All over the world, he noted, men are being forced together into closer union thanks to new media of communications, expanding governmental and business networks, and burgeoning associations for purposes of every kind. It is becoming increasingly difficult to exist, act, or even think alone. In fact, it appears almost as though mankind were turning into a huge superorganism; and this situation is fraught with immense dangers as well as immense opportunities for good. Many, repelled by the threat of depersonalization and enslavement, seek to resist this process of planetary collectivization. Hence the necessity for hope:

> The modern world, with its prodigious growth of complexity, weighs incomparably more heavily upon the shoulders of our generation than did the ancient world upon the shoulders of our forebears. Have you never felt that this added load needs to be compensated for by an added passion, a new sense of purpose? To my mind, this is what is "providentially" arising to sustain our courage—the hope, the belief that some immense fulfillment lies ahead of us.[18]

Elsewhere Teilhard lays down as the essential prerequisite for man's further advance "a great hope held in common." Hope alone, he maintained, can arouse a passionate longing to grow and can overcome all enervating skepticism, pessimism, weakness of spirit, and heaviness of heart. A hope proportioned to our times, moreover, must make for greater synthesis and unity. "Our hope can only be realized if it finds its expression in greater cohesion and greater human solidarity."[19]

As an apologist to the world of science, Teilhard sought to foster "this great hope held in common" by a retrospective panorama of the evolutionary process as it has taken place thus far. In view of the triumphs of biological evolution against almost incredible odds, he thought it necessary to postulate as an explanation a powerful force of attraction drawing the whole process forward toward itself as the point of ultimate convergence. This hypothesis of an "Omega Center," as Teilhard called it, converged remarkably, in his opinion, with the biblical doctrine of the universal Christ. For the Christian, therefore, Teilhard reasoned, Omega was not merely a scientific hypothesis, but a fact to be accepted in faith. The cosmic Christ in Teilhard's system provides the believer with unshakable confidence in the future success of the evolutionary process.

Some have criticized Teilhard's "apologetics of hope" on the ground that it relies too much on merely empirical reasoning regarding the process of biological evolution.[20] There is some basis for this charge, but it should be recognized that biological evolution, as a scientific datum, is not the central feature of Teilhard's apologetic of hope. Instead he is at pains to insist that revelation is needed to set man's hope on a secure basis. The death and Resurrection of Christ, as Christopher Mooney points out, were for Teilhard "the sole guarantee that God's designs for his universe must inexorably succeed in spite of all opposition."[21]

As presently informed, I should be inclined to quarrel with Teilhard's apparent view that the occurrence of the Parousia must depend upon the prior success of man's biological and technological evolution on earth. If he had said only that the generous dedication of men animated by selfless love is a necessary prerequisite, I should have no difficulty in agreeing. By inspiring and demanding such selfless love, Christianity has a mission of eschatological import. By setting forth before mankind the figure of the crucified and risen Lord, the Church can inspire the type of hope most needed by mankind, especially in this crucial period of planetization. Christianity is uniquely adapted to arouse that "great hope held in common" that Teilhard correctly identified as a demand of our times. Thus I believe that there is great value in Teilhard's apologetic of hope.

I do not propose an apologetics of hope as self-sufficient, still less as a substitute for all other forms of apologetics. To show the full credibility of the Christian message it is necessary, today as always, to appeal to the data of history. The story of Jesus of Nazareth cannot be by-passed, for Jesus himself is the most striking sign of the truth of his own message. The Resurrection of Jesus stands as the most powerful expression of God's omnipotent redemptive love. But the Resurrection remains largely inaccessible to the historian, if he follows the conventional methods of scientific research. He has no way of dealing with such a unique phenomenon, in which the barriers between time and eternity dissolve and the end of all history is anticipated. To accept the reality of this event one must already be, or at least one must be disposed to become, a man of transcendental hope. Only he who is prepared to believe in God who finally triumphs over every enemy, not excepting death, can credit the testimonies.

The estimate which one makes of the credibility of the accounts, therefore, depends in great measure on how he hopes. As Moltmann has well said, "the point of the historical debate on the resurrection of Christ was never merely historical."[22] The real question at issue is "a struggle for the future of history and for the right way of recognizing, hoping, and working for that future."[23] Thus the apologetics of history, as it deals with the Resurrection, interlocks with the apologetics of hope. What one makes of the narratives depends in great part on how one answers the question: "What may I hope for?"

To be generally effective in persuading men to accept the gospel, an apologetics of hope would have to be something more than a theory about what Christians ought to be. It would have to be a convincing description of what they actually are. In the world today, the churchgoing public does not always appear as a radiant sign of hope. Christians, like other men, seem to be primarily concerned for those things which, in the words of Jesus, the heathen seek (cf. Mt. 6:32). They are worried about material possessions, honors, and the like. For this reason, more than any other, they are often anxious and disturbed, gloomy and dejected. They do not really put their trust in God. Thus they become, in some measure, a countersign of hope.

Apologetics can at least point out that these attitudes are obstacles to Christian proclamation. Before addressing itself to unbelievers, apologetics has a task with regard to Christians, many of whom are greatly in need of conversion to the gospel. If it can persuade the Christian faithful to accept wholeheartedly the hope that is their rightful heritage, apologetics may perhaps make an important contribution to the future of the Church. An apologetics of hope, therefore, in my opinion, is much to be desired.

II. TEACHERS IN THE CHURCH

— 5 —

Authority and Pluralism in the Church

In the preceding chapters we have considered how the forms of Christian faith, and the rational grounds to which believers appeal, vary in different ages and cultures and are continuing to vary in our day. Although I have not entirely ignored the dimension of community, I have not focused in these chapters on the Church as the community of faith. In the next few chapters, therefore, I propose to consider the Church as a society that lives by, and publicly attests to, the revelation of Christ. We shall particularly consider the role of those whose task it is to articulate the official doctrinal stance of the Church. To what extent should ecclesiastical authority insist upon doctrinal unity, and within what limits should it tolerate diversity within the Church itself? These problems are particularly vexing in an age of swift and radical change—an age, moreover, in which pluriformity and personal authenticity are highly prized.

In the present chapter I shall consider the general outlines of the problems of authority versus freedom and uniformity versus pluralism as they confront all Christian Churches in our day. In the first part of this chapter I shall treat of the nature and functions of authority; then, in a second part, I shall turn to the questions of uniformity and pluralism. Finally, in a brief closing section, I shall call attention to some of the most pressing problems that grow out of the analysis just made, and that, in one way or another, confront nearly all Christian communions in our time.

When we hear the word "authority" most of us spontaneously think of something negative. We think of persons whose role is to impose unwelcome obligations, to restrict free development and inquiry, to pass sentence, to inflict penalties. Our primary image of authority is that of the lawmaker, the judge, the policeman. This coercive notion of authority, I submit, is entirely too narrow and juridical. Viewed in its full dimensions, authority can be seen as an indispensable instrument for promoting freedom and vitality.

If we go back to the root meaning of the term, it seems ironic that a term etymologically connected with creativity (Latin *auctor*, meaning "creator" or "author") and growth (Latin *auctio*, meaning "growth") should have come to suggest inhibition and diminishment. Even today, however, these negative elements do not always predominate. When I say, for instance, that George Lyman Kittredge was an authority on Shakespeare, or that Mahatma Gandhi enjoyed great authority among his people, the implication is that these gentlemen had certain admirable qualities and that people freely accepted their influence as a source of personal or social enrichment. An authority, therefore, is one entitled to respect, whose opinions are presumed to be trustworthy and who is looked to for guidance and direction. The term applies most aptly to a leader of vision and conviction—to one who "speaks with authority."

At this point it may be helpful to distinguish between authority and power. The two may in fact coincide, so that power is exercised by way of authority, and authority makes itself felt as power. But the two terms, considered in their essential meaning, are by no means synonymous. Authority is always a moral interrelationship between free and rational subjects—that is to say, between persons. Power, on the other hand, may be sheerly physical. It can be exerted by dead matter as well as by persons; and it can be used upon lifeless things, animals, or insane and unwilling subjects.

Unlike "power," moreover, the term "authority" generally connotes a moral right or entitlement. It does not on the other hand, necessarily include the capacity to effect what it intends. Thus a person may have authority without power or power without authority.

Because of its importance for what we shall be saying

in later pages, the interpersonal character of authority deserves to be emphasized. Authority does not inhere initially in laws, books, or institutions, but rather in persons. Things, such as laws and books, can become authorities only insofar as they are objectifications of the personal spirit. Authority has its origin in a relationship of respect and trust of persons toward other persons. No man is an authority to himself, but he may be an authority for others, as others may be for him.

Every social organization includes persons placed in authority. A civil society (such as the State) is built upon certain commonly accepted goals and procedures, set forth in constitutional declarations and legal documents which then become recognized as "authorities." These laws and principles, embodying the personal and corporate wisdom of the fathers, are then interpreted and applied by presumptively competent persons, who are also, in their way, "authorities." In civil society certain authorities will be invested with the power to use physical coercion, if need be, for the furtherance of the ends of the society. In a voluntary society, such as a golf club or professional association, the officers will commonly have only moral power, but this too may be, in its way, coercive. The officers can normally bring moral pressure to bear by holding forth the prospect of honors and rewards or, on the contrary, by denying the privileges of membership to those who offend against the principles of the society.

Any religious group will be equipped with a whole system of authorities that are regarded as providing a secure path to the salvation or union with God, which is the aim and goal of religion. Where internal conflicts become severe this is generally a sign of disagreement within the community as to the relative priorities to be assigned to various authorities. Hence, for the preservation and vitality of any religious community, it is important to confront in all seriousness the question of authority.

The religious authorities are, in the first instance, the God or gods recognized by the community. Secondarily, they are the created agencies through which the divine is thought to manifest itself. Some such manifestations are transient and unpredictable; others are stable and habitual. Thus in any religion it is normal to find a certain tension between the charismatic and the sacerdotal, between event and institution.

In the biblical religions the authority par excellence is Yahweh, the God of Israel. A central theme of the Old Testament is that Israel should put its trust in him alone. He is the Creator and Savior of Israel and, indeed, Creator and rightful Lord of the whole universe. "Turn to me and be saved, all the ends of the earth! For I am God and there is no other," runs the refrain of Second Isaiah (see Is. 45:22, etc.). Israel's faith and action as a religious people are totally determined by the word of God.

Even within Israel, however, there are conflicts regarding the locus of authority. How was the word of the Lord to be identified? To the extent that God was felt to be present addressing his people through the Mosaic Law, the Law became authoritative. But in addition to the Law, and in partial tension with it, were other authorities such as the priestly interpreters, who expounded and defended the tradition, and the prophets, who uttered the "word of God" in new and timely revelations. The people were sometimes divided according to which prophets they regarded as authentic and how far they were committed to the Law and the priestly traditions.

What is characteristic of the New Testament is of course that God was thought to have expressed himself fully, definitively, and for all mankind in the life, teaching, death, and Resurrection of Jesus of Nazareth—or, more briefly, in the "Christ event." For Christians Jesus Christ is the living Word of God; and in his case it may be said unequivocally that "the Word is God." Whatever disagreement there may be among Christians regarding the secondary loci of authority, they are at one in looking upon the Incarnate Logos as the authority par excellence.

On the basis of the New Testament, it is undeniable that Christianity is fundamentally a "religion of authority." It comes into the world as a definite message to be believed and proclaimed as the path to truth and salvation. Jesus selects disciples, trains them, tells them what to say, sends them forth as messengers. Where not accepted, they are to "shake the dust from [their] feet" (Mt. 10: 14). For the early community, the gospel unquestionably demands the "obedience of faith" (Rom. 1:5, 16:26). It is not something that can be freely tampered with by men. "Even if we or an angel of heaven should preach to you a gospel contrary to that which we preached to you, let him be accursed." (Gal. 1:8).

After Pentecost, Christ continues to exercise his authority in the Church by means of his Spirit. When Christians appeal to the Holy Spirit, they are looking to a divine authority that can in no way be brought into conflict with Christ or with the Father, provided only that the Spirit be rightly discerned.

While Christians of all ages agree in taking Christ and his Spirit as the supreme authority, this agreement does not prevent the occurrence of serious disputes concerning the secondary loci of authority. Where is the gospel of Christ to be authentically found? Different views on this matter have been a perpetual source of conflict and division within the Christian tradition. In broad strokes one may distinguish between more "catholic" positions, which tend to identify Christ's saving message rather closely with a given ecclesiastical tradition, and "protestant" positions which tend to criticize all created authorities in the name of the Word of God or the Holy Spirit. In a characteristically "protestant" response to the efforts of the Nazis to organize the "German Christian" movement, the Barmen Declaration of 1934 asserted the sole lordship of Jesus Christ. "We repudiate the false teaching that the church can and must recognize yet other happenings and powers, images and truths as divine revelation alongside of this one Word of God, as a source of her preaching."[1]

But even the Barmen Declaration, while rejecting the idea of revelation through secular history, had to refer to some particular places in which the genuine Christ was found. "Jesus Christ, as he is testified to us in the Holy Scripture, is the one Word of God whom we are to hear, whom we are to trust and obey in life and death."[2] But the reference to Scripture immediately raises another question: Where is Scripture rightly heard and interpreted? According to the Barmen Declaration, "The Christian church is the community of brethren in which Jesus Christ presently works in the word and sacraments through the Holy Spirit."[3] Thus the lordship of Jesus Christ, even in this strongly "protestant" interpretation, includes the authority of the Holy Spirit, that of the Bible, Christian preaching, sacramental worship, and finally that of the gathered community. These are "authoritative" insofar as they enable man to find the word of God in its fullness and purity.

In speaking of the secondary authorities we have inevitably raised the long and bitterly debated question of Scripture versus tradition—a question far too subtle and complicated to be dealt with in a satisfactory way in a summary treatment such as this. Suffice it to say here that I see no advantage in setting these two types of authority off against each other, as though what were given to the one were taken away from the other. Tradition is, most fundamentally, the way in which the authority of Scripture becomes manifest and effective for generations who live in post-apostolic times. Tradition lives off Scripture and, at the same time, makes Scripture live.

By Scripture we mean the authentic literary objectification of the faith of the people of God during its formative period—from the earliest times until the end of the apostolic age. This period is "canonical," or normative, for the subsequent life of the Church, and hence its authentic expressions have undying importance. By "tradition" we normally mean the authentic expressions of the life of the people of God in later generations. To ask what expressions are authentic is to raise the question where tradition is to be found; and this is where the Christian Churches seem to disagree. Expressions of the ongoing life of the Church are authoritative only because and insofar as the Holy Spirit is deemed to be active in the community, assisting it to interpret the gospel rightly. Thus the authority of the community can in no way be set up in opposition to God.

In most Christian bodies, several types of authority exist concurrently. On the one hand there is the juridical and public authority of the highest officers—whether pope, bishops, or ruling bodies, such as assemblies, synods, and councils. These officials make their authority felt, normally, by issuing documents, which are regarded as normative for the group. On the other hand, there are private authorities, which in their own way are no less important than the officials. Under this heading one would have to include, first, scholars, who speak on the basis of their research and professional competence. Secondly, there are "charismatic persons" who seem to be endowed with a more than common measure of the true Christian spirit. Like the prophets of old, these charismatics often feel impelled to criticize the officials and scholars, to rebuke them for their infidelity and insensitivity. Finally, there is the authority of consensus. In the Church, public opinion is definitely a force to be reckoned with, especially in this democratic age.

As has been said above, Christianity recognizes only one absolute authority—that of God himself. This means that all the secondary authorities are subject to criticism and correction. Every created channel that manifests God and brings men to him is capable also of misleading men and turning them away from God. If the secondary authorities were absolutized, Christianity would fall into idolatry and thus defect from the "radical monotheism" on which it is based.

Christianity owes its peculiar genius in great part to its delicately balanced system of authorities. If all the authorities are permitted to function within their respective spheres and are prevented from exceeding their proper limits, the Christian faith retains both its continuity with its own past and its ability to adapt itself to new situations. No one of the secondary religious authorities is absolute. As Tillich has shown, not even the most rigid biblicist ever succeeds in making an absolute out of the Bible; the Bible is always read in the light of tradition, even when the tradition adopts the slogan, "Scripture alone." As Karl Rahner, Hans Küng, and others have shown, Roman Catholicism could not make the pope an absolute authority without violence to its own fundamental principles. The authority of the pope is intrinsically connected with other authorities: Scripture, the monuments of tradition, the universal episcopate, and the living faith of the Church as a whole.

In practice, therefore, Christianity lives off a combination of irreducibly distinct but inseparably connected authorities. When the authorities mutually confirm each other, their weight is greater. When any one authority is absolutized at the expense of others, it weakens itself and loses credibility.

Periodically, in the history of the Church, shifts occur in the emphasis given to one or another of the secondary authorities. In some periods, Scripture itself seems to give direct answers to the urgent questions; in others, Scripture does not seem to offer more than a remote foundation for answers that have to be worked out afresh. In some eras, implicit confidence is placed in the hierarchy of office; in others, greater importance is attached to expertise of the scholar, the insight of the prophet, or the consensus of the faithful. In periods of transition, when people are critical of the particular forms authority has assumed in the recent past, it may seem that authority itself is being contested and undermined; but on reflection, and in a wider perspective, it becomes apparent that authority is merely changing its forms. Authority seems to be a permanent feature, which will endure as long as Christianity itself.

At the present moment, the problem of authority confronts different Churches in different ways. In some Churches, such as the Roman Catholic, the vertical authority of office seems to be yielding somewhat to the horizontal authority of consensus.[4] In nearly all churches, including the Roman Catholic, the continuing authority of long-standing tradition is being challenged by the contemporary authority of public opinion. While some are apprehensive that all authority is being undermined, the greater danger is perhaps that the new forms of authority are being too uncritically accepted. For the good of the community, it is necessary to make room for loyal dissent, including the right to stand aloof from the most recent forms of popular enthusiasm. Church structures often serve to safeguard the independence of the scholar, the prophet, the man out of phase with his times. Ecclesiastical authority often protects creative thinkers from the indignation of the uninformed and it often defends minority groups from the encroachments of the majority. Thus our reflections on authority lead naturally into a consideration of unity and diversity in the Church.

Authority, of which we have spoken thus far, is generally, and rightly, regarded as a unitive force. Since every society is a unity of order, a primary function of the social authorities is to co-ordinate the activities of the members for the sake of the common good. In the Christian community, authority is not simply a means of achieving arbitrarily chosen goals, but is constitutive of the Church itself. Because God has spoken authoritatively in Jesus Christ, the Church can and must speak and act decisively. Since there is only one Lord and one Spirit, and one gospel expressive of both, the Church must necessarily be one. The Church, theologically considered, is the one body of Christ and the one temple of the Holy Spirit. The various secondary authorities in the Church solidify and perfect the unity of the Church itself.

Notwithstanding all disagreements about the form that the unity of the Church must take, no Christian can seriously deny that the Church must be one. It stands in the world as a sign that Christ has torn down all barriers and that there is no longer any wall of division between Jew and Gentile, between Greek and barbarian, between bondsman and freeman. The Church must be internally one because otherwise it could not perform its function of gathering together in the name of Christ the scattered children of God. According to Vatican Council II, the Church is a "sign and instrument," that is to say, a "sacrament," of the unity willed by God for all mankind.[5]

Granted the necessary unity of the Church, it must still be asked what form this unity must take. In any society the unity must be a variegated and dynamic one; for a society is by nature a communion of many individuals whose individuality is not lost, but hopefully enhanced, by their mutual association. Each individual in the Church is called to union with God in a fashion proper to himself and has a properly personal contribution to make to the total life of the Church. The Holy Spirit, says Paul, looking toward the common good, "apportions to each one individually as he wills" (1 Cor. 12:7, 11).

According to what we may call the "principle of incarnation," the gospel demands to be realized in distinctive ways in different social contexts. It is therefore proper that local churches should differ from one another: Athens is not Corinth, Rome is not Jerusalem, Bombay is not New York. It is proper, also, that Christianity should adapt itself to temporal changes. As we saw in Chapter 1, Christian history can be divided into a number of major eras— such as the apostolic, the patristic, the medieval, the early modern, and the contemporary. Each major cultural shift has brought about innovations in doctrine, in ecclesiastical structures, in modes of worship, and in ethical patterns.

Without imagining that there is any such thing as a timeless and universal essence of Christianity, which could be predicated univocally of each realization, we must consciously distinguish between Christianity itself and any one of its historical incarnations. Such a distinction is necessary not only for sociological, but also for properly theological reasons.

This is true, in the first place, because Christian faith bears primarily on the ineffable mystery of God himself in his free and loving self-donation to man. The revelation can be thematized in terms of the expressive materials offered by any given culture (its secular experience, its historical memories, its characteristic modes of thought, and its literary usages), but this thematization cannot be communicative to persons who do not—at least by an effort of imagination—identify themselves with the culture in question. Christianity therefore has to be constantly re-thematized; its message has to be translated into the patterns called for by new sociocultural contexts.

Secondly, pluriformity is permitted and demanded by the pilgrim status of the Church, as underscored by the ecclesiology that prevailed both at the Faith and Order Conference at Lund (1952) and at Vatican Council II. Theology, both Protestant and Catholic, today clearly recognizes that the Church has not arrived at its final destination, but is still groping its way through the vicissitudes of history. It must therefore adapt its forms of thought and expression to the successive situations in which faith finds itself.

Thirdly, pluriformity is encouraged by the diversity and mutual tension among the authoritative organs of revelation, as enumerated earlier in this chapter. God's self-revelation in Christ comes to man as refracted through different agencies, all of them humanly conditioned.

The Old Testament contains a multitude of contrasting ideas, sometimes registering doctrinal developments achieved over the course of time, sometimes reflecting tensions between different schools, such as the priestly, the royal, the prophetic, the apocalyptic, and the sapiential.

Similar tensions may be found within the New Testament itself. Ernst Käsemann correctly maintains that "the variability of the kerygma in the New Testament is an expression of the fact that in primitive Christianity a wealth of different confessions were already in existence, constantly replacing each other, combining with each other, and undergoing mutual delimitation."[6] The apocalyptic thinking of Revelation and the Markan apocalypse (ch. 13) contrasts sharply with the "realized eschatology" of the Fourth Gospel; the "faith without works" of Romans is most difficult to reconcile, on the conceptual plane, with the "works-righteousness" of James; nor can

the "adoptionist" Christology of the early chapters of Acts
be easily harmonized, theologically, with the high Christology of the Captivity Epistles of Paul.

The problem of conceptual pluralism is augmented
when attention is given to the non-biblical authorities.
Tradition in its various forms produces formulations of the
Christian faith that have to be combined dialectically with
the affirmations of Scripture—in such a way that neither
suppresses the critical voice of the other. The contemporary Christian, seeking authentic union with God, must
open himself to many influences, past and present—the
reflections of scholars, the admonitions of spiritual leaders,
the affirmations of official Church bodies, and the spontaneous instinct of the faithful.

This plurality of authentic Christian sources protects
the believer from being crushed by the weight of any single
authority; it restrains any one organ from so imposing itself as to eliminate what the others have to say. It provides
a margin of liberty within which each individual can feel
encouraged to make his own distinctive contribution, to
understand the faith in a way proper to himself. And at
the same time it provides the Church as a whole with the
suppleness it needs to operate in different parts of the
globe and in a rapidly changing world.

Some, discontented with the intellectual untidiness gen-
erated by the recognition of such diverse authorities, seek
to reduce everything to unity by arbitrarily exalting one
authority above all the others. For Käsemann, the decisive
elements would seem to be the Pauline doctrine of justification by faith as set forth in Romans and Galatians.
For certain Catholics, the contemporary teaching of the
papacy would seem to be the sole reliable guide. As against
all such simplistic solutions, we should prefer to say that
the "word of God" is best heard when one maintains a
certain critical distance from any given expression of that
word. By holding a multitude of irreducibly distinct articulations in balance, one can best position himself to hear
what God may be saying here and now. To recognize the
historically conditioned character of every expression of
faith is not to succumb to historical relativism, but rather
to escape imprisonment within the relativities of any particular time and place. Unless relativity is recognized for
what it is, it cannot be transcended.

In this age of planetary unification, one might think that

the distinctness and autonomy of the churches would be on the wane. In fact, however, it would seem that within most denominations pluralism is on the increase. Each culture is more conscious than heretofore of its special insights and needs. The growing historical consciousness of Western man, to which reference has already been made, sharply increases our awareness of the rather limited perspectives in which Christianity has been understood and proclaimed in the Western European tradition.

Vatican Council II took giant strides in reactivating the principle of pluralism in Roman Catholicism. Significant in this regard is the omission of the word "Roman" in the designation of the Catholic Church. Where Vatican Council I had spoken of the "Roman Catholic Church,"[7] Vatican II substituted the expression "the Catholic Church, which is governed by the successor of Peter and by the bishops in union with that successor."[8] The Dogmatic Constitution on the Church (*Lumen gentium*), moreover, makes much of the autonomy of the particular Churches within the Catholic family. "These Churches retain their own traditions without in any way lessening the primacy of the Chair of Peter," part of whose task is precisely to "protect legitimate differences."[9] The Decree on Ecumenism (*Unitatis redintegratio*) approves the distinctive heritage of the Eastern Churches as regards customs, modes of worship, and ways of understanding and proclaiming divine things.[10] The Pastoral Constitution on the Church in the Modern World (*Gaudium et spes*) declares that the Church "in virtue of her mission and nature . . . is bound to no particular form of human culture."[11] It teaches that "the accommodated preaching of the revealed word ought to remain the law of all evangelization" so that "each nation develops the ability to express Christ's message in its own way."[12] The Decree on the Church's Missionary Activity (*Ad gentes*), evoking the memory of Pentecost, holds forth the ideal of a Church which "speaks all tongues."[13] The Constitution on the Sacred Liturgy (*Sacrosanctum concilium*), finally, warns repeatedly against the dangers of imposing rigid uniformity and of failing to respect and foster the various gifts of different races and peoples.[14]

In this fostering of greater internal pluralism within the Catholic communion one may see a positive step promoting the restoration of Christian unity. Similar developments have already taken place, or are presently occurring, within many other Christian denominations. When it becomes apparent that the modes of thinking and worship tolerated within a given community differ as widely from one another as from those of other communions, the time has come to ask in all seriousness whether the existing denominational divisions have not outlived their usefulness. Without any suppression of the distinctive heritage of each family, a restoration of communion may become possible, so that Christians of different traditions will recognize each other as members of the same body of Christ.

Conversely it may be observed that a failure to allow for pluralism in the realizations of Christianity has been a major cause of dissidence. Victimized by "non-theological factors"—to use the expression that C. H. Dodd has rendered famous—whole groups of Christians have needlessly anathematized each other. Believers conscious of the inevitable historical and cultural conditioning in man's understanding and practice of the gospel will have reason to be more tolerant of one another's idiosyncrasies. They should be more capable of the empathy required to find Christ in the preaching and worship of cultures alien to their own. Where they do detect real shortcomings, they will be less inclined to judge these harshly, more ready to acknowledge the beam in their own eyes.

Notwithstanding all the merits of pluralism, we must, I think, acknowledge that it has its limits and dangers. If the word of God cannot be totally identified with any particular expression, it by no means follows that every human attitude and expression is consonant with the gospel of Christ. The People of God in every age and locality must constantly labor to find, through an arduous process of "discerning the spirits," what is an apt manner of incarnating the gospel in their own sociocultural situation. And if the People of God are to be a sign of Christ raised aloft among all the nations, there must be some recognizable continuity between the present proclamation of the gospel and the original heralding of the faith in New Testament times. The particular expressions of the faith in different lands, moreover, must not be so diverse that the Church ceases to be a sign of unity. Some manifest unity in faith, in structure, in worship, and in moral teaching is necessary in order that the Church may effectively serve as a sign and instrument of the union and reconciliation of all mankind. Thus it remains an important task of ecclesiastical authority to see to it that the differences between local churches, and the ongoing transformations of Christian life, do not undermine the apostolicity and catholic unity essential to the Church.

This chapter has dealt with the problem of diversity versus unity and with the functions of authority only in the most general terms and has consequently remained on a high level of abstraction. In order to put any of the principles here set forth to practical use, it would be necessary to speak much more concretely of particular problems— and each one of these problems would have to be discussed within the perspectives and possibilities of the various Christian traditions. For the sake of brevity, it may suffice to call attention to some major areas that call for intense investigation and discussion. These may be classified under the rubrics of creedal statement, church structures, forms of worship, and ethical teaching.

1. *Creedal statement.* Do the biblical confessions (such as "Yahweh is God"; "Jesus is Lord") and the early creeds (such as the Apostolic and the Nicene) give us terms and propositions which can and must be accepted by the Church throughout all ages and in all parts of the world? Or could the Church cease to use the name of Yahweh (Lord), desist from calling Jesus the "Son of God," or authorize creeds that do not stand in continuity with those handed down from antiquity? The same problem arises with regard to the dogmatic pronouncements of the early councils and the confessional statements of the major denominations. Could the Church cease to affirm that God is tripersonal or that Jesus Christ is one person with two natures? Could it question or deny the truth of these affirmations in the sense intended by the original authors? Are there any specifiable limits to the doctrinal mobility and variety in the Church?

Some hold that, while the teaching of Scripture and the creeds is irreversible, the terminology and even the conceptual schemes are subject to change in accordance with the thought patterns, customary modes of speech, and vital concerns of various cultures. Is this distinction between affirmation, conceptualization, and language sound and viable? Some distinguish between reformable and irreformable statements, between content and formulation, between what was said and what is meant, etc. Are distinctions of this type dangerous to the continuity of the faith? Do they introduce too much relativity, or do they, on the contrary, tie the Church too much to its own past, preventing creative restatements of the faith? Are such distinctions oversubtle efforts to hang on to both sides of an antinomy instead of either candidly admitting that the faith changes or firmly insisting that it remains constant? To some of these questions we shall return in later chapters.

2. *Church structures.* Are there any structures of "divine institution" that belong inalienably to the essential nature of the Church? Many believe that Christ himself instituted the pastoral office and conferred upon it the task of preaching, teaching, administering the sacraments, and governing the corporate life of the people of God. Some go yet further and hold that the New Testament authorizes and imposes certain specific forms of ministry—e.g., the papal, the episcopal, the presbyteral, the congregational. Some hold that a ministry transmitted by apostolic succession through the imposition of hands is essential to the *esse* of the Church. Roman Catholicism commonly holds that the Petrine office, with its primacy, is a permanent and immutable feature of the Church.

On the other hand, there are some who argue that the New Testament sanctions diversity in the forms of ministry. The fact that different ecclesiastical structures seem to have existed in different local churches is taken as a charter of liberty. Does this mean that the Church is free at any time to institute any form of ecclesiastical government that seems adapted to the times? Or can the Church be bound by the major historical decisions taken in the past and thus irreversibly committed to develop in a certain direction? These are some of the major ecumenical issues for contemporary ecclesiology.

3. *Forms of Worship.* Did Christ institute any definite sacraments, and, if so, can this be proved from New Testament exegesis? The majority of Christians would seem to hold that, in faithfulness to the precept of Christ, the Church must perpetually administer baptism and celebrate the Lord's Supper. Some would insist that the seven sacraments recognized in the later Middle Ages were established by Christ or are a legitimate and necessary development of what Christ instituted, and must always continue to be administered.

Once it is admitted that certain sacraments are divinely instituted and perpetual, questions arise regarding the words and ceremonies attaching to these sacraments. Must the Church in baptizing adhere to the trinitarian formula as given in the finale of Matthew's Gospel? In the Lord's Supper, must the "words of institution" (as given in the Synoptics or in 1 Corinthians) be more or less closely followed? To what extent is the matter of the sacraments immutable? Could saki and rice be substituted for wine and bread? Or coffee and doughnuts?

Is anything essential to the Church by way of liturgical prayer? Must the Church continue to recite the Lord's Prayer?

Even if one admits a great measure of flexibility in theory, how much uniformity is practically desirable in order that the Church may continue to manifest the unity that Christ wills for it? Is a diversity of rites detrimental to the unity of the Church or does it, on the contrary, give added splendor to the spectacle of Catholic unity?

4. *Ethical teaching.* In the past Christianity has closely identified itself with certain codes of conduct. It has insisted on a definite code of sexual morality, on monogamous marriage, and has taken an unfavorable attitude toward divorce, allowing it only under severe restrictions. The "mainline" churches have generally preached obedience and respect toward the civil government, extending even to military service. Radical Christians, on the other hand, have tended to oppose oaths of allegiance and to discountenance military service.

Today some feel that the Church's ethical codes have generally been too closely bound up with the approved social structures of the Mediterranean world at a given stage of its development. They feel that the Church has failed to raise a sufficiently strong voice of protest against war and social injustices (slavery, the class system, economic and political tyranny). Some counsel drastic revisions of the Christian moral code to meet the exigencies of a new era; they call for a theology of revolution, not excluding violence. Demands are also being made for a revolution in Christian sexual ethics, which are considered too inhibitive.

In view of these pressures, Christians must seriously ask themselves whether there are any "moral absolutes"—any objective standards of conduct to which men are universally and permanently bound. Are moral stances by their nature reversible, or can the Church affirm certain laws as immutable? If there are no limits as to what may be regarded as moral in some place or time, it would appear that the Church must disavow an important part of its mission as traditionally conceived. The problem here is similar to the problem of dogma: If there is a single determinate message, it ought to be capable of some kind of unequivocal expression. And yet it is exceedingly hard to win general and permanent acceptance for any given expression, even among those who consider themselves to be committed Christians.

In all four of these major areas, the problem arises as to the degree to which unity can be imposed by the decisions of competent ecclesiastical officers or bodies. When such bodies attempt to settle disputed questions, they almost inevitably find their decisions contested by significant minorities, if not by a majority, among the faithful. The Churches seem to be caught in a dilemma between the paralysis of inaction and the folly of alienating their own members. Now that the Church is generally viewed as a voluntary society, anathemas and excommunications have lost much of their efficacy as sanctions. Can other procedures be devised which will enable the Church to bear witness courageously to the full gospel of Christ without making itself a tragic spectacle of inner division and conflict?

The problem of authority versus freedom, unity versus diversity, affects different Churches in different ways and reappears with distinct modalities in various historical eras. But the problem itself is a necessary accompaniment of an incarnational religion such as Christianity. Every Christian community, large and small, has had to face the quandary: how to reconcile the necessary "obedience of faith" with the equally necessary "freedom of the sons of God"; how to harmonize fidelity to Christ and the gospel with the effective evangelization of a given culture? To the extent that any body of Christians can solve this problem for itself, it will contribute to the vital realization of that unity-in-diversity which must characterize a reunited Church in the future for which all Christians pray.

Doctrinal Authority in the Church

In a satirical essay Ronald Knox, while still an Anglican, argued, tongue in cheek, for the abolition of bishops:

> It has come to be seen that bishops and archbishops are not, as was commonly supposed hitherto, the vehicles of any extraordinary grace, which they passed on one to another, like a contagion, by the laying on of hands, but only another of these obstacles, which make the race of life so agreeable a pursuit. They exist to supervise our doctrines, and find them unscriptural, to control our religious practices, and forbid their continuance, thus enabling us to snatch a fearful joy while we are about 'em: in short, to give the Christian profession that spice of martyrdom, which it has so sorely lacked since the abolition of the amphitheatre.[1]

A certain "spice of martyrdom" has not uncommonly been the lot of theologians in many denominations, even in those that are not episcopally structured. In any Christian group there is a division of doctrinal authority between the highest administrators (bishops, synods, boards, or whatever) and theological scholars. The theologian finds himself in an ambivalent position. As a spokesman for the Church, he considers it his business to understand, explain, and defend its doctrine. But as a competent expert, he must sometimes assume the roles of critic, innovator, and explorer, and in these capacities he is likely to incur official censorship. Although the hierarchy often protects the theologian against unfair charges leveled against him by the laity and by his professional colleagues, sometimes hierarchical power is brought to bear in a repressive way upon the theologian himself.

In Roman Catholicism, the hierarchical magisterium was particularly vigilant in scrutinizing the orthodoxy of theologians in the period from the Modernist crisis until Vatican Council II, and this vigilance resulted in many unfortunate cases of the suppression of ideas which later proved sound and fruitful. In the more liberalized atmosphere of the Church since Vatican II, Catholic theologians have enjoyed an unprecedented degree of freedom in expressing new and revolutionary views. On the whole, public sympathy has been with them rather than with the hierarchy, which still makes occasional efforts to draw the lines between orthodoxy and heresy. The English cardinal, John Heenan, has called attention to the diminishing esteem for papal and episcopal teaching: "Today what the pope says is by no means accepted as authoritative by all Catholic theologians. An article in the periodical *Concilium* is at least as likely to win their respect as a papal encyclical. The decline of the magisterium is one of the most significant developments in the post-Conciliar Church."[2]

The reasons behind this decline of the official magisterium are numerous and complex. We live in a revolutionary age, when the official spokesmen of any group have a hard time winning credibility. Whether in business, in government, or in the Church, people commonly experience suspicion toward, and resentment against, the holders of corporate power. They do not particularly trust the officers of the company as sources of information.

This prejudice against official spokesmen—widespread in all walks of life—is intensified in the case of the Church, since the members of the hierarchy are not chosen by the consent of the governed nor are they commonly noted for outstanding capacity in doctrinal matters. The gulf between intellectual competence and decisive power has become, at times, too wide for comfort. Why, people ask, should the right to commit the Church publicly be placed in the hands of officers who notoriously lack the requisite skill?[3]

In this situation little is gained by passionate insistence on "religious submission of mind and will." The precise point at issue is whether such submission is morally responsible and whether the alleged charisms of the episcopal office (to which appeal is commonly made) can in fact compensate for the apparent lack of professional competence. The plea for obedience often fails to answer the question, for it overlooks the fact that assent to teaching cannot normally be a matter of sheer voluntary obedience. As an intellectual act, it demands grounds for honest conviction.[4]

On the basis of this preliminary delineation of the problem, I should like to discuss the problem of doctrinal authority in the Catholic Church under three main aspects: first, the existence in the Church of unofficial or non-hierarchical teaching; secondly, the importance of official or hierarchical teaching; and thirdly, the desired relationship between these two types of teaching.

As a basic paradigm of the Church, the validity of which can scarcely be challenged, let us take the Pauline image of the Body of Christ. In 1 Corinthians 12, Paul insists that the life of the Church is sustained by a great variety of ministries and competences, including those of apostles, prophets, teachers, and administrators. While these ministries are not all on the same level of dignity, none of them is so exalted that it has no need of the rest. Just as the eye cannot say to the hand, "I have no need for you," so too, Paul implies, the apostle cannot do without the prophet nor the teacher without the administrator. There is a reciprocity of dependence of each upon the others. Again in Ephesians, Paul returns to the same theme, listing the ministries of apostles, prophets, evangelists, pastors, and teachers. All of these ministries, he says, contribute to the building up of the entire body in love (cf. Eph. 4:11–16).

Applying this doctrine to the modern situation, one might say that the bishops, as one order in the Church, cannot claim for themselves the totality of teaching power. Providence ordains that there should be other teachers, including charismatics (such as prophets) and scholars (such as theologians). Each type of minister has his own gift and must be allowed, as the phrase has it, to "do his thing."

In the documents of Vatican II, this organically diversified view of the Church was accepted. *Lumen gentium*, in Chapter 2 (no. 12), declared that the People of God as a whole is a living witness to Christ and shares in his prophetic office. In Chapter 4 (no. 31) this was further specified by the statement that the laity are sharers in the "priestly, prophetic, and kingly offices of Christ,"[5] and that they should exercise their freedom as sons of God in expressing themselves about things of concern to the Church, making full use of their "knowledge, competence, or outstanding ability."[6]

The Pastoral Constitution, *Gaudium et spes*, frankly recognized that humanity is entering a new age and thus intimated that new styles of teaching authority are to be expected. Fresh avenues of knowledge, it stated, have been paved by the rapid advances of the human and social sciences, as well as by natural science and technology.[7] Theological inquiry must keep in close contact with these other sciences and seek to collaborate with them in the better understanding of the faith.[8] In the complex world of our day, said the Constitution, it would be a grave mistake to imagine that the hierarchy is omniscient: "Let the layman not imagine that his pastors are always experts, that to every problem which arises, however complicated, they can readily give him a concrete solution, or even that such is their mission."[9] In order to cope with the rapid changes presently occurring, the Church has to rely on laymen well versed in various specialties: "With the help of the Holy Spirit, it is the task of the entire People of God, especially pastors and theologians, to hear, distinguish and interpret the many voices of our age, and to judge them in the light of the divine Word."[10] For this reason, continued the Constitution, "It is to be hoped that many laymen will receive an appropriate formation in the sacred sciences."[11] Finally, echoing *Lumen gentium*, the Pastoral Constitution declared: "Let it be recognized that all the faithful, clerical and lay, possess a lawful freedom of inquiry and thought, and the freedom to express their minds humbly and courageously about matters in which they enjoy competence."[12]

It seems evident, therefore, both from Scripture and from the official documents of the modern Church, that sound doctrine does not in every case flow down to the theologians and the laity from the top officials in the Church. If the Spirit dwells in the entire Body, enlivening all the members and breathing as he wills, doctrinal initiatives can begin from below as well as from above. Alert Christians, listening to the many voices of our age, may be expected to have something intelligent to say to the hierarchy.[13]

The theologian, then, cannot be rightly regarded as a mere agent of the hierarchical teaching authority. His task is not simply to repeat what the official magisterium has already said, or even to expound and defend what has already become official teaching, but, even more importantly, to discover what has not yet been taught.[14] He must seek to discern and to formulate "what the Spirit is saying to the Churches" (Apoc. 2:7). Paul VI, after alluding to this biblical phrase, went on to speak of the theologian's task of interpreting "the general mental outlook of our age and the experiences of men" and his duty to transmit his insights to the hierarchy for the enrichment of the entire Church.[15]

The second problem with which I wish to deal grows out of the points already made. If the Church is not a purely juridical society, in which all sound teaching flows down from the highest officers, but a Spirit-filled Body such as I have described, is there really any need or room for an institutional hierarchy? Cannot the society allow itself to be directed by the various movements stirred up here and there, now and again, by the Holy Spirit, and learn to live with both the tensions and agreements that seem to be the lot of such a Body? Does the Church really need a juridical power to adjudicate conflicts of opinion? Can any juridical power, in fact, effectively settle such conflicts?

Questions such as these cannot be solved by purely abstract reasoning without some attention being given to the kind of basic constitution which was historically given to the Church. Yet even without appealing to such historical evidences, one may properly note that the nature of the Christian faith would seem to call for some official teaching authority in the Church. The Church is not simply an association for the advancement of religious knowledge. As a witnessing community, it differs radically from a professional group, such as the American Historical Association. It is bound together not simply by a common method but by a common creed. Its corporate existence and its life of witness, worship, and service are premised on what God is believed to have revealed in Jesus Christ.

The Christian faith was communicated in the first instance not to any particular individual but to the

Church as a group. Any individual person, even though he be a pope or a bishop, is capable of losing the faith. Only the Church as a society enjoys the divine promise of indefectibility.

For the Church to perdure in the world as Christ's authentic witness it must have some way of publicly expressing its faith. From the earliest centuries, it has repeatedly had to define itself against heretical distortions, such as Gnosticism in its various forms. In modern times this danger of falsification continues to haunt the Church. For instance, the "German Christians" in the 1930s sought to popularize a Nazified version of the gospel. In our own country some have sought to find biblical warrant for white or black racism. Or, to take a less extreme example, some have understood the axiom "Outside the Church, no salvation" in a harsh and unacceptable way, apparently consigning to perdition all but Roman Catholics. Against aberrations such as these, the Church needs ways of authentically expressing its genuine faith. At the present time, when the stresses and strains on traditional faith have grown to new intensity, the Church, if it lacked a doctrinal authority, would rapidly cease to stand for anything determinate. It might be overrun by the forces of public opinion. Thus the times call not for a dismantling but for a rehabilitation of the magisterium.

The difficult questions about the magisterium, for most Catholic Christians, relate not so much to its existence as to its nature. It is not easy to say what persons are entitled to speak for the Church, what matters lie within the scope of their competence, how great is the binding force of their decrees, and what are the rights and duties of those who find themselves in disagreement. In this chapter I shall focus my attention on the first question: Who constitute the members of the magisterium?

The primary members, it would seem, are those who exercise the pastoral ministry on the highest level. The bishops, since they are charged with the supervision of the preaching and sacramental life of the Church, became involved in doctrinal questions in the early centuries. It was their task to admit or exclude from the sacraments, to license preachers, and to regulate catechetical schools. Thus it was natural that doctrinal disputes were referred to them for adjudication. Especially after the conversion of Constantine in the fourth century their position in the

Church was assimilated to that of senators in the Roman Empire.[16] Since that time they have always been regarded as the supreme spokesmen of the official teaching of the Church.

Vatican Council II, far from restricting the teaching authority of bishops, raised it to unprecedented heights. Partly to offset the excessive papal centralization of the preceding century, the Council invoked the principle of collegiality and assigned to the universal episcopate the supreme jurisdictional and magisterial powers which Vatican I had recognized in the Roman pontiff: "The order of bishops is the successor of the college of the apostles in teaching authority and pastoral rule."[17] "The episcopal order is the subject of supreme and full power in the universal Church."[18] By thus extending to the bishops collectively the powers previously ascribed to the pope, the recent Council inevitably raised the question no longer of papal but now of episcopal absolutism. But this threat was averted. As we have seen earlier in this chapter, the Council made it clear, in numerous documents, that the public teaching of the official magisterium is only one of many elements in the total witness of the Church. The hierarchy does not have exclusive, absolute, or unlimited doctrinal authority.

The primary task that faces the post-Conciliar Church is to find a proper relationship between the juridically supreme teaching power of the bishops and the equally undeniable right of the faithful in general, and competent experts in particular, to exercise their doctrinal responsibility. The decline of the magisterium, to which Cardinal Heenan refers, is partly due to the fact that the universal episcopate has not yet achieved a satisfactory working relationship with the intellectuals and prophets in the Church. Reserving the question of prophecy for later treatment, I should like to concentrate for the moment on the scholars.

Lest the relationship be totally misunderstood from the outset, it must be recognized that there is a qualitative difference between the authentic magisterium of the hierarchy and the doctrinal magisterium of the scholar. The bishop and the theologian, while they are both teachers, have different roles. The bishop's task is to give public expression to the doctrine of the Church and thus to lay down norms for preaching, worship, and Christian life. His concern, therefore, is primarily and directly pastoral. The theologian, on the other hand, is concerned with reflectively analyzing the present situation of the Church and of the faith, with a view to deepening the Church's understanding of revelation and in this way opening up new and fruitful channels of pastoral initiative. To be faithful to his vocation, the theologian often has to wrestle with unanswered questions and to construct tentative working hypotheses which he submits to the criticism of his colleagues. His goal is not to spread doubt and confusion—though he is often accused of seeking to do so—but rather to face the real questions and to pioneer as best he can the future paths of Christian thought and witness.[19]

Because of this difference in vocation it is clear that the theologians should not seek to substitute themselves for the public teaching authority in the Church, nor should the bishops turn over their teaching responsibility to the theologians. Only the bearers of the official magisterium can formulate judgments in the authoritative way. They may of course accept and approve the work of private theologians, but when they do so it is they—not the theologians—who give official status to the theories they approve.

The bishop's task, therefore, does not require him to be a theologian in his own right. He is not supposed to reduplicate, on a higher and more authoritative level, what the theologian does in a less official way. Still less is he supposed to decide doctrinal questions without paying any heed to what theologians are saying. He has no charism that operates mechanically or magically, even though he fails to take measures to avoid mistakes. In order to make good doctrinal decisions the magisterium has to bring the best and most creative available theological talent to bear upon the problem that is to be decided. It must listen to what the professional thnkers are saying, direct the dialogue, engineer a measure of consensus, discern the spirits at work, and render pastorally sound decisions.

Speaking of ecclesiastical government in general, Yves M.-J. Congar remarks that the Church has traditionally been governed by conciliar procedures, not by solitary personal decisions.[20] Cyprian, who was a theologian, a bishop, and a saint besides, enunciated the principle: "I have made it a rule, ever since the beginning of my episcopate, to make no decision merely on the strength of my own personal opinion, without consulting you [the priests and deacons] and without the approbation of my people."[21] In another letter Cyprian wrote: "Bishops must not only teach but also learn, for the best teacher is he who daily grows and advances by learning better."[22]

In his address to the International Congress on the Theology of Vatican II, in 1966, Paul VI acknowledged the dependence of the magisterium on the work of theologians:

> Without the help of theology, the magisterium could indeed safeguard and teach the faith, but it would experience great difficulty in acquiring that profound and full measure of knowledge which it needs to perform its task thoroughly, for it considers itself to be endowed not with the charism of revelation or inspiration, but only with that of the assistance of the Holy Spirit . . .
> Deprived of the labor of theology, the magisterium would lack the tools it needs to weld the Christian community into a unified concert of thought and action, as it must do for the Church to be a community which lives and thinks according to the precepts and norms of Christ.[23]

Occasionally the magisterium issues pronouncements without adequate theological consultation. In spite of all efforts to enforce acceptance by appeals to the authority of office, these pronouncements become an embarrassment to the Church. Some years later they have to be corrected or retracted and as a result the general confidence of the faithful in the magisterium is undermined. An obvious case in point would be the series of responses issued by the Pontifical Biblical Commission during the aftermath of the Modernist crisis. Many of these decrees are now dead letters. In the long run it would have been better for the authority of the magisterium if more liberal Scripture scholars had been called in to share in the drafting of these responses. The same may be said of certain encyclicals of the anti-Modernist period, such as *Spiritus Paraclitus* and even sections of *Humani generis* that have, in retrospect, proved unduly restrictive and were not reaffirmed by Vatican Council II.

As Karl Rahner has noted, there is nothing in the nature of the case that requires that the episcopate should always be a conservative force and that the theologians should represent the radical or critical wing.[24] Ideally, bishops and theologians should appear as brothers in a single unified community of faith and witness. The highest officers, no less than the theologians, should be concerned with adapting the Church to the needs of the times and with leading it forward into God's future. This is an important part of the pastoral office, which too often conceives of its task in a negative and restraining way. On the other hand the theologians, no less than the official magisterium, should be concerned with faithful obedience to the word of God as it comes to us through the Bible and the monuments of tradition. In recent times theologians have tended to become increasingly venturesome in advancing new and untried theories. Not surprisingly, the bishops, conscious of their responsibility to safeguard the ancient Christian heritage, have become increasingly suspicious of creative theology. Many bishops habitually consult only the more conservative theologians—those who are likely to represent the state of theology a generation ago.

As a result, a vicious circle has been set up. Theologians, distrustful of the procedures by which official decisions are reached, are increasingly critical of the magisterium. Often they feel that they cannot conscientiously defend one or another of its pronouncements. If they are not permitted to voice their dissent within the Church, they turn increasingly to secular publications and news media. Some theologians, feeling that they cannot operate successfully under the aegis of the hierarchy, prefer to pursue a purely academic kind of theology in secular institutions.

The increasing independence of theology from the magisterium, while it is not entirely bad, could seriously weaken the corporate witness of the Church. While preserving its scientific integrity and autonomy, theology should be conscious of its ties with the magisterium. The theologian cannot properly perform his task unless he is solicitous of keeping his solidarity with the Church, to which the Christian revelation has been primarily committed. He must feel co-responsible, as Léon Joseph Suenens would say, for its teaching and therefore anxious that his personal charisms of wisdom and knowledge should redound to the benefit of the whole Church, making it better able to articulate its faith.[25]

In order to restore a proper working relationship it might be desirable to institutionalize to some degree the participation of theologians in the Church's decision-making processes. Some interesting models for such institutionalization can be found in the Middle Ages, when the theologian was considered to have quasi-hierarchical status. In many medieval texts, as Congar points out, the *ordo doctorum* is listed after the *ordo cardinalium*, the *ordo episcoporum*, and the *ordo praelatorum*, i.e., as an instance of the hierarchy.[26] The university theology faculties played a normal role in the settlement of theological disputes and in the formulation of official doctrine. Thus the decrees of the Council of Vienne (1311–12), by order of Pope Clement V, were not made official until they had been submitted to the universities.[27]

It might be profitable to study anew the medieval conception of the general council with a view to assessing its positive value for our times. Of many medieval councils one may say what Brian Tierney says of the Fourth Lateran Council (1215)—that it "was not simply a synod of bishops but an 'assembly of estates' to which all the constituent elements of the Church were summoned either in person or through representatives."[28] Not infrequently at the medieval councils non-bishops in attendance were given the right to exercise a deliberative vote. When some opposition was voiced to this procedure at the Council of Constance (1414–18), Cardinal Pierre d'Ailly, among others, argued for the view that eventually prevailed. In the course of his famous speech, delivered in 1415, he particularly urged that theologians should have the power to vote:

> One cannot exclude from decisive vote the doctors of sacred theology, civil and canon law, especially the theologians, who have received the authority to preach and teach everywhere. This is no small authority over the faithful. It greatly exceeds that of an individual bishop or an ignorant abbot or titular.[29]

In the later Middle Ages the papacy was in danger of being excessively enslaved by the magisterium of theologians and by the interventions of secular princes. Since the sixteenth century, the Church has been understandably anxious to keep the freedom of the magisterium to go against the desires and opinions of any particular group. In some non-Catholic bodies, the highest officers have so little doctrinal power that the group as such can hardly utter anything but platitudes. The prophetic freedom of the magisterium in the Catholic Church is an asset that should not be lightly bargained away under pretext of democratization. It is good that the Church, through its highest officers, should be able to take a strong stand, if necessary, against the tide of public opinion. If the Church could no longer champion an unpopular cause, the salt would quickly lose its savor.

Without introducing complicated juridical procedures that would paralyze the magisterium, the modern Church should seek better ways of assuring that official doctrinal decisions are regularly made in the light of the best theological advice available. In practice the bishops cannot fulfill their teaching office without wide consultation and consensus on the part of scholars and intellectuals of various schools of thought. Vatican Council II achieved splendid results because the most talented theologians of many nations were involved in the drafting of the more important documents, and because the successive drafts were submitted to the criticism of numerous experts, including Protestant, Anglican, and Orthodox theologians, before being brought on the Council floor.

To recommend how the theologians of a particular country might relate themselves more effectively to its national hierarchy demands careful thought and creative experimentation. In principle it might be possible to send theologian representatives, chosen by professional societies or by university and seminary faculties, to take part in national synods or bishops' conferences. It might also be possible for the draft declarations of such meetings to be submitted to criticism and review by the theological community, or by other competent experts, before being formally promulgated. Such procedures would not, in my opinion, undermine confidence in the value of such declarations; it might, on the contrary, win them added support.

There is no reason in principle why the names of theologians who collaborate with the hierarchy on official statements should be kept secret, as though only the words of bishops were graced with the unction of the Holy Spirit. Nor is there any good reason why disagreements among bishops on doctrinal questions should be concealed. In American political life the conflicting views of senators and congressmen are public knowledge, and this does not result in any disrepect for duly established laws.

Whether voting powers should be given to non-bishops when they meet with bishops in ecclesiastical councils is a question that cannot be answered in the abstract. In the last analysis, voting in Church councils is valuable as a means of discerning the existence of a consensus. For some questions it might be important to find out whether the consensus is present not simply among bishops but among theologians and other experts. Since Church councils do not ordinarily operate on a basis of simple majorities, one could provide against the contingency that a majority of the bishops might be voted down on some doctrinal question by a majority of theologians together with a minority of bishops. The fact that the deliberative vote, even in modern ecumenical councils, has never been confined to the bishops, indicates that theologians and others could be invited to express their adherence by a deliberative vote. In this way they would become more evidently participants in the magisterium of the Church.

In conclusion, then, who constitute the magisterium? If we think of the magisterium as a function, rather than as a determinate body, we can leave the answer somewhat vague. The highest officers of the Church—the pope, the other bishops, and perhaps certain other prelates—by virtue of their office, have general charge of the Church's teaching as well as its worship and discipline. But these prelates are not, by themselves alone, the teachers. In order to teach effectively they must "tune in" on the theological wisdom that is to be found in the community and bring it to expression. Thus the theologians are not totally external to the magisterium considered as a function or process.

All of this could perhaps be summarized in a metaphor. One may say that in the Church of God there is an abundance of light provided by the gospel of Christ and the inner illumination of the Spirit. In the total Church this light is widely diffused among individuals and groups which are differently gifted. The task of the hierarchy in any given region, and in the world at large, is to gather up all this radiance of light and bring it into focus. The official teaching of the Church emanates indeed from the episcopate, but not from the episcopate alone. The popes and bishops are, rather, the lens by which the light, issuing from all who are competent by faith and scholarship, is brought to a focus and expressed. By gathering up and concentrating the diffused light, the hierarchy intensifies its splendor and enables it to be refracted, with greater power, into the world. All the members of the Church, and especially those who seek to understand and teach the faith, must contribute, in their distinctive ways, to the public doctrine of the Church in order that the Church may continue to be, in this troubled and divided world, the light of the nations and the catalyst of reconciliation.

The Magisterium in a Time of Change

The reception accorded to *Humanae vitae* in 1968 brought to the surface a relatively new phenomenon in the Catholic Church. There are elements in Catholicism capable of publicly criticizing and rejecting the pronouncements of the highest authorities. The official teaching office, or magisterium, no longer enjoys the implicit and unquestioning confidence of the vast majority of the priests and faithful in the way that it did a decade or two ago. Even bishops differ among themselves in assessing the binding force of a papal encyclical. This phenomenon indicates that the Church is not the monolithic authoritarian society it was recently thought to be. Sophisticated Catholics today have other criteria of truth by which they sometimes judge even the teaching of the hierarchy.

The 1970–71 president of the Catholic Theological Society of America, Father Richard McCormick, aptly summarized the present situation when he declared in June 1969: "I believe it is safe to say that the hierarchical magisterium is in deep trouble. For many of the educated faithful it has ceased to be truly credible."[1] While some may rejoice in the greater freedom of individuals, one should not overlook the darker aspect of this development. As we have noted in the preceding chapter, the Church needs an effective teaching office. To function as a living society of faith and witness, the Church must be able to say within certain limits what views and attitudes are required, permitted, and excluded by Christian revelation. It must therefore have some organ or organs for officially articulating its corporate stance. I would even go so far as to add that the Church must have the power to disassociate itself from—to excommunicate—those who pertinaciously hold positions deemed repugnant to the gospel and destructive of its own existence as a community of faith. Even the most liberal thinkers of our day—or perhaps they most of all—would insist, for example, that the Church should repudiate idolatry, superstition, and poisonous doctrines such as racism.

To admit the necessity of the magisterium is one thing; to endorse the particular form which the magisterium has taken at any given moment of history is quite another. Lest we identify the magisterium itself too closely with the forms familiar to us from the recent past, it is important to approach the question with a wide historical perspective. There is no possibility here of investigating the multitudinous shapes that the magisterium has assumed in the past, but we should refer at least briefly to some of them. The brevity of these remarks will inevitably entail some oversimplification.

In apostolic times there was relatively little concern for developing a consistent body of doctrine. There was, however, a variety of ministers of the word who witnessed in various ways to God's revelation in Christ. We read in the New Testament of apostles, prophets, evangelists, teachers, and administrators. All of these functionaries, according to Paul, need each other, in view of the law of mutual dependence that binds together all the members of the body of Christ. The apostles, of course, exercised a uniquely authoritative ministry, but they did not consider themselves masters of the word of Christ or sovereign rulers of the Church. While rebuking deviations from the clear meaning of the gospel, they took pains not to "lord it over the flock" (cf. 1 Pet. 5:3). In the pastoral letters we find evidences that the apostles, as they reached the end of their earthly career, turned over some of their governing and teaching functions to colleges of bishops or presbyters.[2]

In early patristic times the apportionment of teaching authority is complex and confused. We find a tension among three groups: the prophets, who speak as they feel themselves impelled by the Spirit; the teachers, who form catechetical schools and make the first groping efforts toward a Christian theology; and the pastors—the presbyters and bishops, who preside over the worship and discipline of the local communities. From the early third century, after the condemnation of Montanism, the prophets cease to be an effective force in the community. The teachers, in turn, are progressively subordinated to the bishops, who, as cultic leaders, have charge of the discipline of the sacraments. As a justification for the doctrinal prerogatives of bishops, Irenaeus submits that the apostles entrusted their doctrine to those to whom they entrusted their churches, so that the presiding officers of the apostolic churches may be presumed to have the surest access to pure doctrine. But the view of Irenaeus is not universally accepted. Clement of Alexandria and Origen, for instance, consider that in strictly doctrinal matters, the teachers (*didascaloi*) stand, in their own way, in the apostolic succession and therefore need not look exclusively to the hierarchical magisterium for pure apostolic doctrine. Tertullian, in his Montanist period, reduces the role of bishops to a purely disciplinary one.[3]

The hegemony of the bishops over the other teachers was promoted by various developments of the third and fourth centuries. The need to cope with new heresies compelled the Church to devise ways of unequivocally determining its official stance and thus contributed to the delineation both of the biblical canon and of church structures. Emperor Constantine after his conversion wanted to have a well-organized body to which he could turn for an authoritative statement of the doctrine of the Church; he treated the bishops as the ecclesiastical counterparts of the Roman senators. Even before Constantine, former lawyers such as Cyprian, when they rose to prominence in the Church, looked to the Roman senate as a model for episcopal synods. Francis Dvornik has shown how closely the early councils, beginning with Nicaea, followed the procedures of the Roman senate.[4] Since many of the leading theologians in the patristic period were bishops, the faithful looked naturally to the episcopate for guidance in doctrinal matters. Generally speaking, juridical authority and intellectual competence were found in the same class of persons.

In the Middle Ages the bishops as a group lost some of their pre-eminence. Laymen, especially kings and princes, played a major role in church affairs. From the tenth to the thirteenth century the papacy, in combination with the religious orders, assumed the upper hand. Beginning with the thirteenth century, the university faculties of theology began to exercise a scholarly magisterium of their own. The term "magisterium," in the usage of St. Thomas Aquinas and his contemporaries, normally designates the function of professors, but it is recognized that the prelates have a responsibility to supervise the preaching of the Church and thus to exercise what we might today call a pastoral magisterium. According to the conciliar theory, which exerted great influence in the later Middle Ages, the general council was a kind of "Estates General" representing the various classes of persons in the Church, rather than simply a meeting of bishops. At the Council of Constance, for example, abbots, monks, friars, and lay leaders were given the same voting rights as bishops and cardinals.[5]

In the Counter Reformation period, Catholics brought into high relief the very elements denied by the Protestants. The magisterium was accordingly juridicized and clericalized. The very idea of church teaching underwent a transformation: it was identified less with giving insight and enlightenment than with the authoritative imposition of certain officially approved formulas. In the majority of the Scholastic manuals of the early twentieth century the magisterium is treated as an aspect of the power of jurisdiction. The proper response is looked upon as obedience rather than personal assimilation. Quite naturally, therefore, the teaching office was increasingly reserved to those possessing jurisdiction in the Church—especially the pope and the bishops. No longer did the laity participate actively in ecumenical councils; even priest-theologians were, for the most part, present only as advisers. The Church was viewed as a society consisting of two unequal classes: a "teaching church," which ostensibly did not have to learn, and a "learning church," which ostensibly could not teach.

To foster unquestioning acceptance of papal and episcopal utterances, even in cases where little or no evidence was offered, a certain mystique of magisterial authority was promoted. Efforts were made to show that the bishops, without recourse to the normal tools of research or consultation, could nevertheless have privileged insights into the truth of revelation. This marvelous power was traced to their grace of office, which allegedly included a special "charism of truth." While some such grace of office in the case of bishops, as in the case of other responsible Christians, need not be denied, one may legitimately question the mythical terms in which this grace was sometimes interpreted. In the popular imagination, confidence in the hierarchy was fortified by fanciful speculations, such as the idea that if a pope were about to sign a document containing error, the pen would be miraculously swept out of his hand or he would suddenly fall dead. Educated Christians of our day can scarcely be expected to accept magical explanations of this type. The credibility of the magisterium must be defended not by myths and fantasies but by solid theological principles.

Before we turn to such principles let me add one reflection to our historical survey. The present collapse of confidence in hierarchical teaching would seem to be attributable, in great part, to the growing discrepancy between the current style of operation of the Catholic magisterium and the decision-making processes that have come into general usage in modern secular society. Since the sixteenth century, and especially between the two Vatican Councils, Catholicism moved in a direction diametrically opposed to modern thought. The Church in the nineteenth century was restorationist, and after the Modernist crisis it became self-consciously antimodern. To illustrate this I should like to focus on four points of contrast between the ecclesiastical and secular mentalities as commonly found in the early twentieth century.

In the first place, while society as a whole was becoming democratic and self-critical, the Church became progressively more oligarchic and authoritarian. The control of doctrine was concentrated in the hands of a small class of teachers, who were alleged to have mysterious charisms denied to others. The procedures of public criticism, dialogue, and consensus, which were establishing themselves in political and academic life, were systematically excluded from the Church. Pius X spoke for the Catholicism of his time when he declared in 1906: "In the pastoral body alone reside the right and authority necessary to direct the members towards the end of the society. The duty of the multitude is to allow itself to be led and to follow its rulers obediently."[6] At a time when authority in worldly disciplines seemed to be losing its supernatural sanctions, many turned to the Church for divine oracles. Special stress was given to the pope, whom some theologians situated on a lonely pinnacle, as if he were infallible all by himself, rather than, as is more commonly held today, in fellowship with his brother bishops. Through reverent submission to the magisterium and to the papacy in particular, Catholics found it possible to give expression to their interior self-surrender to the authority of the revealing God.

Connected with this authoritarian development was a second trend: the swing toward absolutism. In a period when secular scholarship was coming to the conclusion that all human statements are profoundly conditioned by historical, cultural, sociological, and psychological factors, and hence limited in their validity, the Church gave unprecedented emphasis to the absolute value of its solemn pronouncements. It was as though absolutism, banished from every other area, found a final place of refuge in Roman Catholicism. In the century between the two Vatican councils the Church neglected no occasion for insisting on its power to compel acceptance of its own dogmatic formulations in the name of divine faith and to forbid any doubt or denial under pain of eternal damnation. In an era when the historicity of human knowledge was becoming a commonplace, Roman Catholicism dared to proclaim that its solemn teaching was universally and perpetually valid and thus "irreformable." This gave Catholics an enviable feeling of religious certainty at a time when most other Christians felt torn by inner doubts.

Thirdly, the very concept of truth implicit in the Catholic teaching on the magisterium as this developed in the nineteenth century was antithetical to the increasingly concrete and contextual view current in modern philosophy. Certain isolated statements were tagged as "revealed truths," as though truth and revelation could be predicated of abstract formulas in a purely objective state. The utterances of the magisterium were transmitted by the most impersonal forms of communication—chiefly in the form of carefully chiseled written statements in solemn, curial Latin. This abstract, metaphysical, propositional view of truth was out of harmony with the new philosophies. It conflicted, for instance, with dialectical materialism, which insisted that truth is always concrete, that phenomena must always be understood organically in reciprocal relationship to one another. It ran counter to pragmatism which focused, as William James put it, on "the distinctively concrete, the individual, the particular, and effective, as opposed to the abstract, general, and inert."[7] It differed likewise from instrumentalism, which saw knowledge as existing in the service of action. In an age immersed in the ambiguities of dialectical thinking, Catholics were almost the lone defenders of Aristotle's syllogistic logic.

Yet a fourth point of contrast between post-Tridentine Catholicism and the modern world may now be mentioned. At a time when Western culture was coming to look at the past as a mere point of departure for progress toward the future, the Catholic Church in its official teaching became anxiously conservative. Revealed truth was conceived to reside wholly in a deposit handed down from the apostolic age. The primary function of the magisterium thus became not to find new answers to new problems but rather to defend the inherited patrimony against the attacks of modern infidelity. The pronouncements of the Church were invariably legitimated by an appeal to the venerable antiquity of the doctrine in question—and, if historical evidence was lacking, the mere fact that the magisterium pronounced on the point was considered proof that the doctrine must have come down from apostolic times. Under the circumstances, Catholicism became a favorite haven for those who nostalgically longed for the splendors of patristic or medieval Christendom.

In summary, the Catholic doctrine of the magisterium as it developed from the nineteenth century until the mid-twentieth represents a progressive alienation from the modern world. In proportion as the thinking of secular society became self-critical, relativist, concrete, and future-oriented, the magisterium became more authoritarian, absolutist, abstractionist, and backward-looking.

For a large group of Catholics this alienation was not unpleasant. It gave them a feeling of secure and easy access to the divine. But there was a price to be paid. Catholics found it increasingly difficult to enter sympathetically and wholeheartedly into the concerns of their Protestant and secular contemporaries. They were being edged into an intellectual ghetto. John XXIII, with prophetic clarity of insight, recognized this situation and in his brief pontificate brought a remedy. He shifted the course of the Church in a radically new direction, toward dialogue with, and involvement in, the modern world. In so doing he unquestionably contributed to the present crisis, which squarely poses the question: How can the Catholic who wishes to think critically and progressively as a modern man accept the Catholic notion of "magisterium" as it has evolved in the past few centuries?

In my opinion there are aspects of this post-Tridentine development that should not be accepted. The times call for an "epochal" reinterpretation of the very notion of "magisterium," not less radical than the previous shifts to which I have alluded. Unless the style of the magisterium is reshaped to meet the demands of our time as effectively as it has met the demands of other times, we may expect the present loss of credibility to intensify. Modernization would not be a mere concession to the requirements of the times but, more positively, a way of taking advantage of the new ecclesiological possibilities that our age affords. Contemporary techniques of government, teaching, and communications would seem to harmonize at least as well with the demands of the gospel as do the feudal and absolutist patterns of the past. In the remainder of this chapter I should like to illustrate this with regard to the four problem areas already mentioned.

With reference to the first area, democratization, it may be asked whether the Church should regard itself, as it did in the time of Pius X, as being by divine constitution a hierarchical society in which all decisive power regarding doctrine and discipline is placed in the hands of a governing class. The affirmative answer could be defended by appeal to a few biblical texts that seem to give total authority to the apostles, whose status in the primitive Church might be analogous to that of the bishops in the Church today. But there are other New Testament texts, no less important, that accord doctrinal authority to the whole Church and recognize the special charisms of prophets and teachers.

Peter's Pentecost sermon, as reported in Acts 2, clearly teaches that the Holy Spirit has been poured forth upon the entire community of the new people of God. Paul repeatedly admonishes administrators to be respectful of the testimony of teachers and prophets. Several Johannine texts insist that each and every one of the faithful is taught by God himself (Jn. 6:45) and is interiorly anointed by the Holy Spirit, so as to be no longer dependent, in any fundamental way, on human authorities (1 Jn. 2:20). In the early centuries of the Church, bishops were generally careful to exercise their teaching functions in respectful dialogue with the presbyters and faithful; and in the Middle Ages, as we have seen, the professors of theology exercised an important doctrinal magisterium.

Relying on data such as these, the more creative Catholic theologians of the past generation have sought to recover some of the democratic elements that belong to the fundamental constitution of the Church. In a number of learned works, Yves Congar protested against the modern transformation of ecclesiology into what he called "hierarchology" and sought, through studies such as his *Lay People in the Church*, to show how active a role the laity can take and have at various times taken in the teaching office. Karl Rahner, in his brochure *Free Speech in the Church*, spelled out certain implications that he discerned in Pius XII's declaration that something would be missing from the life of the Church if the force of public opinion did not operate within its ranks.

Vatican II, following up on these studies as well as on the previous insights of scholars such as Newman, did much to reactivate the democratic principle within Catholicism. This is particularly evident in the Council's two longest documents, *Lumen gentium* and *Gaudium et spes*. *Lumen gentium* laid the theoretical groundwork by setting the teaching office of pope and bishops within the total context of the People of God as a dynamic communion in the life of grace. Thanks to the anointing of the Holy Spirit, it declared, the entire Church is infallible in belief and witness. The hierarchy therefore exists not to supplant the witness of the faithful but to help them carry out their divinely given mission. In its chapter on the laity, *Lumen gentium* called upon pastors to recognize the freedom, dignity, and responsibility of all members of the Church.

Gaudium et spes in its statements on the secular order laid down certain democratic principles that seem applicable, with the necessary adjustments, to the Church. It declared, for example: "Praise is due to those national procedures which allow the largest possible number of citizens to participate in public affairs with genuine freedom."[8] In the preceding chapter we noted how *Gaudium et spes* seemed to favor similar participation by the laity in church affairs. For instance, it expressed the hope that "many laymen will receive an appropriate formation in the sacred sciences"[9] and enunciated the principle, "Let it be recognized that all the faithful, clerical and lay, possess lawful freedom of inquiry and thought, and freedom to express their minds courageously about matters in which they enjoy competence."[10]

These principles, if consistently followed out, can offset the imbalances in the recently prevalent opinion that the bishops alone constitute the "teaching church." Vatican II recognized at many points that the bishops and other pastors in the Church are not omniscient and that they depend on the expertise of scholars and upon the discernment of charismatically gifted leaders. Since the Holy Spirit inspires and directs the whole People of God, public opinion in the Church can be a true theological source. The teaching Church and the learning Church, therefore, are not two separable parts. The faithful as a whole, and especially those who have scholarly competence or charismatic insight, participate in the magisterium. Conversely the bishops are part of the learning Church. In the words of Cyprian, already quoted: "Bishops must not only teach but learn, for the best teacher is he who daily grows and advances by learning better."[11]

What, then, is the special contribution of bishops? In line with the contentions of our previous chapter, it should be understood not as some arcane source of new knowledge, but rather as an aptitude to draw upon and to bring into focus the wisdom resident in the entire Church. The bishops, if they are to be true to their calling, must seriously consult before they decide. They cannot effectively say the last word unless they have allowed competent persons, in full freedom, to say the next-to-last word. They may on occasion feel conscientiously bound to reject the prevalent views of the community, but it is important that they should not do so without giving evidence of having understood, appreciated, and gone beyond the best reasoning that can be adduced for the position they are rejecting. If the hierarchy fails to utilize the human means at hand, one may, as Father McCormick observes, wonder to what extent they may still lay claim to the assistance of the

Spirit.[12] We must be on guard against a primitive and magical view of the charisms of office.

A second problem area to which I have referred is that of relativity versus absolutism. In recent centuries there has been a great concern on the part of Catholics to rise above historical relativities and to articulate the faith in timeless formulas. This concern, however, is a peculiarly modern one. In biblical times there was as yet no thought of "freezing" revelation in ideas and expressions that would be valid always and everywhere. The New Testament writings propose the Christian message in terms of a variety of patterns of thought, none of them simply reducible to the others. The early Church likewise found it possible to achieve unity of faith amid a pluralism of confessional formulas. The modern concern to find concepts and terms that could be imposed on all the faithful is itself, paradoxically, conditioned by a particular historical crisis. In the nineteenth century, when historical consciousness broke through in the secular disciplines, exposing the radical historicity of human thought, the Church made itself the defender of some of the most cherished theses of eighteenth-century rationalism. Theologians took the view that the truths of revelation, at least, were indubitable, universal, and immutable. They claimed unrestricted currency for that select body of axioms which, in the nineteenth century, came to be called "dogmas."[13]

In the 1940s the *nouvelle théologie* of Henri de Lubac, Henri Bouillard, and others pointed out that man's religious knowledge is necessarily embedded in contingent notions that depend upon particular cultural circumstances. From this it followed quite logically that the dogmas of the faith are subject to reconceptualization. The permanent validity of the dogmas—which these theologians did not contest—ought not to be identified, they maintained, with the contingent representations involved in any given formulation. The *nouvelle théologie*, of course, was vigorously attacked by conservative theologians and met with some disfavor in the encyclical *Humani generis*. Even in our own day, some theologians continue to insist on the immutability of the concepts and terms employed in dogmatic formulations.

John XXIII, however, opened the door to the more liberal position when he declared that Vatican II should study and expound authentic doctrine "through the methods of research and through the literary forms of modern thought. The substance of the ancient doctrine is one thing, and the way in which it is presented is another."[14] This thought, quoted practically verbatim in several conciliar documents, is in basic accord with the doctrine of the Church set forth in *Lumen gentium*. Here the Church is described as a mystery, even to itself, and is portrayed as God's pilgrim people pressing forward amid the darkness and vicissitudes of history toward a goal not clearly seen. Its task therefore is not to define everything with perspicuity, but rather to declare the mystery of the Lord "in a faithful though shadowed way, until at last it will be revealed in total splendor."[15]

The Pastoral Constitution, *Gaudium et spes*, took account of the cultural and historical relativities inherent in the human situation. It asserted that the Christian message must be expressed in diverse ways adapted to various times and cultures. "For God, revealing himself to his people to the extent of a full manifestation of himself in his incarnate Son, has spoken according to the culture proper to different ages."[16] From this it followed that "theologians are invited to seek continually for more suitable ways of communicating doctrine to the men of their times" and of understanding Christianity in the light of new scientific advances.[17]

The idea that revealed truth must be continually poured into new human vessels does not involve any disrespect for, or diminution of, the role of the magisterium. On the contrary, it is precisely here that the necessity of a living magisterium becomes most evident. A primary task of the magisterium is to see to it, in every generation, that Christian teaching is suitably recast so that the gospel still appears as the good news that it must always remain. The content of the Christian message is in danger of becoming stale unless it is restated in a challenging way for every time and culture. Such restatement involves changes not only in language and imagery, but also in the conceptual structures underlying older formulations. Such changes are in no way contrary to infallibility. On the contrary, as Gregory Baum points out, "The gift of infallibility means that the Church is able to remain faithful to the past and is yet free to reformulate Christian teaching as the Good News for the contemporary world."[18]

Thirdly, I spoke of the development toward abstractness and impersonality characteristic of the magisterium in the modern period. Quite evidently this trend runs counter to the general tendency of modern thought, which views truth in a more concrete and operational manner. More importantly, perhaps, it seems scarcely faithful to Jesus who said of himself most concretely, "I am the way, the truth, and the life." Jesus did not teach in technical and abstract terms but by parables and symbolic actions that vividly embodied the mission he had to accomplish. He did not address himself to speculative and theoretical questions but to the pressing questions bearing upon the salvation of the individuals present before him. The New Testament for the most part is content to express the message of Christianity quite unsystematically through fragments of sermons, homely stories, and letters dealing predominantly with the practical problems of local communities.

In the patristic period the Church had to change its style to some extent in order to resist the incursion of Gnostic systems, which would have dissolved the substance of the Christian message. This rejection involved adopting some technical and non-biblical language. But the dogmatic pronouncements of the patristic period remained close to the fundamental themes of Christian revelation. Only in the later Middle Ages do the official pronouncements of popes and councils become burdened with recondite technicalities so that formulas savoring of university theology are imposed on the faithful at large. Something of this Scholastic mentality continued to dominate the Roman magisterium in the nineteenth and early twentieth centuries.

Here again John XXIII adopted a new style. He asked that the declarations of Vatican II be proportioned to the needs of "a magisterium which is predominantly pastoral in character."[19] To a great extent the Council carried out this wish. *Dei Verbum*, for instance, makes it clear that revealed truth is by its very nature a participation in divine life and that therefore a purely theoretical type of knowledge could not possibly be revealed. The truth of Scripture, says this constitution, is that which God wanted written down "for the sake of our salvation."[20] The Council here broaches the notion of what we might call "salvation truth," a truth not univocal with the purely speculative truth of classical philosophy.

In its treatment of the magisterium, *Lumen gentium* restores the primacy of preaching over teaching of a scholarly sort. The bishops are authentic teachers, we are told, inasmuch as they "preach to the people committed to them the faith they must believe and put into practice."[21] Preaching, as distinct from academic teaching, is an existential event that transpires within a living community of faith. Christian doctrine, being essentially aimed at faith and conversion, is not intended primarily to communicate exact concepts about God and religion, but rather to bring men into effective communion with God, so that their lives may be transformed and renewed by the Holy Spirit. The preference for abstract and metaphysical language in the hierarchical pronouncements of recent centuries does not represent an irreversible development, as Vatican II well showed. The Church might well adopt a more concrete and symbolic type of proclamation, more akin to its style in the earliest centuries. The use of evocative, rather than scientific, language is appropriate, for Christian teaching must strive to arouse and intensify the religious experience of men in communion with the living and risen Lord. The privileged locus for magisterial teaching, as Baum observes, is the liturgical assembly. Here the word of proclamation serves to direct the faithful toward a sacramental encounter with the God of grace.[22]

As the pastoral role of the magisterium is restored, the disproportionate emphasis on the judgmental function will presumably be corrected. The magisterium exists not simply to settle debated questions but, even more importantly, to inspire, encourage, stimulate and sensitize the minds of men. It aims not to restrict or suffocate creative thinking, but rather to make the Church an authentic home of courage and responsible freedom. Education in the modern secular world is conceived less as the imparting of a certified body of information than as a participation in an ongoing quest. In like manner the teaching office of the Church may be expected to concern itself progressively less with closing debate and dictating definitive solutions and progressively more with bringing light to bear on the religious questions that agitate the modern world. It must aim to pinpoint the most urgent problems, to open up new horizons, and to stimulate new initiatives.[23] This view of the magisterium corresponds with the image of the pilgrim Church to which I have already referred.

My last point concerning the divorce between the magisterium and the modern world relates to the antinomy between past and future. That the hierarchy should be concerned with preserving incorrupt the patrimony of Christ and the apostles is of course right and proper. Even in New Testament times Paul exhorted the Corinthians and Galatians to remain steadfast to the gospel that had been preached to them; he anathematized all who might attempt to preach another gospel. The pastoral epistles insist on the duty of bishops to "hold firm to the sure word as taught" (Tit. 1:9). But in recent centuries the magisterium has been almost totally concerned with preserving what is old and with guarding against "profane novelties," as they are called. The Church has been affected by an anxious conservatism more reminiscent of the servant who buried his talent in the ground than of those who invested their master's capital so as to bring in interest.

Among all human movements, Christianity should be conspicuous for its thrust toward the future. The central theme of Jesus' preaching was the promised Kingdom of God. Paul looked upon all creation as groaning in eager expectation of the redemption promised to the sons of God (cf. Rom. 8:18–25). The Church, as he saw it, was pressing forward toward the achievement of deeper faith and knowledge, "to mature manhood, to the measure of the stature of the fulness of Christ" (Eph. 4:13). Of himself Paul said: "Forgetting what lies behind and straining forward to what lies ahead, I press on toward the goal." Only then did he add, almost as an afterthought: "Let us hold true to what we have attained" (Phil. 3:13–16).

In the language of the magisterium since the Middle Ages, this note of eager anticipation has become muted. Especially since Pius IX, the papacy has been wont to eulogize the past and to lament the evils of "these calamitous times." Too little heed has been paid to the possible movements of the divine Spirit in contemporary events.

As in other areas, here too Pope John XXIII reversed the trend. In his opening allocution at Vatican II, he admitted that there is in our day no lack of "fallacious teaching, opinions, and dangerous concepts to be guarded against and dissipated."[24] He mentioned the importance of defending the patrimony of divine revelation, but then immediately added: "Our duty is not only to guard this precious heritage, as if we were concerned only with antiquity, but to dedicate ourselves with an earnest will and without fear to that work which our era demands of us."[25] Explicitly repudiating the sentiments of those "prophets of gloom" who see in modern times nothing but prevarication and ruin, he affirmed his conviction that "in the present order of things, divine providence is leading us to a new order of human relations" in which, according to God's inscrutable designs, things will work out for the greater good of the Church.[26] The Council, he predicted, would be "like daybreak, a forerunner of most splendid light."[27]

The conciliar documents, to some extent, reflect this vision of John XXIII. *Lumen gentium* described the Church as the initial budding forth of the Kingdom of Christ. "While she slowly grows, the Church strains toward the consummation of the Kingdom and, with all her strength, hopes and desires to be united in glory with her King."[28] At Pope John's request, the Council inserted into the Constitution on the Church an entire chapter on "the eschatological nature of the pilgrim Church," in which the most important Scripture texts concerning the hope of future glory were splendidly arrayed.

As the Church becomes newly oriented toward the future and reanimated by intense hope in the fulfillment of God's promises, the magisterium may be expected to take on new and unfamiliar forms. Its primary task will be less to preserve what is already explicit in the teaching of the past—although this must of course be done—than to make men sensitive to the breathing of the Spirit in the world today and to open their minds to the future to which God is beckoning his people. The magisterium must, with the help of all who can contribute light, "decipher authentic signs of God's presence and purpose in the happenings" of our age.[29] This discernment cannot take place except against the horizon of the promised Kingdom. Our hope for the future is constitutive of our understanding of the present; our vocation to the Kingdom first tells us what we really are—and what God is.

The magisterium must continue to be concerned, as it

always has been, with authentic tradition; but the very idea of tradition has to be newly understood. Taking issue with Josef Pieper, Jürgen Moltmann has drawn a vivid contrast between the Greek concept of tradition, which presupposes a golden age in the past, and the Christian idea, which prophetically announces what is to be. In the Old Testament view, Moltmann declares, the promised future lures us forward:

> This tradition of promise turns our eyes not towards some primaeval, original event, but towards the future and finally towards an *eschaton* of fulfillment. We do not drift through history with our backs to the future and our gaze returning ever and again to the origin, but we stride confidently toward the promised future. It is not the primaeval ancients who are near the truth and dwell nearer to the gods, but it is to future generations that the promises are given, in order that they may see the fulfillment.[30]

In basic continuity with the Old Testament, Christian tradition points forward. It constantly propels the Church to move into the promised future and prepare for eschatological life that is to come.

Once tradition is reinterpreted in this dynamic sense, it becomes possible to overcome the restrictive and repressive conception of magisterium now current. The pastors of the Church may properly regard it as their prime responsibility to direct the Church into God's future. Theirs is a prophetic function. As true shepherds, they must seek to walk ahead of the people of God and not to be the last defenders of a vanishing status quo.

Can we realistically hope for a magisterium such as I have sought to describe? To some, discouraged by recent and well-publicized events, the program I have sketched may seem unduly idealistic. But I think it is too easy, by concentrating on momentary difficulties, to overlook the enormous progress that is being made. What future historians, I suspect, will most remember about the Church in the 1960s is not the inevitable hesitations, failures, and delays, but rather the bold measures that have been taken. In the five years since the Council we have witnessed many steps in the directions outlined in this chapter.

Collegiality is rapidly establishing itself on every level.

Early in October 1969 the International Commission of Theologians held its first session in Rome. In the following two weeks the Episcopal Synod met in an important special session with the pope. The internationalization of the Roman Curia is well under way. Nearly every region of the Church has an effectively organized Episcopal Conference. On the national and diocesan level there have been innumerable synods, senates, and pastoral councils with wide participation on the part of both clergy and laity. While much remains to be done, powerful forces have unquestionably been set in motion.

To a great extent the preoccupation of the magisterium with recondite points of doctrine has been abandoned. Pope John and Pope Paul have shown no interest in new dogmatic definitions, and the Second Vatican Council refused to issue any new infallible pronouncements. The magisterium has adopted a more pastoral style and has addressed itself to the pressing practical problems of the Church and the world today.

Striking too is the new manner of leadership of the last two popes. Unlike their predecessors since 1870, neither of them has been content to remain immured in Vatican City. They have gone out to the world to visit not only churches and shrines but factories, hospitals, and prisons. They have taught not simply by what they have said but by their attitudes and actions. Pope John, radiating joy, compassion, mildness, and optimism, presented a new image of the Church and in so doing caught the imagination of the world. Paul VI has likewise taught most effectively by his inspired dramatic actions. History will long remember his journey to Jerusalem and his cordial encounters with the Patriarch Athenagoras; it will remember too his voyage to Bombay, so expressive of the breadth of the Church's concern for the poor; his address to the United Nations in which he so clearly identified the Church with the cause of human peace and international justice; his trip to Geneva, so significant for relations both with the labor movement and with the Protestant world; and his journeys to Uganda and the Far East where he underscored the importance of regional autonomy for the churches of the developing nations.

If difficulties have arisen about certain documents emanating from the Holy See, this is, from one point of view, a proof of the distance we have come. There is a new breath of freedom in the air. Catholics are no longer prepared to submit blindly to teaching that seems at odds with the liberalizing and modernizing tendencies of which I have spoken. The criticism shows not that the magisterium is on the verge of collapse, but that certain forms of the magisterium, long in honor, are becoming unacceptable. Instead of feeling dejected about this, we ought rather to lift up our eyes and contemplate the emerging possibilities. New and imaginative styles may be expected in the magisterium of the Church tomorrow.

The Permanence of Prophecy in the Church

In accordance with the scope and purpose of this work we have concentrated mainly, in the past few chapters, on the doctrinal aspect of the ministry of the word. Several times, however, we have alluded to the role of the charismatics, and, in particular, to that of the prophets. During the past decade a remarkable number of seemingly prophetic Christian leaders have made their appearance on the scene, radiating new hope and enthusiasm, and condemning, sometimes with passionate intensity, the conservative elements in the Church and in secular society. While it would take us too far afield to assess the various messages of these "prophets," or the means which they have seen fit to adopt—both violent and non-violent—our treatment of the magisterium would be one-sided unless we were to consider the abiding importance of the prophetic ministry in the Christian Church.

In apostolic times the ministry of the word was exercised by different classes of persons, including apostles, evangelists, teachers, and various charismatic figures. Among the charismatics the place of highest dignity belonged to the prophets (1 Cor. 14:1–5), who are regularly ranked second after the apostles and thus above the teachers (1 Cor. 12:28; Eph. 2:20, 3:5, 4:11). If the Church of today is the continuation of the apostolic Church, one might expect to find in her persons having the same or equivalent gifts. That bishops are successors to the apostles has long been an accepted Catholic thesis. But have we sufficiently attended to this problem: Who, if anyone, has taken over the functions of the prophets and teachers?

The problem of succession in the prophetic lines seems to offer special difficulty, since prophecy is by its nature a charismatic gift, distributed by the Holy Spirit when and as he wills. Yet it seems clear that charismatic gifts have not died out in the Church. Up to most recent times, visionaries and ecstatics have made their appearance, and there have been periodic outbursts of glossalalia resembling the biblical "gift of tongues." As the magisterium itself teaches, the completeness of the Church in every age demands both hierarchical grades and charismatic gifts, so that charismatically endowed persons will never be wanting to the Church.[1] Thus we ought to consider seriously whether there are not, or should not be, successors of the phophets in the contemporary Church.

According to Acts 2:16–17, St. Peter interpreted the miracle of Pentecost as evidence that the whole Church was a prophetic community, animated by the Holy Spirit. God had fulfilled Joel's oracle, "Your sons and your daughters shall prophesy." But from the New Testament as a whole it is clear that certain individuals were specially called to exercise the prophetic ministry (Rom. 12:6; 1 Cor. 12:4–10, 28–29).[2] While these prophets were in some cases itinerant preachers (e.g., Judas Barsabbas, Silas, Agabus), the majority seem to have been leading figures in the local communities. According as the Spirit gave them, they would utter words of praise or condemnation; they would summon to penance or to renewed hope. The effects of prophecy are described as edification, encouragement, and consolation (1 Cor. 14:3).

For the sake of accuracy, one must distinguish the prophets from the apostles, evangelists, teachers, and ecstatics. They differ from apostles in that they do not speak as official witnesses of the risen Christ, but give more particular admonitions on the basis of what the Spirit teaches them. Unlike evangelists, they are not missionaries; they proclaim not the basic news of God's salvific deed in Christ, but its further implications for life and conduct. Thus they speak within the Christian community. They differ also from teachers, since they are concerned not with general points of doctrine, but with urging, on the basis of an inspired insight, the course to be taken in the present concrete situation. In connection with their admonitions, the prophets not infrequently predict things to come, especially in the proximate future (e.g., Acts 11:28, 21:9–10). They differ, finally, from the ecstatics, because they are not rapt out of their senses. They speak with full self-possession in a language that all can understand (1 Cor. 14:6–25).

Although the author of the Apocalypse, imitating the style of some Old Testament prophets, claims unquestionable authority for his message (Apoc. 22:18–19), the New Testament prophets are usually regarded as subject to critical scrutiny. Their message is to be rejected if it contradicts the Church's Christological faith (1 Cor. 12:3; 1 Jn. 4:3) or fails to harmonize with orthodox teaching (Rom. 12:6, according to one interpretation). But these doctrinal tests, valid though they may be, are insufficient. Nor are miracles, taken by themselves, a sure criterion, for false prophets are able to deceive by signs and wonders (cf. Mk. 13:22). The good or evil fruits of the prophet's teaching are a third type of sign (Mt. 7:15–23). None of these signs, however, gives automatic certitude. The final assessment requires prudence and insight. The entire community should normally play a part in the process of discernment (1 Cor. 14:29–33; cf. 1 Thess. 5:21; 1 Jn. 4:1), but some are gifted with a particular charism to discern with divine assurance (1 Cor. 12:10).

Building on the experience of the apostolic Church, the Fathers of the first two centuries took it for granted that the charism of prophecy was a permanent endowment of the Church. In the *Didache* (nos. 11–13) elaborate rules are laid down for the reception of visiting prophets and for distinguishing genuine prophets from their counterfeits. Some have seen in these prescriptions an indication that certain communities, having no prophets of their own, had to depend on visitors to fill their role. About the middle of the second century, Justin argues in his *Dialogue with Trypho the Jew* that "from the fact that even to this day the gifts of prophecy exist among us Christians, you should realize the gifts which resided among your people have now been transferred to us."[3] Miltiades, who was probably a pupil of Justin, was heavily engaged in the struggle against Montanism. He set it down as a rule that a true prophet does not speak in ecstasy.[4] Notwithstanding

the aberrations of the Montanists, Miltiades is convinced
that, according to the doctrine of St. Paul, "it is necessary
that the charism of prophecy should be present in the
whole Church until the final parousia."[5] Irenaeus, who
was likewise concerned with the growing combat with false
prophets, felt it necessary to defend true prophecy. Some,
he observed, in their excess of zeal against the pseudo-
prophets, go so far as to reject the grace of genuine prophecy in the Church.[6]

By the third century charismatic prophecy begins to be
viewed as a thing of the past. Origen in his controversies
with Celsus so treats it.[7] As the Church becomes increasingly a society of law and doctrine, the magisterium and
theologians gain fuller control of the ministry of the Word.
This trend continued in the Middle Ages, when prophecy
fared best in what Ronald Knox calls the "Christian underworld."

St. Thomas Aquinas, from his intellectualist point of
view, is concerned with prophecy as a supernatural mode
of knowledge. It interests him principally as a means by
which the deposit of faith was built up in biblical times.
At the end of his treatise on prophecy he adds, almost by
way of concession, that even after apostolic times "there
were not lacking some endowed with a spirit of prophecy, not indeed for declaring any new teaching of faith,
but for the direction of human actions."[8] While acknowl-
edging that postbiblical prophets may be useful insofar as
they serve to correct men's behavior, he seems to give them
no role in casting light on what people should believe.[9]
For the lacunae in St. Thomas' doctrine of prophecy one
may assign three main factors, all rooted in the mental
climate of his day: a sharp dichotomy between the speculative and practical intellect, an inadequate realization of
the importance of postbiblical history,[10] and a spirituality
intensely focused on man's hope for eternal life hereafter.

As the mere mention of Bernard of Clairvaux, Francis
of Assisi, and Catherine of Siena should suffice to prove,
prophetism remained in lively tension with sacerdotalism
throughout the Middle Ages. But the increasing fre-
quency with which prophetic spirits ended up as heretics or
martyrs—we all recall in this connection figures such as
Joan of Arc and Savonarola—seems to indicate that the institutional Church was becoming continually less recep-

tive to prophetic criticism. Several Catholic ecclesiologists have seen the ecumenical significance of this development. The history of the Reformation might have been quite different if the Church in the sixteenth century had been more open to searching scrutiny in the light of the gospel.[11] In post-Reformation times, the history of western Christianity is dominated by the struggle between the prophetism of the Reformation churches and the sacerdotalism of the Catholic tradition. In a separation that ought never to have occurred, churches of the word were arrayed against churches of the sacrament. From the standpoint of Russian Orthodoxy, Vladimir Solovyev and Nicholas Berdyaev added their own prophetic protest against the priestly bent of Roman Catholicism. "More than all other Christianities," writes Knox, "the Catholic Church is institutional."[12]

In Catholic theological literature since the Reformation, prophecy was progressively demoted to the point where it came to be regarded primarily as an extrinsic sign validating the authority of persons claiming to speak in the name of God. In this view, the content of prophecy was deprived of intrinsic interest. It was enough that the prophet should predict some unknowable future contingency. All attention was focused on the material correspondence between what was foretold and what subsequently came to pass. In order to achieve its purposes, prophecy had to be a prediction of verifiable historical occurrences. Little attention was paid to prophecy in the traditional sense of a disclosure of God's plans and purposes in history.

A certain renewal in the theology of prophecy began with the deeper study of ecclesiology in the past century. But Catholic authors, defensively oriented against Protestant positions, were reluctant to admit any real friction between the prophets and the official magisterium. Many, on the contrary, took the view that prophecy was nothing more than the discharge of what they called the "prophetic office" of the Church—an office identified, for all practical purposes, with the magisterium.

There is a profound sense in which the Church has succeeded to the prophetic role of Christ and has become, in Newman's phrase, "God's prophet or messenger" in the world. As Newman goes on to explain, a prophet is one who comes from God, who speaks with authority, who is ever one and the same, who is precise and decisive in his statements, who is equal to successive difficulties, and can smite or overthrow error. Such has the Catholic Church shown herself in her history, and such is she at this day. She alone has the divine spell of controlling the reason of man, and of eliciting faith in her word from high and low, educated and ignorant, restless and dull-minded.[13]

Newman the convert and archenemy of Liberalism might well be impressed by these aspects of the Church. But one may question whether his view does justice to the full biblical concept of prophecy, especially as we find it in the Church of the New Testament. From the standpoint of the twentieth century, moreover, Newman's ecclesiology seems excessively monolithic and triumphal.

Vatican Council II registers a further advance in the rehabilitation of prophecy. Its Constitution on the Church, in an idiom more congenial to our times, teaches that the Church as a whole has a prophetic function (Chapter 2, no. 12). Chapters 3 and 4 go on to explain how the prophetic office is exercised both through the authoritative teaching of the hierarchy (no. 25) and through the unofficial witness of the laity (no. 31). Christ, we are told, fulfills his prophetic office through the laity insofar as he "made them his witnesses and gave them understanding of the faith and the grace of speech (cf. Acts 2:17–18; Apoc. 19:10), so that the power of the Gospel might shine forth in their daily social and family life" (no. 35). But in spite of the biblical allusions, the conception of prophecy here advanced seems to be only a pale reflection of the rich and dynamic charism described in the New Testament. The discussion of charisms in Chapter 1 (no. 7) makes no special mention of prophecy. Nor does the Decree on the Apostolate of the Laity, in its treatment of the laymen's "prophetic role," come any closer to the biblical conception outlined above.

The Council's principal contribution toward a renewal of the theology of prophecy is to be found in passages other than those that deal expressly with the charisms and the prophetic office. The Decree on Ecumenism and the Pastoral Constitution on the Church in the Modern World have far-reaching implications in this regard.

The Decree on Ecumenism, without expressly mentioning the gift of prophecy, makes ample room for prophetic criticism of the Church by those inside and outside her membership. It calls attention to the urgent need for Catholics to "make an honest and careful appraisal of whatever needs to be renewed and achieved in the Catholic household itself" (no. 4). A little later (no. 6) it declares that "Christ summons the Church, as she goes on her pilgrim way, to that continual reformation of which she always has need, insofar as she is an institution of men here on earth." In the following paragraph (no. 7) the Decree embodies a humble confession of sins against unity. All this contrasts strikingly with the previous tendency of Catholics to justify all the ways of their own Church and to dismiss ecclesiastical reformation as a Protestant preoccupation.

The Constitution on the Church in the Modern World deals in a genuinely prophetic manner with the crucial task of "scutinizing the signs of the times and of interpreting them in the light of the gospel" (no. 4). In an important topic sentence, the Constitution goes on to state various presuppositions of prophetic activity, especially the twofold confidence that the Church is led by the Spirit of God and that God manifests his presence and purposes in events of the present age (no. 11). Recognizing the complexity of contemporary developments, the Church freely confesses that she does not always have at hand a solution to particular problems (no. 33), but feels the need of "special help, particularly in our day, when things are changing very rapidly and the ways of thinking are exceedingly various" (no. 44). Only through the assistance of all who may be favored with light and understanding can the Church hope successfully to "hear, distinguish and interpret the many voices of our age and to judge them in the light of the divine Word" (no. 44).

Through documents such as those just mentioned, Vatican Council II expressed the Church's need for prophetic guidance and in so doing faced up to the needs of our day. The demand is not for ecstatics caught up into another world, but for men capable of discerning God's hand in the history of our times. Prophecy in this sense must, in Rahner's words, "contain concrete and timely imperatives for our day, deriving from the general theology of the fu-

ture and of history which Scripture already gives us."[14]
The Israelite prophets of the classical period spoke in this
way. Even in their predictions they did not appeal to clair-
voyance: "The contents of these predictions are always related to contemporary historical circumstances and may
be explained as the result of a normal faculty of observa-
tion combined with an intensified insight into the religious
and moral situation of Israel."[15] Conscious of the new
and urgent demands of God's word, they castigated the
deficiencies of a religion that was in danger of formalism
and superstition. They issued a ringing challenge to repentance and reform.

The current demand for prophets in the Church is due
in part to the revolutionary changes in our time. Under
pain of irrelevance the Church can no longer ignore the
course of world history. The rapidly evolving secular culture of our day puts questions to the Church for which
there are no ready-made solutions. Scrutinizing the signs
of the times, Christianity must reinterpret its own doctrine and goals in relation to the world of today. To effect
this transposition without loss of substance is a task calling for prophetic insight.

Churchmen are always tempted to suppress prophecy,
for it is a disturbing element. By upsetting men's settled
views and destroying their complacencies, it continually
threatens the unity and stability of the institutional
Church. Yet the Church needs prophecy. "A Church in
which the prophets have to keep silent declines, and becomes a spiritless organization" and its pastors degenerate
into mere bureaucrats.[16] In such a Church, men would be
suffocated by the fumes of a decaying sacerdotalism. As
George Bernard Shaw once declared, a fruitful tension
must be maintained among the regal, sacerdotal, and prophetic powers: "We must accept the tension and maintain
it nobly without letting ourselves be tempted to relieve it
by burning the thread."[17]

St. Paul exhorted his communities to have deep respect
for prophecy (1 Thess. 5:20) and to aspire to prophetic
gifts (1 Cor. 14:1, 39). Subsequent history has shown that
when prophets are not given their say within the Church,
they rise up to condemn it from outside. Vatican Council
II therefore acted wisely in exposing the Church to harsh
winds of prophetic criticism from within its own ranks.

If the priest needs the prophet, the reverse is also true.

A Church governed by prophets alone would be no better than one without prophets. When the ostensible prophets disagree, others must meditate between them. When they go beyond the bounds of practicality, as prophets are wont to do, others must stress the values of moderation, compromise, and civility.

The two gifts of priesthood and prophecy, far from being antithetical, require each other. At times they are even found in the same individual. Several of Israel's greatest prophets, including Ezekiel, were priests. Christ himself, who eminently fulfilled the role of eschatological prophet, is the eternal high priest. And in our own time, one of the most truly prophetic figures in the Church, John XXIII, was a pope. The prophetic priest is sometimes torn by painful conflict between loyalty to the institution that he serves and discontent with its present condition. But is this not the inescapable fate of one who accepts a ministry in the Church that was born on Pentecost? While working within the institutional framework to which he owes his message and his forum, the priest must be conscious of the defects and limitations of institutional religion. Otherwise he would turn into a mere functionary.

If the prophet and the priest are not one and the same person, let them at least, like Moses and Aaron, be brothers. For their ultimate goals are the same. The prophet, unless he is to undermine the basis of his own protest, must stand in solidarity with the Church. And his goal must ultimately be constructive. Since all the gifts of the Spirit are bestowed "for building up the body of Christ" (Eph. 4:12), the prophet as well as the priest must "strive to excel in building up the Church" (1 Cor. 14:12).

III. THE REVISION OF DOGMA

— 9 —

Doubt in the Modern Church

In the concluding portion of this book I wish to address myself to the problem of doctrinal change. To many Christians, especially in the Catholic tradition, such change is restricted within very narrow limits because the Church is viewed as a divine oracle that must always continue to teach with absolute certitude the truth revealed in Jesus Christ. Christian faith, on this view, is unalterably shaped by the immutable dogmas of the Church. Although there is some validity in the approach reflected by this objection, deeper inquiry should make it clear that there is ample room for doubt and revision even with regard to the dogmas of the Church. Before concentrating specifically on dogma, I should like to set forth some general reflections on the dialectical relationship between certitude and doubt in the act of faith.

The title of this chapter is admittedly scandalous. In most Christian traditions, doubt in the area of religion is equated with sin. Catholics, when examining their consciences for confession, are advised to consider whether they have entertained doubts about matters of faith and to seek absolution for those doubts that may have been voluntary. While an individual Christian might be thought likely to fall victim to doubt, it seems hardly proper to ascribe doubt to the Church itself. Since doubt is viewed as separating man, at least partly, from the Church, some would think it absurd to attribute doubt to the Church. And yet I shall here attribute it to the Church —at every level.

Most laymen can be brought without difficulty to acknowledge that they or other laymen can be assailed by doubt, but they are inclined to think that the clergy have some higher form of faith, immune to such corrosive influences. Or if they come around to admitting that a priest might have doubts, they still assume that bishops have some charism of certain knowledge about all truly important religious issues. Or at least—to take the most obvious case—they would think it clear that the pope can have no doubts.

Pope Paul VI's long hesitation and evident anguish in reaching his decision about birth control, combined with his refusal to invoke his infallible teaching authority in issuing an encyclical on the subject, shattered the illusions of many of the faithful regarding the pope's immunity to doubt. They began to suspect that even the "Vicar of Christ" might be uncertain as to what is or is not essential Catholic doctrine. The very fact that a possible change of doctrine was long and carefully considered—and that such a change was advocated by a majority of the papal commission on birth control, and in fact may still be in the offing—gave rise to doubts about the rectitude of the present teaching. Many commentators found it hard to see how the papal press secretary, Monsignor Fausto Vallainc, could say that if the Church changed its position on birth control, this would not imply doubt at any moment; it would be a change from one state of certitude to another.[1] Whoever admits the possibility of such a change can hardly be certain, in the normal sense of the term, that the current official teaching is correct.

At first sight it seems difficult to understand why so many Christians are convinced that doubt in the province of religious truth is out of place. Experience seems to indicate that there is as much room for groping and uncertainty in this area as in science, history, or other fields of knowledge. If I have no sufficient warrant for taking a definite stand, I ought to keep an open mind. To whip oneself up to an unfounded and merely subjective state of certitude is not faith but fanaticism. And to pretend to a certitude that I do not possess is hypocrisy. Fanaticism and hypocrisy, although they have often existed in the Church, are certainly not Christian virtues. Jesus, as we know from the Gospels, rejected the fanaticism of the Zealots and denounced the hypocrisy of the Scribes and Pharisees.

I should be prepared to argue, in fact, that doubt is

often an authentic Christian virtue. Men do not commonly like to face important issues that call their previous convictions into question. Many people never come to faith because they ask too few questions, not too many. When the mind is full of its own certitudes it has no room for God. But one who has accustomed himself to radical questioning, and who realizes the utter insecurity of every human answer, has one of the main prerequisites of faith. Unbelievers, for the most part, refuse to ask the great and serious questions—for example: Is there anything in existence beyond ourselves and the world we experience? Is there any goal of human life that can be attained in spite of poverty, sickness, isolation, death? Is it better to receive than to give? Is there anything worth living and dying for? To ask questions of this kind implies a serious concern for truth, high idealism, readiness to sacrifice. For in changing our ideas you always sacrifice something of yourself. You have to be humble enough to admit that you were previously wrong.

Christian theologians do not seem to have reflected sufficiently on the theology of the question. Have we ever seriously asked ourselves the reason why, from a purely grammatical point of view, there are so many questions in the Gospels and so few direct answers? Innumerable questions are put to Jesus, but he often answers evasively and sometimes not at all. He frequently refuses to say, in response to questioning, whether he is or is not the Messiah, the King of the Jews. He does not tell the curious questioner whether many or few will be saved. Nor does he inform the subtle disputant what is required for someone to be his neighbor. Nor does he answer the persistent questions of the disciples regarding the time when the Kingdom of Israel will be restored and the Son of Man will return. On the other hand, Jesus himself asks many searching questions: Who do you say that I am? Which of the three was neighbor to him who fell among the robbers? If I cast out devils by Beelzebub, by whom do your children cast them out? When the Son of Man comes, do you think that he will find faith on earth? Why do you call me good? Was John's baptism from heaven or from men? If David calls him—the Messiah—Lord, how is he his son? Why are you troubled? Why are you anxious? Why are you afraid?

All of this suggests that the life of faith consists in constant probing. Easy answers are not faith, and faith is no answer except to the man who questions deeply. If faith puts us in communion with the absolute mystery we call God, there is a sense in which faith does not answer anything. Its chief task, perhaps, is to preclude superficial and premature answers, which give the impression of having mastered the unfathomable.

Quite evidently, neuroticism is possible in the realm of doubt as well as in that of certitude. While some people compulsively claim to have absolute certitude about everything really important, others are mortally afraid of admitting that anything is certain. They are torn by anxiety about whether they really exist, whether the whole world is just a dream, whether their best friend really likes them, and so forth. Both these groups of neurotics succeed pretty well in making themselves and everybody around them miserable. In a way, they are both victims of the same obsession. Straining for a kind of evidence that is humanly unattainable, they fail to see and to respond appropriately to the evidences that are at hand. Indubitable certitudes are few and far between.

Many readers doubtless would be prepared to concede that religious doubt and questioning are praiseworthy were they not convinced that faith involves unshakable certitude. We must therefore face the problem whether the full commitment we call "faith" is compatible with doubt. Doubt seems to imply openness and lack of commitment, and thus lack of faith. Thus there seem to be two clearcut alternatives. If faith, no doubt, and if doubt, no faith.

Now I should concede that if doubt excludes certitude, it also excludes faith. But I deny that doubt excludes certitude. As Augustine pointed out in his refutation of skepticism,[2] every doubt includes some certitude, or rather many certitudes: Whenever I doubt that something is true, I am certain that I exist, that I doubt, that there is such a thing as truth, that I may be wrong, that I ought not to assent rashly, etc. If you analyze any particular doubt, and especially a doubt that involves real anxiety (for example, whether a given war is just or unjust), you will see that it implies a multitude of strong convictions —e.g., that there is a war going on, that some wars are unjust, that one has a duty to inquire before taking part in a possibly unjust war, and so forth. It often happens that men with the deepest convictions are those who suffer the most from doubt, whereas the thoughtless and the superficial have neither conviction nor doubt.

We have seen that he who seriously doubts one thing is necessarily certain about many others. A more difficult point is whether we can simultaneously be certain of and doubt the same thing. In some areas of knowledge, the answer is clearly "No." My certitude that I am presently at my typewriter excludes a simultaneous doubt about the same matter. So, too, my certitude about some self-evident maxim, such as that the whole is greater than any of its parts, does away with any doubt about the truth of that maxim. In general, whatever is immediately evident or strictly demonstrable admits of a certitude that excludes real doubt.

But if something is indubitable, it cannot be an object of faith either. The content of faith is always something that we do not see and cannot strictly prove. This can easily be illustrated from the Old and New Testaments. Ancient Israel lived by the conviction that its God, Yahweh, would keep his covenant promises and would make the fortunes of the country prosper if the people trusted and obeyed him. The people knew about Yahweh and his promises, not by having personally seen and heard him—this can scarcely be affirmed even of the prophets, notwithstanding the biblical imagery of how the "word of the Lord" came to them—but primarily because he had given signs of his power and mercy in their history. On the strength of these signs, interpreted by the prophets, the Israelites placed their faith in the Lord of the Covenant.

In the New Testament, faith for the Christians meant acceptance of Jesus as the Messiah (Christ), Lord, and Savior. Those who heard and believed the good news that God had raised Jesus from the dead and constituted him Lord of the universe had what the Christians called "faith." The first Christians did not actually see that Jesus was Messiah or Lord, but they found signs in their own lives, and in the history they witnessed, which provided a sufficient basis for believing these things. Their belief had certitude in the sense that they voluntarily put full trust and confidence in Jesus. For his sake they were willing to face poverty, persecution, and death. But faith did not give clear evidence of a sort that would exclude intellectual doubt. The Christian walks—as Paul expressed it in 2 Cor.

5:7—by faith, not by sight. And so faith is defined in his Letter to the Hebrews as "the evidence of things not seen" (11:1).

From these biblical examples it should be clear that the certitude of faith is different in kind from the certitude of vision or that of mathematical or syllogistic demonstration. These other kinds of certitude exclude doubt, but faith is open to doubt in the sense that any believer is aware that at any moment he could, without absurdity, stop believing. His faith is suspended over a void of non-evidence. This consciousness of the lack of compelling evidence renders faith internally vulnerable to doubt.

Does this imply that the believer, while he believes, can simultaneously doubt the very things he believes? Many theologians would answer in the negative, as Newman did, for instance, when he coined his famous phrase that "ten thousand difficulties do not make one doubt." "Difficulty and doubt," he continued, "are incommensurate. . . . A man may be annoyed that he cannot work out a mathematical problem, of which the answer is or is not given to him, without doubting that it admits of an answer, or that a certain particular answer is the true one. Of all points of faith, the being of a God is, to my own apprehension, encompassed with most difficulty, and yet borne in upon our minds with most power."[3]

Newman's statement is true enough, but still we must, I think, recognize that sometimes the assent of faith is accompanied not simply by difficulties but even by doubts. We have positive reasons for denying the affirmations of faith, and these reasons gnaw away at the assent itself. For example, while we believe that Jesus Christ was truly the Son of God, we are aware of many grounds for holding that no man could have a claim to this title in anything but a metaphorical sense. So, too, we believe that Jesus rose from the dead in spite of abundant evidence that men who die remain dead. Because of the contrary evidence, our minds are internally torn; our assent is a restless one. What we confidently profess on the strength of the Scriptures and the creeds we are inclined to deny when we attend to other considerations. Like the distressed father in the Gospel story we cry out in prayer: "Lord, I believe, help my unbelief" (Mk. 9:24).

Because of the complexity of the human psyche, it is possible for a man to believe on one level what he disbelieves on another. As Karl Rahner puts it, man is normally somewhat schizophrenic.[4] Since we live in a world largely populated by non-Christians, we are inevitably affected by the prevailing disbelief. Something of it rubs off on us, with the result that, often enough, we are not sure to what extent we can call ourselves "believers." Do we assent with the depth and intensity really required for personal commitment? Are we convinced in the inmost core of our being? Are our hesitations merely fleeting and peripheral, or is our profession of Christianity vacillating, even insincere? We cannot tell, with evidential certitude, whether or not we belong in the category of true believers. We hope that we believe, and because we lack introspective insight into the inner recesses of our own minds, that is the best we can do. Even God cannot ask more of us.

In the popular opinion, doubt, if it co-exists with faith, is an evil. We may tolerate it, but we should seek to be rid of it. An ideal act of faith would be unaccompanied by doubt. Such is the popular opinion, but is it correct? Paul Tillich argues, in my view correctly, that a certain type of doubt—he calls it "existential doubt"—is necessarily present in the structure of faith, insofar as there is an element of insecurity in every existential truth. If we acutely experience the doubt, as occasionally happens, this is not to be regarded as abnormal or evil. "If doubt appears," Tillich says, "it should not be considered as the negation of faith, but as an element which was always and will always be present in the act of faith. Existential doubt and faith are poles of the same reality, the state of ultimate concern."[5]

Existential doubt does not exclude the personal commitment of faith, but rather calls for it. Faith is an act of courage, by which we pin the meaning of our lives on something we do not see and cannot prove. In any such act of daring, Tillich explains, there is a real possibility of failure, but the risk is worth taking because unless we make an act of faith the ultimate meaning of our life escapes us.

History affords ample evidence that every really great human life is based on faith. A man without faith is dragged about by the hope of worldly pleasure and the fear of pain, the expectation of success and the dread of failure, and all sorts of motives that inhibit his freedom and blunt his purpose. Faith gives a freedom and a rock-like strength that cannot be attained in any other way. Because the man of faith chooses what really counts for him, and accords supreme value to something greater than any force within the world, he can move ahead without being distracted by passion and fear. The lives of the saints vividly demonstrate that faith is productive of assurance, peace, joy, confidence, and energy. Even those who feel unable to believe cannot help feeling somewhat envious of the man of faith. Such a man is not immune to doubt, but he is able to go on believing in spite of doubt. Realizing that, humanly speaking, he has no security, he accepts his perilous condition and pins his security on the God in whom he believes. His faith is not blind, but fully cognizant of its own condition. Thanks to the purifying influence of doubt, the mature believer keeps his own commitment under constant criticism and thus avoids the pitfalls of superstition and fanaticism. Because he is keenly aware of all the reasons for not believing, he is able to enter a meaningful dialogue with the confident unbeliever whom he meets in the world, the troubled believer whom he meets in the Church, and the secret unbeliever who lurks in the consciousness of the most committed Christian.[6]

Now that we have explored somewhat the relationship between doubt and certitude in the individual's act of faith, we may turn to the second major question raised by the title of this chapter: What is the place of doubt in the Church? Many Christians would concede that faith would be the kind of venture I have thus far described except that Christ instituted an authoritative Church, capable of removing the element of doubt from faith.

Too many Christians, especially Roman Catholics, look upon the Church as though it were a great infallibility machine. You grind in the problem, deposit a coin, and out pops an infallible answer. By a kind of instinct, and not a wholly good one, people are inclined to look to the Church for all the security they find lacking in their own lives. Far from being pleased when they are told that they are free to doubt or deny certain teachings of the Church, anxious believers become angry and disappointed. They cannot abide the idea of a Church that is not always protected against error. This is one of the factors that complicates the continuing crisis regarding the Church's teaching on birth control. Some of the faithful want the doctrine to change in a direction that will give them greater freedom. But others would feel let down if it were admitted that in such an important matter the Church could change her teaching, thereby admitting, in effect, that she had been wrong.

In point of fact, theologically educated Catholics have always known that the vast majority of the Church's teaching is fallible and therefore subject to error. In all the thousands of pages of encyclicals issued by the popes of the last hundred years, there is not to my knowledge a single sentence of infallible teaching. In the 800-odd pages of the documents of Vatican II, there is not one new statement for which infallibility is claimed. But if a given doctrine is not infallible, it is fallible; in other words, it could be wrong. Having once conceded that their teaching could be wrong, Church authorities should not be afraid to admit, when the occasion requires, that they have been wrong.

If you went through the whole history of Church teaching, you could find a multitude of questions on which the Church has actually reversed its teaching. In the Middle Ages taking interest on money loans was considered sinful, and many theologians taught that sexual intercourse between husband and wife was always somewhat sinful.

In the seventeenth century Church authorities condemned Galileo for teaching that the sun did not go round the earth and forced him to retract. At a later stage the theory of evolution was condemned, and Catholics were obliged to hold strictly to the historical character of the creation story in Genesis. The Biblical Commission, on behalf of the pope, made countless decisions regarding the text and interpretation of the Bible that have since been found to have been mistaken.

A more recent example would be Vatican II. In all honesty it is not possible to say that Vatican II speaks about the other Churches, the other religions, or religious liberty in the same way as earlier popes and councils had spoken. The ancient doctrine "Outside the Church, no salvation" has been so drastically reinterpreted by Vatican II that the meaning is almost the opposite of what the words seem to say. Modern Catholics take a very different view of this matter than their ancestors in the Middle Ages.

In many cases the faithful are not aware that the doctrine is being changed. Roman documents have a way of making it appear, whenever they say something new, that they are just clarifying what has always been taught. For this reason most of the faithful are still unaware of how fallible most of the Church's guidance really is.

You might ask why the Church is so reluctant to admit that its doctrine really changes. I can think of two reasons. One is that, as mentioned above, the faithful want the consolation of feeling that the Church gives guidance without any risk of error. The other is that ecclesiastical authorities are afraid that if they admit their vulnerability to error the faithful will become disrespectful and insubordinate.

I myself am convinced that both these motives are unworthy. In the present democratic age, adult people should be able to get along without fostering illusions of infallibility in areas where there is no infallibility. And the faithful should be able to accept a religious authority that could, on occasion, fall into error. Some Catholics ask petulantly, "What is the use of a fallible teaching authority?" To that question one can best reply with another: "What is the use of a fallible doctor, lawyer, judge, or professor?" In every field of knowledge except religion people have grown accustomed to recognizing the value of experts and officials who make no pretense of being immune to error.

Nothing that I have said should be taken as a denial that the Church does have a certain measure of infallibility. I am convinced that it does. According to the Gospels, Christ promised that the Church would last till the end of time and that the powers of death would never triumph over it; he said he would be with his apostles, or their successors, for all the centuries to come. If the Church lost sight of the essential content of God's revelation in Christ and definitely committed itself to a false understanding of the gospel, the world would be in effect deprived of the benefits of Christ's coming. Thanks to the Church, God continues to make the truth of Christ available from one century to the next.

While the Church does not understand everything with complete clarity, it has never lost sight of the essential message of the gospel, and Catholics, at least, believe that it never will. At certain decisive turning points of its history, the Church has spoken with complete unanimity and unclouded assurance about life-and-death issues. For example, when certain Christians in the fourth century denied the divintiy of Christ, and in the fifth century of the Holy Spirit, the Church, in several ecumenical councils, spoke out confidently on these points and forged the glorious creeds that are recited to this day. Not only Catholics but most Protestant and Orthodox Christians agree that the Church took the only position on these points that it could have taken, under pain of denying its own essential heritage.

On the basis of these observations, let us return to the question of doubt in the Church. Can a loyal Catholic, without wishing to leave the Church, doubt any of its teachings? The answer to this question is plainly "Yes." Quite evidently, the fallible teaching of the Church may and should be doubted whenever there is good reason to suspect that it is wrong and that it should be changed.

With regard to infallible teaching, the question is more complicated, but still there may be place for doubt. This is true for several reasons. In the first place, there is no clear line of demarcation between fallible and infallible teaching. There is no infallible list of what the infallible teachings are. We have to rely on the agreement of theologians in this matter, and they sometimes disagree. In some periods of history the zone of infallibility is understood very widely; at other times it is contracted. In the nineteenth and early twentieth centuries we went through a period when some theologians were claiming infallibility for all sorts of statements that could hardly, by any stretch of the imagination, be found in the original Christian revelation. For example, it was taught that the Church could infallibly pronounce that a given saint was really in heaven. Today most theologians speak far more cautiously. Tomorrow they may be more cautious still. Whenever there are grounds for doubting that a given teaching really is infallible, one may, for sufficient reasons, doubt whether it is true.

Finally, let us consider those cases where we can be quite sure that the Church has exercised infallible teaching power—for example, the doctrine that there are three divine persons: Father, Son, and Holy Spirit. Is there room for doubt even here? Again, I should answer "Yes." For as I said earlier in this chapter, faith by its very nature is subject to doubt; its certitude cannot be the tranquil and untroubled certitude of clear vision. Even while mak-

ing the free commitment of faith, we may be troubled by
anxiety. Because of the complexity of the human mind,
with its many levels of consciousness, we can wholeheartedly assent to something while at the same time we are inclined to disbelieve it. We are conscious of the risk of
faith.

One thing that stands in the way of an untroubled assent to much of the Church's teaching is the difficulty of
understanding just what it means. When we are told, for
example, that Christ descended into hell or that he
ascended into heaven, it is hard to determine the real content of these statements. No one today would understand,
as earlier Christians did, that heaven is up above the stars
and hell down beneath the earth. Different individuals
understand the same dogmas in different ways. When one
person says he does not believe that God is personal and
another asserts that God is personal, we cannot immediately assume that they are contradicting each other; perhaps they understand the word "personal" in two different
senses. And so likewise other key terms, such as "Incarnation," "Resurrection," and "Redemption," admit of a variety of meanings, which makes it difficult for people to decide whether they accept these doctrines or not. Until they
perceive what they are being asked to believe, they may
legitimately be in a state of indecision. After all, nobody
can really assent to something he does not even understand.

The difficulty of assent is even greater when the doctrines seem to mean something incredible. Some ways of
stating the doctrine of the Trinity are so paradoxical that
they seem to demand a sacrifice of reason itself. When we
are told that God is completely simple and that one and
the same God is three distinct persons, it sounds as though
we were being asked to believe, in effect, that one is three
and three is one. No matter how hard he tries, no one can
believe an internally contradictory statement. Until the
statement is explained in such a way that it does not seem
to involve a contradiction, the Christian is within his rights
in withholding an assent. At best his act of faith will have
to take the form of believing that the Church will be able
to explain the proposition in a coherent manner. Until this
explanation is offered, belief must take the form of hope
that one will eventually be able to believe what is really
meant.

My conclusion, then, is that there is lots of room for legitimate doubts on the part of faithful members of the Church. They may doubt fallible Church teaching as soon as they have reason to suspect that it is wrong. They may withhold assent from infallible teaching when they are not sure that it really is infallible, or when they do not understand what they are being asked to believe, or when it is proposed to them in a way that is apparently absurd and incredible. Finally, even when one does assent, the very nature of faith allows for the possibility that the believer may simultaneously doubt the very thing to which he is assenting. There is no reason why Christians should have a bad conscience regarding doubts that seem to them reasonable or unavoidable. A desperate attempt to suppress doubts of this kind can have disastrous effects both for one's religious and for one's psychological life.

In the next and final portion of this chapter I should like to take up the question of doubt in the *modern* Church.[7]

There are special circumstances in the contemporary world that make for a vast increase of doubt. For brevity's sake, let me limit myself to three. First of all, the modern era lives under the sign of science, which owes its progress to its persistent use of deliberate, methodic doubt. In the eyes of scientists, all laws and theories are regarded as merely tentative and as subject to continual testing and modification in the light of further evidence. Secondly, partly as a result of scientific progress, we have entered into an era of ever-accelerating change. The world-views of ancient and medieval man are hopelessly obsolete, and we have no assurance that our own world-view will stand up for any length of time. We seem to have no stable screen upon which to project our ideas, or, to change the metaphor, no abiding principles upon which to base our thoughts and actions. Everything is in a dizzying state of flux. Thirdly, we live in a time of unprecedented pluralism. Almost every day we are exposed to the clash of mutually conflicting ideologies and religions. This makes it very hard for the individual to claim that his point of view —or that of his own religious group—is certainly right and that the rest are certainly wrong.

These three factors—or others that might be mentioned —do not, in my opinion, make faith impossible, but they may make it more difficult, and they unquestionably affect the quality of faith when it does arise. Contemporary faith is almost bound to be mingled with a larger ingredient of doubt than was considered admissible by Christians of an earlier generation. But since faith and doubt are not mutually exclusive, the presence of doubt is not necessarily destructive of faith. A faith that does not feel itself to be threatened is scarcely an authentic faith at all.

To illustrate the change that has taken place, we might consider the attitude that our forefathers several generations ago took toward the Bible. On the ground that it was the word of God, they considered themselves bound to accept every statement in the Bible as literally true. The creation narrative in Genesis convinced some of them beyond all shadow of controversy that God had created the world in six days (neither more nor less), and that he had fashioned man directly out of the slime of the earth. They assumed that all the miracles of the Old and the New Testaments took place almost exactly as described: that the Israelites crossed the Red Sea dry shod, that the Jordan flowed backward in its course, that the sun stood still over Gibeon for a full day while Joshua fought against the Amorites, that Jonah lived three days in the belly of the great fish, and so forth.

Modern scientific criticism of the Bible has undermined this naïve faith. Although it lives on in some sections of our country, especially in the "Bible belt," and still claims large numbers of adherents, it is unquestionably moribund. We need not regret its demise, for it was a superstitious kind of faith, unworthy of adult and educated men in our time. We are called to a faith that is neither naïve nor credulous, but severely critical of its own affirmations. While we are, hopefully, open to the word of God, we must recognize that God's word never comes to us except through human words, which are subject to the personal and historical limitations of their heralds. The whole biblical revelation is formulated in terms of the prescientific world-view of ancient Semites. If we are to accept and appropriate the revelation, we must somehow manage to divest it of its obsolete form and translate it into concepts that make sense to modern man.

To some extent, the teaching of the Church in successive ages has kept the faith of Christians abreast of man's expanding scientific and philosophical knowledge.

The early Church translated Christianity from the Semitic thought-forms of the Bible to those of the Hellenistic world. Medieval theology kept restating the faith as the progress of knowledge required. But in modern times, the Church—at least the Catholic Church—has almost ceased to be a progressive force. Threatened by fear of heresy, it has been inordinately concerned with conserving and defending the ancient deposit. Too often it has taken a hostile attitude toward new ideas and has discouraged the faithful from participating in the forward thrust of the human spirit. We may to some extent understand and excuse this undue conservatism, but we must regret it and in any case not imitate it. Vatican Council II belatedly recognized that if faith is to have a future, it must not cling timidly to its own past forms.

The Church today, partly because of the courageous initiatives of Vatican II, is torn by doubt. It is groping for a better way to understand and express the faith for our own time. To translate the traditional formulas of the Bible and the creeds into meaningful contemporary language is no easy task. There is a real risk of distorting or diluting the gospel itself. But this risk must be boldly taken in order to avoid what would otherwise amount to sclerosis and eventual death. Christianity cannot make a vital impact on the contemporary world unless it speaks credibly and powerfully to the concerns of our day.

As I have contended in Chapter 1, faith in our day is undergoing a major transformation. This is not surprising, for faith has gone through many metamorphoses in the past, and we live in an age in which change is apparent everywhere. From the Counter Reformation until the present generation, Catholics have generally looked upon faith as a submission of the mind to the teaching of the Church. Compared with the biblical view of faith, as I have briefly described it above, this was an impoverishment. In biblical times faith did not mean the acceptance of a collection of dogmatic formulas on the authority of an institutional Church, but rather the liberating recognition that the God of love was present and active in the ongoing life of his people.

Today men are once again concerned with the movement of history. They are disturbed by the proliferation of fratricidal conflicts that threaten the very survival of man-

kind. The world seems to be increasingly torn by prejudice, strikes, recriminations, protests, and wars. Many feel,
with desperate urgency, the need for a power that can
draw mankind together into love and solidarity, for a mag-
net that can extricate them from private and collective
egoism, for a compass that can give them stable goals amid
the all-engulfing kaleidoscopic changes. Faith, once it addresses itself to these deep human aspirations, can revitalize itself. It can free itself from excessive bondage to its
own past forms and meet the urgent demands of our time.

Much of the Church's teaching and practice has become somewhat obsolete, but this need not discourage
us. Beneath all its ancient forms it continues to possess a
priceless treasure. All its doctrines, institutions, and ceremonies are but vessels of clay, intended to preserve, describe, and transmit the gospel itself. New doctrines, institutions, and ceremonies must be devised, not in order
to replace the gospel, but to keep it alive and bring it to
bear on the problems of the present age.

What is ageless is the gospel itself, or, perhaps better,
the person of Jesus Christ, who lives on in the Church insofar as we will let him. In him the values of universal
love, disinterested service, and courageous sacrifice have
become manifest in a divinely perfect way. These values
our age needs as much as any age in the past. If our theological vocabulary has become trite and questionable, the
love of God, as shown forth in Jesus Christ, has lost none
of its power. The Church must find new ways of understanding and expressing that love in order to save the men
of this age from falling into hatred and despair.

Is the Church, then, in doubt? Clearly, yes. It is in
doubt as to what to say to the modern world, and how to
make the love of God, shown forth in Jesus Christ, the
vital and life-giving force it ought to be. But, for all its
doubts, the Church still remains the home and hearth of
living faith. Those who have learned to be patient with the
Church, and to identify themselves with it in its struggles
and confusion, find evidence enough that God has not de-
serted it. When they are tempted to turn their back on
the Church, they feel as if they were hearing again the
question put by Christ himself: "Will you also go away?"
And like the apostles, they are prompted to reply: "Lord,
to whom shall we go? For you have the words of eternal
life" (Jn. 6:68–69).

Dogma as an Ecumenical Problem

If there is any validity in the familiar dictum that "doctrine divides but service unites," it might well be expected that dogma would be an obstacle to reconciliation among the Churches. Experience seems to show that this is the case. According to Edmund Schlink, "At any ecumenical gathering it may be observed that members of divided Churches find it much easier to pray and witness together than to formulate common dogmatic statements."[1] At the Roman Catholic-Protestant Colloquium held at Harvard in 1963, Cardinal Bea addressed himself quite forthrightly to this point. With regard to the future possibilities of the ecumenical movement, he felt obliged to warn:

> First and foremost the fundamental teaching of the Catholic Church will not be changed. Compromise on points of faith which have already been defined is impossible. It would be quite unfair to our non-Catholic brethren to stir up false hopes of this nature. Nor is there a possibility that the Church—even in its zeal for eventual union—will ever be content with a recognition only of "essential dogmas," or that she will reverse or withdraw the dogmatic decrees drawn up at the Council of Trent. Again it would be simply dishonest to suggest that there is any likelihood that the dogmas of the primacy or the infallibility of the Pope will be revised. The Church has solemnly proclaimed all these doctrines to be of faith, that is to say, truths revealed by God himself and necessary for salvation. Precisely because of these solemn declarations made under the guidance of

the Holy Spirit, the action of the Church in this field is severely limited. She must guard these truths, explain them, preach them, but she cannot compromise them. For the Church founded by Christ cannot tamper with the Word of God which he preached and entrusted to her care. She must humbly subject herself to him with whom she is inalterably united.[2]

These remarks by Cardinal Bea, reflecting the candor, prudence, and reserve of a great churchman, call attention to a very serious ecumenical problem. To understand its full import, one must have some awareness of the notion of dogma which Bea here presupposes. In current Catholic usage, the term "dogma" means a divinely revealed truth, proclaimed as such by the infallible teaching authority of the Church, and hence binding on all the faithful without exception, now and forever. To doubt or deny a dogma, knowing that it is a dogma, is heresy; it involves an implicit denial of the teaching authority of the Catholic Church and therefore automatically excludes one from the Church.

Nobody has ever undertaken to draw up a complete list of the Church's dogmas, and the effort would be futile, because there are many borderline cases. Any such list would presumably include the declaration of Nicaea that the son is consubstantial (*homoousion*) with the Father; the definition of the First Council of Constantinople that the Holy Spirit is worthy of divine adoration; the affirmation of Council of Chalcedon that Jesus Christ has two complete natures, divine and human; the listing of the seven sacraments by the Council of Trent; papal infallibility as defined by Vatican I; and two Marian dogmas of 1854 and 1950—the Immaculate Conception and the Assumption. This is not a complete list, or even a selection of the most important, but a mere sampling to indicate the kind of thing we are talking about when we speak of dogmas.

Although many Protestants would recognize some of these dogmas as unquestionably true, and perhaps even as divinely revealed, dogma does raise serious obstacles to Christian unity; for the various Churches do not agree about what the dogmas are. The Catholic Church, in particular, has defined a number of dogmas since the great divisions between the Eastern and Western Churches in the Middle Ages and between Protestantism and Catholicism in the sixteenth century.

The problem of dogma, as an ecumenical issue, arises chiefly from the side of the Catholic Church, since it would seem that the Catholic Church must require, as a condition for reunion, that the other Churches accept the Catholic dogmas. Having taken irreversible steps on its own, Catholicism must demand that others take the same steps. If Christian reunion is conceived of in this light, it seems to be a one-sided affair. The other Churches would have to come to where the Catholic Church now is, while Catholicism, apparently, would not have to make any corresponding concessions. No wonder that many Orthodox, Anglican, and Protestant Christians are suspicious that Roman Catholic participation in the ecumenical movement is merely a disguised effort to convert other Christian bodies to the Catholic version of Christianity.

If this impression is allowed to stand, the ecumenical progress of the past few decades may lead to a dead end. It is imperative, therefore, to take a new look at the Catholic understanding of dogma. Catholic theology in the past few years has been reassessing the status of dogma, with the result that the Church's position appears less inflexible than is generally thought to be the case.

The concept of dogma, explained above, though widely prevalent, is of relatively recent vintage. Neither in the Bible, nor in the writings of the Fathers, nor in medieval Scholasticism does the term have this technical meaning.[3] In ancient and medieval times "dogma" sometimes denotes simply an opinion or tenet of some philosophical or religious group—not necessarily true, let alone revealed. The term was used also in a juridical sense, to designate an official edict or decree. Even in the sixteenth century, as Piet Fransen points out, the Council of Trent "could 'define a dogma' while remaining perfectly conscious of the fact that the content of this *dogma* was not necessarily immutable."[4]

While there were obviously anticipations in earlier centuries—especially perhaps in the medieval concept of the *articuli fidei*—the current notion of dogma was forged in the controversial theology of the Counter Reformation. Walter Kasper attributes the emergence of the term, in its precise modern significance, to the Franciscan Philipp Neri Chrismann. In his *Regula fidei catholicae* (1792),

Chrismann declares "that a dogma of the faith is nothing other than a divinely revealed doctrine and truth, which is proposed by the public judgment of the Church as something to be believed by divine faith, in such wise that the contrary is condemned by the Church as a heretical doctrine."[5] Chrismann's narrow definition of dogma was assailed by many as too minimalistic, and his work was placed on the Index of Prohibited Books in 1869[6]; nevertheless it continued to exert great influence.

In the latter part of the nineteenth century, when the faith was threatened by attacks in the name of reason, Chrismann's authoritarian view of dogma was found to be a handy weapon. At least in substance, it reappears in the official Roman documents of the period, such as the Syllabus of Errors of 1864, the Constitutions of Vatican I, and the anti-Modernist documents of 1907–10.

The notion that there could be doctrines immune to historical limitations and capable of being imposed by the sheer weight of extrinsic authority reflects the non-historical and juridical type of thinking prevalent in the Church of the Counter Reformation. The roots of this mentality may be traced to Greek intellectualism and Roman legalism. More proximately, the absolutistic view of dogma reflects the characteristics of Catholic theology in a rationalistic era. To ward off naturalistic rationalism, orthodox theology adopted a supernaturalistic rationalism in which revelation was conceived of as a divinely imparted system of universal and timeless truth entrusted to the Church as teacher.

Vatican II, to a great extent, broke with the concept of revelation that had been prevalent in the previous century. The constitution Dei Verbum, without turning its back on previous Church pronouncements, depicted revelation primarily as a vital interpersonal communion between God and man.[7] In so doing, it paved the way for the reconsideration of dogma that has been going on in the theological literature of the past five years. Post-Conciliar theology calls into question at least four important features of the Neo-Scholastic notion of dogma: its identity with revelation, its conceptual objectivity, its immutability, and its universality. Let me comment briefly on each of these four points before I proceed to the question of ecumenical applications.

Regarding the first point, contemporary theology is conscious of the need of re-examining the relationship between revelation considered as a salvific event and those propositional formulations we call "dogmas." It is commonly conceded today that revelation does not actually exist except when it is being apprehended by a living mind. Dogmatic statements serve an important, and in some ways indispensable, function in the "self-becoming" of the individual believer and in the creation of Christian community; they bring to explicit realization essential aspects of man's prepredicative encounter with God. But revelation itself cannot be limited to spoken or written words, nor do such words of themselves constitute revelation.

To illuminate the paradoxical relationship between revelation and dogma, some modern theologians have made use of the Heideggerian analysis of truth. The term both in the Latin form, *revelatio*, and in the Greek equivalent *apo-kalypsis*, means "unveiling." It therefore has close affinities with the Greek term for "truth" (*a-lētheia*, unconcealment). According to Martin Heidegger, truth is the event of the luminous self-donation of the mystery of Being. He therefore comes close to the theologian's notion of revelation as the attesting Word of uncreated Truth.[8] If truth itself is, as Heidegger insists, at once the revealment and the concealment of the plenitude of Being, the theologian might well look upon divine revelation as the gracious self-disclosure of the immeasurable Plenitude that faith calls God.

Following this line of thought, several modern theologians have sought to clarify the relationship between dogma and revelation by applying analogously what Heidegger has to say of the relationship between beings and Being. Being itself, according to Heidegger, is interior to all beings, lighting them up for what they are, and yet is not itself a being. This paradoxical diversity within unity Heidegger calls the "ontological difference." Kasper, extending this concept, speaks of a "theological difference" between gospel and dogma.[9] The truth of revelation, he maintains, is neither separate from dogma nor, in every respect, identical with it. Dogma has the value of revelation if, and only if, it is grasped by a mind presently influenced by God's active self-bestowal. (In classical terms, we may translate: There can be no revelation, and

hence no faith, without the interior illumination of grace.)
When the event of revelation occurs, there is a kind of
dynamic identity between revelation and dogma. The
revelatory truth is present in the dogmas through which
it comes to expression and yet continues to exceed them
insofar as it surpasses man's powers of comprehension. In
the words of William Richardson, "Every human effort to
utter the ineffable is constricted by the law of finitude
and therefore leaves something unsaid."[10]

This notion of truth is modern but, as Kasper shows,
it bears close analogies with the biblical conception of
God's truth as his life-giving presence in and through his
word. Even Scholasticism preserved something of this dynamic notion of revelatory truth. According to the well-
known axiom, fruitfully exploited by Albert the Great,
Thomas Aquinas, and Bonaventure, *articulus fidei est
perceptio divinae veritatis tendens in ipsam*.[11] In the
formulas of faith we catch fleeting glimpses of the divine
truth toward which our whole being is tending. The truth
of the revealing God cannot be reduced to the dead letter
of any doctrinal affirmation, yet such an affirmation may
become God's revelatory word.

The second question raised by contemporary theology
has to do with the supposed objectivity of dogmatic discourse. Some have depicted the definitions of popes and
councils as if they were capable of exactly circumscribing
the content they affirm. But from what we have already
said it is evident that the content shatters our ordinary
framework of discourse and demands a unique type of
assent. From the form of dogmatic language it can easily
be shown that this is the case. Schlink, in the study already referred to, calls attention to the structural complexity of creedal and confessional statements.[12] They
combine elements of repentance, faith, worship, and witness. The creed is composed with a view to being uttered
in the presence of God and as a testimony before men.
The recitation of the creed aims to bring about a situation
in which believers, gathered in worship, can better apprehend and respond to the revealing presence of the divine.
Most of the early Christian confessions, which form the
basis of later dogmatic statements, were framed in a
liturgical context and are doxological in form.

Wolfhart Pannenberg, after paying tribute to Schlink's

analysis of the doxological character of dogmatic statements, calls attention to a closely related feature—their proleptic character. Since they have reference to a new creation and a new life to be fully realized at the end of the world, dogmatic statements transcend our present experience and power of conceptualization. Of necessity, therefore, they speak provisionally and metaphorically.[13] Pannenberg illustrates this with respect to the Christological titles—"Son of Man," "Son of God," and "Kyrios" —and with respect to the Christian way of speaking about the "resurrection of the dead." We have to use approximative imagery, Pannenberg says, to describe what lies beyond our power of clear apprehension. Because revelation is eschatological, dogma always points to a future disclosure beyond all history.

Ian Ramsey shows the futility of treating dogmatic statements as though they were intended as descriptive or scientific statements. Building on analogies from various types of non-religious discernment, Ramsey establishes beyond doubt that "the language of Christian doctrine is likely to bristle with improprieties" and "logical oddities."[14] In this connection he points out that in titles used of Jesus (e.g., "the eternal Son," "the only-begotten of the Father") the adjectives are not further descriptions of something previously designated, but intrinsic modifiers that enable the notion of sonship to "do justice to what is 'disclosed' in worship."[15] The norm of correct usage is derived from a situation in which the mystery of the divine is efficaciously evoked and encountered. It would be a fatal error, says Ramsey, to imagine that the dogma of the hypostatic union describes some fact in the way that ordinary language describes its objects. This would lead to such absurdities as the equation "Godhood+manhood=Jesus Christ."

The Catholic Karl Rahner speaks in much the same terms as the Lutherans Schlink and Pannenberg and the Anglican Ramsey. Dogmatic statements, he holds, are not merely subjective; they intend a definite content and do not wish only to express the attitudes of the speaker. On the other hand, the realities of God and his grace, according to Rahner, do not admit of any simply objective presentation.[16] Dogmatic discourse, therefore, must somehow contrive to point the way to an existential confrontation with the mystery itself. Theological dogmatic language, he asserts, is "mystagogical," insofar as it conjures up the gracious presence of the divine. It has an almost sacramental function, transmitting not the idea but the reality of God's generous self-outpouring. The truth of symbol is existential insofar as it transcends the subject-object schema of ordinary propositional discourse and cannot be rightly apprehended without personal appropriation.[17]

Nothing here said about the peculiarities of creedal language ought to be taken as undermining its truth value. On the contrary, these peculiarities stem from its task of conveying a truth greater and more serious than ordinary language is able to bear. Thus dogmatic speech, while it is irreducible to scientific or descriptive language, is by no means equivalent to mere subjective fantasy. The propositions of dogma, as Hans Urs von Balthasar has remarked, "are true insofar as they are a function and expression of the Church's understanding of the Christ-mystery, as given to it by the Holy Spirit. They cannot be taken out of this setting; therefore, they do not have any *purely* theoretical (i.e., non-experiential, non-existential) truth."[18]

A third development in the Catholic understanding of dogma has reference to its supposed stability. Once a dogmatic formula is hammered out, it must, according to the popular conception, remain forever. If it states a revealed truth, why should it ever be changed?

One answer, of course, is that the meaning of words shifts according to varying circumstances of time and place. When the original language ceases to be well understood, it may prove necessary or expedient to change the words for the sake of conveying the original ideas more effectively. This much is obvious and may be abundantly illustrated from the history of dogma.

Surprising changes in the verbal tests of orthodoxy have occurred in the course of time. For example, a local Council of Antioch, in 268, ruled that the Son was not *homoousios* (of one substance) with the Father.[19] Half a century later the Council of Nicaea declared that he was *homoousios*. Had the Church changed its mind? By no means. The term *homoousios* taken in one context implied Unitarianism and in another context became a touchstone of the Church's authentic Trinitarian faith.

Many similar lessons may be culled from ancient history. The Councils of Nicaea and Sardica accepted the view that there was but one hypostasis in God. Constantinople I and Chalcedon, however, took the view that there were three divine hypostases.[20] Once again, neither formula is necessarily better than the other. What is vital is the meaning, not the words. The term "hypostasis" does not have some one pre-established meaning, but receives its precise meaning from general usage and from the particular context in which it is used.

All this has evident applications for the faith of Christians today. Many of them recite the orthodox formulas with so little understanding that their thoughts may well be heretical. When the modern Christian declares that there are three divine persons, he may well have in mind the modern psychological concept of "person" as an autonomous subject endowed with its own proper consciousness, intellect, and will. Such a concept, consistently followed out, would lead to tritheism. God might be conceived of as Siamese triplets! To safeguard Trinitarian orthodoxy, one might raise the question whether it would not be preferable to call God a single person with three modes of being. Whatever may be thought about this particular case, the principle of variability in language seems unassailable.

Many Christians, neglecting the lessons of history, fall into the error of imagining that orthodoxy consists in adhering rigidly to consecrated formulas. To reject these is considered heresy, as is suggested by the familiar expression "si quis dixerit . . ." in the conciliar canons. But the more one studies language, the more obvious it becomes that words are a poor test of right thinking. What some people call "orthodoxy" really ought to be called "orthology" or "orthophony"; it has to do with right speech rather than right ideas. While right speech has its value, the rightness of speech depends on a great variety of circumstances, some of which are not within the control of the Church. Thus the Church may be forced to change its canons of right speaking.

It would be a gross oversimplification, however, to imagine that the reformulation of dogma consists simply in changing words. Revelation always comes to men within some definite sociocultural situation, and this necessarily affects the manner in which they articulate the revelation conceptually. The biblical peoples inevitably expressed their experience of God in terms of their own central concerns, with the help of concepts derived from their own physical and cultural world. The content of the Bible is therefore permeated with ideas and images borrowed from the agricultural and patriarchal society of the ancient Israelites. The subsequent history of doctrine in the Christian Church has been deeply affected by the societal forms, the customary attitudes, and the philosophical heritage of the Greek, Roman, feudal and baroque worlds.

In interpreting biblical and ecclesiastical pronouncements, therefore, we must be alert to distinguish between the revelation itself—i.e., the divine meaning which is coming dynamically to expression in human concepts and words—and the culturally conditioned manner in which the revelation is expressed. A competent interpreter of any doctrinal statement will have to examine the entire historical and cultural context out of which it arose in order to discern its true significance. The modern believer cannot and should not be asked to accept the world view of ancient or medieval Christians. He should be encouraged to think as a man of his own day. To the extent that traditional statements of the faith are conditioned by a cultural situation no longer our own, they must be reinterpreted for modern man. Otherwise they will seem meaningless, incredible, or at least irrelevant.

This process of reinterpretation cannot be a matter of stripping away the human conceptual vesture until one reaches some timeless and unquestionable kernel of pure divine truth. The pursuit of such an unconditional grasp of revelation is an illusion, betraying a serious ignorance of man's fundamental historicity. We ourselves are just as historically conditioned as our ancestors and hence cannot hope to achieve supracultural formulations. The hermeneutic process by which we reinterpret past dogmatic formulations will involve a concrete logic of proportionality. We begin by noting that the revelation (R) was expressed in a certain way (a^1) by men in a cultural situation (a^2). Our problem is to devise a new statement (b^1) appropriate to our own cultural situation (b^2). The process of finding the right formula involves more than mere deductive logic. It calls for a living sense of the faith and for a realistic grasp of the world in which we live. To validate new and appropriate expressions, suited to the mentality of the times, is primarily the responsibility of the Church's magisterium. But the theologian has the function of exploring new possibilities and of seeking in this way to be of service to the Church.

Such reconceptualization has been occurring throughout the history of the Church. It may be illustrated, sufficiently for our purposes, by the axiom "Outside the Church, no salvation" (*Extra ecclesiam nulla salus*). This ancient maxim, with a venerable patristic pedigree, was affirmed in the strongest terms by popes and ecumenical councils in the Middle Ages.[21] And there can be little doubt but that many who proclaimed the principle understood it in a harshly literal sense. In our time the ancient understanding of the formula is repugnant to practically all Catholics. As Gregory Baum has written, "the conciliar documents . . . make it quite clear that this sentence is no longer taught *eodem sensu eademque sententia*. According to the repeated teaching of Vatican Council II there is plentiful salvation outside the Church."[22] Many contemporary theologians would prefer to see the formula used as little as possible in preaching, since it will almost inevitably be misunderstood.[23]

What is here in question is no mere change of words. The formula must be changed because in the mental and social structures of the contemporary world there is no longer any room for an exclusivist concept of the Church as a society of the saved. The old formula was not totally wrong. It was based on a valid insight into the ecclesial character of all Christian salvation; it called attention to the inseparability of the grace of God from the Church of Christ. But the modern conception of the relationship between the Church, as a visible community of believers, and the saving grace of God must be more nuanced than the axiom "Outside the Church, no salvation" would suggest.

It is an oversimplification, therefore, to say that dogmas are irreformable. In principle, every dogmatic statement is subject to reformulation. At times it may be sufficient to reclothe the old concepts in new words that, for all practical purposes, have the same meanings. But in other cases the consecrated formula will reflect an inadequate understanding. In order to bring out the deeper and divinely intended meaning, which alone is inseparable from faith, it may be necessary to discard the human concepts as well as the words of those who first framed the dogma. When men acquire new cultural conditioning and mental horizons, they have to reconceptualize their dogmas from their present point of view. There are signs that this process is now going on with respect to many Catholic dogmas, such as original sin, transubstantiation, and perhaps the virginal conception of Jesus. This prompts us to ask whether those doctrines which have traditionally divided the Churches might not be capable of an equally radical reinterpretation.

Before developing the ecumenical implications of this point, let me make my fourth and last remark about the emerging concept of dogma. Modern theologians have generally taken it for granted that a dogmatic formula, once it is sufficiently authenticated, ought to be professed by all believers everywhere. But this has not always been assumed. The New Testament displays a proliferation of creedal affirmations traceable to various segments of the primitive Church. And in the early centuries, as a glance at the opening pages of Heinrich Denzinger's *Enchiridion* will show, the several churches were content to possess their own local creeds. At least until the conversion of Constantine, when Christianity became the general law of the Roman Empire, the recitation of identical creedal formulas was not considered essential to Christian fellowship. The churches had other ways of testing the genuineness of one another's apostolic faith.[24]

In the Middle Ages the Latin West, excessively isolated in its own theological world, began to make additions to the ancient creeds and to formulate new dogmas without regard to the rest of Christendom. The addition of the *Filioque* to the Nicene Creed, of course, was one of the major factors leading to the tragic schism between East and West. The Council of Florence, which in the fifteenth century temporarily patched up this schism, showed an exemplary breadth of understanding.[25] It affirmed that the unity of the Church should be built not on particular doctrinal formulas, but rather "on the cornerstone, Christ Jesus, who will make both one." In the union then decreed, there was no question of compelling either Church to accept the devotional practices of the other. The Western and Eastern Churches were allowed to follow their own liturgical calendars and to worship their own saints (which might seem to imply some acknowledgment of each other's canonizations).

More importantly for our purposes, an agreement based on mutual tolerance was reached regarding the crucial question of the procession of the Holy Spirit. Both East and West were permitted to follow the long-standing tradition of their own Churches. The Latins, therefore, could continue to declare—and to recite in their creed —that the Spirit proceeded from the Father and the Son, while the Greeks could omit the *Filioque* from the creed and subscribe to the formula "from the Father through the Son."

Superficially it might seem that the discussion concerned only the use or omission of certain words. Were the Latins justified in continuing to recite the creed with the added term *Filioque* and the Greeks in adhering to the more ancient usage of the Church? The council's decision to answer both these questions in the affirmative was an implied recognition that diverse thought-forms, as well as diverse modes of speech, could be tolerated without impairing the catholic unity of the Church. For the difference of terminology, as Kasper notes, was rooted in irreducibly diverse forms of thought.[26] The Eastern and Western formulas were different in their formal conceptual content and hence not synonymous, yet, according to the council, they designate, under different aspects, one and the same divine mystery. If "dogma" is taken to mean "dogmatic formula," one may say that the Council of Florence implicitly rejected the equation "one faith—one dogma." It acknowledged that conceptually diverse formulations may co-exist in different sections of the Church. The mere fact that a formula, rightly understood, is true and orthodox does not necessarily mean that it should be imposed as a confessional test upon all members of the Church.

The valid principle of dogmatic pluralism, after prevailing at Florence, became obscured during the Counter Reformation, and even more so in the past century when the Church felt obliged to take stringent measures to stave off various forms of relativism. But in Vatican Council II pluralism managed to reassert itself, as several passages from the Decree on Ecumenism[27] will attest:

> The heritage handed down by the apostles was received in different forms and ways, so that from the beginnings of the Church it has had a varied development in various places, thanks to a similar variety of natural gifts and conditions of life. [no. 14]

> In the investigation of revealed truth, East and West have used different methods and approaches in understanding and proclaiming divine things. It is hardly surprising, therefore, if sometimes one tradition has come nearer than the other to an apt appreciation of certain aspects of a revealed mystery, or has expressed them in a clearer manner. As a result, these various theological formulations are often to be considered complementary rather than conflicting. [no. 17]

> After taking all these factors into consideration, this sacred Synod confirms what previous Councils and Roman Pontiffs have proclaimed: in order to restore communion and unity or preserve them, one must "impose no burden beyond what is indispensable" (Acts 15:28). [no. 18]

A similar regard for pluralism may be found in the Dogmatic Constitution on the Church, which strongly emphasizes the value of the distinctive contributions of individual local churches to the many-splendored spectacle of Catholic unity. The unity of the faith, we are told, is all the more radiant when refracted in the variety of many traditions (cf. no. 13).

As a result of the current reassessment of dogma, briefly surveyed in the preceding paragraphs, we may be in a position to moderate somewhat the apparent rigidity of Cardinal Bea's statement quoted at the beginning of this chapter. It is far from obvious that the dogmas of the Church, having been "revealed by God himself," cannot be revised by the Church, or that they are unconditionally "necessary for salvation," or that they can in no sense be subjected to compromise. Our findings suggest that the Catholic dogmas as presently formulated and understood may be significantly changed and that positive acceptance of all the dogmas may not be absolutely necessary for communion with the Roman Church. Let me explain each of these two points in greater detail.

With regard to the "irreformability" of dogma, I have endeavored to show that, as our total fund of knowledge increases and as our perspectives change, dogmatic formulations must be kept under constant review. Without failing in due reverence for the past, we may frankly admit that an increasing number of dogmatic statements are showing the kind of inadequacy already noted in the axiom "Outside the Church, no salvation." This may be readily illustrated regarding several ecumenically disputed dogmas.

If the Church were today in a position to speak for the first time about the institution of the sacraments, it would not be likely to declare without qualification, as the Council of Trent did, that the seven sacraments of the New Law "were all instituted by Jesus Christ our Lord."[28] A contemporary scholar familiar with modern biblical and historical studies would see the need of important distinctions that would scarcely have occurred to a sixteenth-century theologian.

So too, in speaking of the origins of the papacy, we should be unlikely to use the concepts and terms of Vatican I, which forbade anyone, under pain of anathema, to deny "that Blessed Peter the Apostle was constituted by Christ the Lord prince of all the apostles and visible head of the entire Church militant" or that Christ invested him "directly and immediately with the primacy not of honor alone, but of true and proper jurisdiction."[29] These statements embody important principles regarding the unity of the Church, and to these the contemporary Catholic feels strongly committed. But the formulation reflects the religious "style" of the baroque Church and the exegesis of an age less sensitive to historicity. If someone were being asked to become a sharer in the belief of the Church as of 1970 rather than 1870, it would not be desirable or necessary to hold him to anachronistic or triumphalistic declarations of this kind. The path toward Christian unity would be greatly facilitated if Catholics abandoned any thought of obliging other Christians to submit to outmoded and admittedly deficient expressions of the faith, even though these expressions are to be found in documents of the highest authority. To demand this type of submission would contravene the principle of Florence, reaffirmed by Vatican II, that one must "impose no burden beyond what is indispensable."

Not only must outworn formulations from previous centuries be clearly distinguished from revelation itself; the same must be said of contemporary statements that may have to be corrected at some future date. As stated above, we never receive the revealed truth except in fragile human vessels. Thus even the most current dogmatic utterances must be questioned. The true test of orthodoxy is not whether a man accepts the official statements at their face value, but whether he has sufficient confidence in the tradition to accept its formulations, in spite of all their human deficiency, as vehicles of a divine truth that lies beyond all formulation. The Catholic may agree, at least in part, with the conjectures of the Lutheran Carl Braaten:

> . . . we cannot now foresee the terms on which our churches might agree on those important doctrines which now divide us. It seems likely, however, that the dogmas concerning papal infallibility and Mary will have to be so reinterpreted that many people will scarcely recognize their continuity with the older traditions. Mere traditionalists who cling to ancient formulae will be unhappy. Equally radical reinterpretations of those protestant affirmations which give offense to Roman Catholics will be demanded. We cannot say a priori that this is impossible or improbable. Dogmas are things of history; they arise in history, they have a history; and they generate a history of interpretation in which earlier meanings are transcended through incorporation into new and quite dissimilar formulations. . . . Neither the trinitarian and christological dogmas, which we share with Roman Catholics, nor the papal and mariological dogmas, which we do not share, are exempt from new interpretations in an age of radical historical consciousness.[30]

The current ecumenical dialogue imposes a task upon all the Churches engaged in it. The effort to explain our positions to others compels us to re-examine what we ourselves have been saying. At many points we shall doubtless find that our views have not been accepted because they are in some respects unacceptable. This should accelerate the process of dogmatic development that history, to some extent, forces on us anyway. It should help us to amend the distortions in what we have hitherto been saying and thinking about our own faith. In this way divided Christians who are committed to the same gospel and who invoke the same Holy Spirit may hopefully converge toward greater solidarity in confession.

The question still remains whether total unity in confession is a prerequisite for full ecclesiastical communion. From what precedes, it should be clear that simultaneous dogmatic pluralism is sometimes admissible without prejudice to church unity. If one and the same faith can be differently formulated for different historical epochs, a similar variety may be tolerated for different cultures in a single chronological period. In view of the literary form of confessional statements, as described above, creeds may be regarded as resulting from the inner exigencies of a lived faith; they should not be forcibly imposed, by external authoritative action, upon peoples not prepared for them by their corporate historical experience. The Christians of the early centuries were orthodox in their faith, but they probably could have made no sense of some of the dogmas which Bea would regard as "necessary for salvation." Why could not the same liberty be granted to culturally diverse peoples living contemporaneously? In line with the teaching of Vatican II, it might be fairly asked whether Christianity would not even stand to gain from a greater diversity in its creedal formulations.

The unity within difference permitted by the Florentine Decree of Union might prove paradigmatic for Protestant-Catholic relations. The Reformation Churches, if they were ever to enter into communion with Rome, could contribute many riches from their own traditions. In this connection one thinks especially of the great Reformation watchwords such as *sola fide, sola gratia, sola Scriptura,* and *soli Deo gloria* and phrases such as *simul iustus et peccator* and *ecclesia semper reformanda.* These are the nearest Protestant equivalents to the new dogmas of post-Reformation Catholicism. Just as Protestants would do well to try to find some religious value in the distinctively Catholic dogmas, so Catholics should seek to relate themselves positively to the key principles that have sustained Reformation Christianity for the past four centuries.

Until recently it was common for Catholics to polemicize against the Reformation slogans, which can surely be understood in ways incompatible with the Catholic vision of the Christian dispensation. But in the past generation many Catholic theologians, including some of the most prominent (Karl Rahner, Hans Küng, Louis Bouyer, W. H. van de Pol . . .), have been pointing out that these formulas admit of a Catholic interpretation. Vatican II practically adopted the last two of these expressions. In the Decree on Ecumenism it declared: "Christ summons the Church, as she goes her pilgrim way, to that continual reformation of which she always has need, insofar as she is an institution of men here on earth" (no. 6). And in the Dogmatic Constitution *Lumen gentium*, the term *simul iustus et peccator* is in effect applied to the Church, which is described as being "at the same time holy and always in need of being purified" (no. 8).

As in the case of the Catholic-Orthodox discussion about the procession of the Holy Spirit, so with regard to these Protestant slogans, we should not imagine that words alone are involved. Behind the formulas lies a very definite style of thought, characteristic of Evangelical Christianity. The question is whether Catholicism can absorb this without diluting its own witness.

Otto Pesch, O.P., in a lengthy treatise on the subject,[31] has shown that the Lutheran formula *simul iustus et peccator* rests upon a mode of thought that may be called "existential"—one that corresponds to what the believer is prompted to utter in a situation of prayer, when he comes into the presence of his God. No matter how just or holy he may be, he still has to declare: "Lord, have mercy upon me, a sinner." Normative Catholic theology, as represented by Thomas Aquinas, for example, has taken a more objective or, in Pesch's term, a more "sapiential" point of view. It therefore seeks to analyze the process of justification from a more detached standpoint. These two theological styles, according to Pesch, lead to verbally contradictory formulas. Aquinas will have to say that once a man is justified, he is no longer in a state of sin; Luther will have to say the contrary. These statements cannot be harmonized; yet they are not strictly contradictory, any more than are the theologies of Paul and James, or John and the

Synoptics. Since they stem from different points of view, the same words do not have identical meanings. Thus Pesch can conclude:

> If one does not antecedently give absolute value to Luther's form of existential theology and exclude every other form as deceptive, then there is a presumption that the difference we have discussed, and likewise all other differences traceable to it, can find a home within the same walls; that the two modes of theology need each other as critical insurance against falling into mistaken forms, and that the Church of all times needs both, in order to preserve the full tension of the Christian reality.[32]

Can logically irreconcilable dogmas, as Pesch here suggests, be admitted within one and the same Church? If one recognizes the logical anomalies of religious language, to which reference has already been made, it is difficult to see why not. It would be a bold man who would try to make a neat logical system out of the dogmas of a single Church. Catholic theology today abounds in apparent antinomies, such as, for example, the twofold assertion that God's dominion is absolutely sovereign and that man remains free in working out his salvation. The affirmations seem to be mutually repugnant, and no one has really succeeded in showing why they do not conflict, but Catholics are convinced that in the real order both truths are compatible. In the same way it might be possible to hold with Aquinas and the Council of Trent that in justification the sinner is truly cleansed of his fault, and yet, with Luther, that he remains in some real sense guilty and sinful. At every point religious language has to do with truths that it cannot fully comprehend.

I do not wish to imply, of course, that in religion anything goes, or that all the formulas of all the Churches can be thrown together into some great theological mishmash. There are statements that suitably express what Christian faith perceives, and others that fail to do so. Before Christians with irreducibly diverse confessions can acknowledge their mutual solidarity in faith, they must find a way of ascertaining that neither group has substantially departed from the gospel. As Schlink points out, it is uncommonly difficult to decide under what conditions to give recognition to a formula that we do not appropriate as our own.[33] He recommends a careful study of the literary forms and a reinsertion of the disputed formula into the precise confessional context out of which it arose. The tools of exegetical and hermeneutical science must be skillfully brought to bear.

In the last analysis, I suspect, there are no adequate extrinsic norms for measuring the validity of confessional statements. They cannot be tested against other biblical or creedal utterances by merely syllogistic logic. The norm must be to some extent existential. It is necessary to enter into the spiritual world of the other Church with true empathy and in this way to assess its declarations in relation to one's own sense of the Christian reality. Christian reunion therefore presupposes a certain sharing of religious experiences on the part of believers of different denominations. It also presupposes that the Churches themselves assess and ratify the judgments of individual Christians.

For those who with sufficient preparation engage in the task, religious contact with another tradition cannot fail to be immensely rewarding. It affords a new perspective on both the other tradition and one's own. While one must keep open the possibility that either or both traditions may be found to have forsaken the pure wellsprings of divine truth, one will probably find, more often than not, that the different confessions are surprisingly convergent in purpose. The manifest diversity of their confessions often conceals an inarticulate unity at a deeper level.

The aphorism "doctrine divides but service unites" is therefore not the last word. Dogma is not in the first instance a source of division but rather a badge of unity. It expresses what some relatively large body of Christians see together, and find the strength to affirm in unison, by the light of their common faith. The fact that the dogmas of different Christian groups seem to conflict should not turn us against dogma itself. The conflicts are partly due to the faultiness of the ecclesiastical statements, many of which are in urgent need of reformulation, and partly also to the ineffable richness of revelation, which defies compression into compact formulas. Ecumenical confrontation can serve the double function of making us critical of the formulations we accept from our own tradition and of awakening us to the authentic values in other confessional families.

No attempt has been made in this chapter to solve any of the substantive doctrinal issues presently dividing the Churches. My concern has been only with method. If my thesis is correct, it may take decades of ecumenical experience before any far-reaching doctrinal consensus between the Catholic Church and other Christian bodies can be achieved. But it should be clear at least that the objection put in the opening pages if not fatal. Christian reunion should on no account be conceived of as if it were a mere matter of convincing Protestant, Anglican, or Orthodox believers to adopt all the Catholic dogmas presently "on the books." Nor can it consist in a simple abrogation of distinctively Catholic dogmas or in a passive acceptance by Catholics of the present views of other denominations. Each participant in the ecumenical discussion must be seriously critical of its own traditions and genuinely anxious to receive enrichment from the heritage of the other Churches. Through this process of mutual teaching and learning we can progressively rediscover one another—and deserve to be rediscovered by one another—in Christ. As we do so, we shall undoubtedly find Christ himself in a new and richer way. For he wills to be acknowledged not simply as the head of various separate sects and denominations, but as the bond of mutual union among all who have life in his name.

The Hermeneutics of Dogmatic Statements

Especially perhaps within Roman Catholicism, a doctrinal crisis is going on. Nothing had been more characteristic of Catholicism in the past than a high degree of certainty about a multitude of doctrines. Gradually over the centuries the zone of certitude increased, as more and more doctrines became officially endorsed, even defined, by the magisterium. In the past few centuries it began to appear as though the positions of Thomas Aquinas on most points were destined to become the positions of the Church for the rest of time. With its high degree of systematization and its tenacity in adhering to the patristic and medieval tradition, Catholicism became par excellence the Church of historical continuity and of organic development. It claimed to offer its members a complete and reliable map of life, together with all the desired aids of navigation.

In the past decade, especially since the end of Vatican II, the uniformity in Catholicism has shown signs of breaking up. It is as though the neatly woven fabric were becoming unraveled. More and more of the accepted doctrines have begun to be questioned or even contested within the Church. Some begin by asking "Do we still have to believe in angels?" Then they question the Immaculate Conception and the Assumption, then transubstantiation, then the virginal conception of Christ, then papal infallibility, and so on—until the anxious faithful begin to ask, as many do today, what doctrine is exempt from questioning within the Church? What can one believe with full and unhesitating conviction?

What is happening? Is it that a spirit of unbelief has been let loose in the Church? Are the skepticism and incredulity of the modern world seeping into the Church and eroding the structures of faith? If so, we should discountenance these new developments, adhere stanchly to the ancient heritage, and remain loyally by the side of Christ even though the majority of his disciples should desert him.

It would be a mistake, however, to make a facile identification of the present questioning with unbelief. Some of the most radical probing is being done by men who are deeply committed to Christ and to the Church. They feel that in criticizing ancient formulations of faith, and in rejecting what seems to be inadequate or false, they are performing a loyal service to the Church. They even claim authorization from John XXIII and from Vatican Council II. Hence the present conflict is not so much between belief and unbelief as between different shades of opinion within the Church. Some tend to be conservative and traditional, others liberal and progressive, in the manner in which they formulate their faith.

Terms such as "conservative" and "liberal," of course, are only relative. Every Christian is somewhat conservative, for Christianity means understanding one's life in terms of a past event—the event of Jesus Christ which forms the central theme of the New Testament. If this event were denied or ignored, a man would have no reason to call himself a Christian. On the other hand, no Christian can be completely conservative, for what he understands in the light of Christ must be precisely his own life and his own world. This is something that did not exist for the biblical authors. The contemporary believer must ask new questions that had not arisen, as such, in biblical times; and new questions demand answers that are in some respects new.

The problem of the old and the new arises out of the historicity of man. Man is a being who lives out of a remembered past, in a transitory present, toward an anticipated future. To what extent must Christian faith, then, retain the forms that it had in the past? To what extent is it legitimate and necessary to construct new formulas of faith that correspond to our experience and hope today?

Some Catholics would appeal at this point to the distinction between fallible and infallible teaching. They would say that we are free to form new opinions on all those points that have not been settled by unanimous consent of the Fathers or by a solemn definition of a pope or general council. Since there are relatively few irreformable pronouncements, this approach seems to provide a large measure of maneuverability.

But this distinction between infallible dogmas and the rest of church teaching is not as helpful for our purposes as one might think. In the first place, there is no agreed list of irreformable decrees, and therefore the distinction does not really tell us what may, and what may not, be questioned. Secondly, the interpretation of admittedly dogmatic statements is not always clear, and thus what one person regards as the very core of the definition will seem to another to be an excessively narrow interpretation of it. Thirdly, many dogmas are as great a stumbling block to the contemporary believer as the non-dogmatic statements. Several of the disputed points I mentioned earlier (Immaculate Conception, transubstantiation, infallibility, etc.) have to do with dogmas. If it is not permitted to ask questions about these matters, the "liberals" have lost their case without a hearing. On the other hand, there are so few statements of unquestionably dogmatic status, that to say that they alone constitute the binding content of faith would excessively narrow down the import of Christianity. Thus I do not think that the distinction between fallible and infallible teaching is the true key to our problem.

As a more fruitful approach, I suggest that we focus our attention on the historical relativity of all doctrinal statements. If we recall that the truth of revelation is never known in its naked absoluteness, but is always grasped within the perspectives of a sociocultural situation, we shall have a useful tool for finding out what may be conserved in an unquestionably antiquated formulation and what ought to be revised in an indubitably authentic expression of the faith. The fact that men in the past expressed the Christian revelation in a manner suited to their own times does not mean that we should reject what they said; nor does it mean that we ought to speak the same way. Our task is to "appropriate" what they said—to make it our own—and to express it in a contemporary form.

This program of modernization is, however, too obvious to be instructive and too vague to be practical. It merely raises the question of how we are to distinguish between what some would call the "form" and "content" of an ancient doctrinal statement. Are there any criteria by which we can separate the good grain of revelation from the chaff of historical relativity? Unless such criteria can be found, we shall not get beyond the present impasse, in which the very thing that one theologian regards as a time-conditioned interpretation represents, in the eyes of another, the very substance of the faith.

In this chapter, I have no intention of discussing the total problem of religious truth and its expression. I shall have to presuppose certain positions that cannot be defended here. I assume, for instance, that revelation is salvific truth; that it necessarily has to do with the redemption of mankind and of the world. Merely historical or scientific information, considered in itself, cannot possibly be the true content of revelation. Furthermore, I take for granted that the salvific truth is, most centrally, the mystery of God's vital self-communication, which comes to us as a call to transcend our limited self-interest and to entrust ourselves to God. This mystery of the divine self-communication cannot be spoken of with the same clarity and objectivity that we seek when discussing things familiar to us from our ordinary experience. I presuppose, moreover, that when a man speaks about the themes of revelation, he necessarily has to use concepts and terms drawn from his experience in the world. We cannot designate the saving mysteries except with the help of ideas and terminology supplied by the culture in which we live. In Scripture, in Christian tradition, and in the contemporary Church the word of God comes to us in and through the culturally conditioned words of men. Finally, I shall assume that church teaching over the centuries has been, by and large, an accurate, though not always a fully balanced, articulation of the Christian faith.

As regards the binding force of church teaching, there are several pertinent principles that have no particular connection with the problem of historical relativity, but which should be kept in mind in connection with all that follows. In the first place, as already mentioned, not all church documents have the same degree of authority. The extempore remarks of the pope at an audience in the Vatican may represent simply his personal feelings at the moment and need not be always taken as official teaching. Even when a pope or bishop intends to make use of his power as an authoritative teacher, it is not to be presumed that the utterances are infallible definitions. Only very rarely does the magisterium invoke its defining power.[1]

Secondly, it should be clear that in any magisterial statement, however authoritative, a distinction must be made between the point of the affirmation and the supporting statements. There is nothing new or unusual about this principle. Lawyers, for example, often distinguish between the decision of the court, which constitutes a normative precedent, and the reasoning of the court, which is as valid as the arguments proposed. *Obiter dicta* are in no way binding. Scripture scholars have ably distinguished between the degrees of affirmation in the Bible. "Here is the definite affirmation, there is also the statement of a probability, or of a possibility, even of a mere conjecture or of a doubt."[2] So, too, in documents of the Church, any skilled theologian must know how to distinguish between what the Church was intending to teach, and the statements introduced merely for the sake of clarification, persuasion, or edification. The standard manuals of theology, in their treatment of the "notes" or "censures," give some helpful rules of thumb, but it cannot be said that this problem has generally received the attention it deserves.[3]

As regards the interpretation of authoritative statements, the true point of the affirmation is often best discerned by studying the historical context. One must know why the magisterium was speaking, what error it was rejecting. As Piet Schoonenberg remarks, "If a pronouncement is issued against a certain opinion, its positive statements should be interpreted in the first place as a defence against the condemned opinion and not as the only possible definition of the mystery which is being defended."[4] Generally speaking, this principle is an excellent guide, though it may happen that the positive statement is the only conceivable alternative to the condemned opinion— as the divinity of the Christ is the only possible alternative to the condemned proposition that the Son is a creature.

With these preambles in mind, let us now turn to the specific question that presently concerns us: how to distinguish between the truth of revelation and its time-bound formulations. The following six principles are, I believe, important.

1. *In the interpretation of doctrinal statements, heed should be paid to variations in literary conventions.*

This principle, obvious though it may sound, has frequently been violated in traditional theology. For centuries efforts were made to force the Bible into the framework of Greek and Western literary forms and to treat apparently scientific and historical statements in Scripture as though they had to conform to what a modern European might mean if he made the same statements. In Catholic teaching, an immense step forward was made when the encyclical *Divino afflante Spiritu* (1943) officially acknowledged that the authors of the Bible employed the forms and modes of speech in use among the people of their own place and time and that therefore the exegete, instead of deciding a priori what forms ought to have been used, should base his decision on the evidence of what the biblical authors actually did do.[5] Largely as a result of this encyclical, confirmed by the teaching of Vatican II,[6] Catholic exegesis today has no hesitation in recognizing in the Bible metaphor, hyperbole, pseudonymity, and the conventional use of prophetic and apocalyptic imagery.

This principle of literary forms has important implications for theology. The biblical scholar today feels free to admit discrepancies that would formerly have been regarded as scientific and historical errors. Further, he does not feel obliged to take literally many statements that were previously thought to refer to miraculous divine interventions. For example, the fact that a biblical book begins, "The word of the Lord came to the prophet X, saying . . ." does not necessarily imply that the words that follow are the direct discourse of Yahweh himself.

What has not yet been done, in sufficient detail, is to subject official church documents to form-critical analysis.[7] We too often forget that popes and councils sought to speak in ways common for high officials of their time and that they were aiming not simply to communicate a content, but to do so in a manner that would evoke a suitable emotional and practical response on the part of the faithful. Ecclesiastical pronouncements from the Middle Ages until the First Vatican Council (inclusively) commonly were phrased in a majestic, even triumphalistic, style that would not be considered appropriate today. In order to arouse feelings of awe and confidence, the Church presented her doctrine as "most certain," "most evident," and branded the contrary views as blasphemous and absurd. Erring Christians were accused of being proud, stubborn, and shameless in their adulteration of the word of God and were threatened with eternal penalties if they failed to submit. Vatican II, speaking to a twentieth-century audience, avoided the pyrotechnics of dogmatic definition and anathematization. When we go back to earlier church documents, we should not read them as if they were written yesterday. We must be on guard against mistaking merely rhetorical superlatives for substantive teaching. If hyperbole is to be admitted in the Bible, who is to deny that it may also be found in ecclesiastical pronouncements?

2. *An antiquated world view, presupposed but not formally taught in an earlier doctrinal formulation, should not be imposed as binding doctrine.*

As far as the Bible is concerned, this principle was the heart of Rudolf Bultmann's demythologizing program. In his famous essay "New Testament and Mythology"[8] he argued that the New Testament, in its presentation of the events of redemption, presupposes an essentially mythical view of the world as a three-storied structure, with the earth in the center, the heavens above, and the underworld beneath. In such a world view, he says, it was taken for granted that the earth was the scene of the supernatural activity of God and his angels and of Satan and his demons. Possession and miracles were deemed to be common occurrences. The New Testament writers did not invent this world view; they did not teach it; they simply took it for granted as something accepted by the milieu in which they lived. They presented the gospel in terms of the accepted ideas of their time.

In order to preach the gospel today, it would be pointless to try to force twentieth-century men to accept a first-century cosmology. We ought to be able to present the biblical message in terms of a modern world view. Otherwise we would be illegitimately adding to the content of the gospel by requiring people to accept a strange and incredible world view that was not part of the original gospel, but simply an unquestioned presupposition at the time the New Testament was written.

To some extent Christians always have modified the biblical world view in accordance with the accepted ideas of their own time. The medieval theologians, nurtured on Greek philosophy, took it for granted that God must be pure spirit, immutable, impassible, etc. When they found statements in the Bible about God changing, or becoming angry, or repenting what he had done, they took these to be metaphors. A writer such as Thomas Aquinas conceives of God and of God's relationship to the world in a way quite foreign to biblical thought, but we have become so habituated to the Thomistic conception that it no longer strikes us as a daring innovation. Today the cosmology of Aquinas is almost as antiquated as that of the Bible, and it is necessary to restate the Christian message in terms of a contemporary world view. Teilhard de Chardin made one attempt to do so, and we may expect that there will be others. As these efforts are made, many classical theological conceptions will no doubt be transformed. It is hard to predict what may happen to the currently accepted ideas of creation, inspiration, miracle, resurrection, etc. We must be prepared for revisions insofar as the traditional notions are to some extent bound up with an obsolete cosmology.

3. *Technical terms should be interpreted in terms of the systematic framework presupposed by those who used them.*

A great deal of Christian doctrine in the patristic era and in the Middle Ages is based on conceptual structures taken over from Greek philosophy. While Christian theology refined the categories of Greek philosophy, it did not essentially change them. It continued to presuppose the dichotomies of time and eternity, spirit and matter, substance and accident that had prevailed in Platonic and Aristotelian philosophy. If a theologian today were to accept a radically different philosophical system, such as one finds in modern personalistic phenomenology or process philosophy, he would have to transpose many of the Christian doctrines in a manner that might sound like a rejection. But to try to introduce these doctrines unchanged into a new philosophical framework would be impossible or would amount to an even greater deformation.

As a case in point, one might cite the recent dispute about the term "transubstantiation." In terms of a common-sense substance philosophy, it is meaningful to say that Christ takes the place of the "whole substance" of the bread. But if one denies that there ever was such a thing as the "substance of the bread" or that physical realities are made up of substance and accident, it becomes almost necessary to speak of the "real presence" in a new way. To find satisfactory equivalents in other philosophical systems is a task of creative theology.

4. *In the interpretation of biblical and theological terms, cognizance should be taken of connotation as well as denotation.*

The terminology of the Bible is concrete, imaginative, and conceptually imprecise. A great deal has been lost when theologians have tried to pick out terms from the Bible and give them exact, abstract definitions. When we read in the New Testament, for instance, that we have been redeemed by the blood of Christ (Rom. 3:25; Heb. 9:13–14, 13:12; 1 Pet. 1:19), we are not dealing with terms that admit of any simple definition. They are laden with connotations from the Exodus, the Temple worship, and the Mosaic Law. In general it may be said that redemption by the blood of Jesus did not mean to the New Testament authors what it spontaneously suggests to the modern Western mind. Especially since Anselm, the terms "redemption" and "blood" have taken on new significances and have largely lost the significance they had to the ancient Semite. The notion of making reparation to the offended honor of God by offering up the blood of an innocent victim is more medieval than biblical.

Today, when the biblical conception of redemption has become almost unintelligible and the Anselmian doctrine repugnant, there is urgent need for forging a new vocabulary of redemption. One might well begin by so immersing himself in the biblical tradition as to grasp what the New Testament authors meant by their soteriological terms. In order to find suitable equivalents, one would probably have to come at the whole problem of sin, salvation, and new life in God from a new direction. The biblical and medieval terms are so imbedded, respectively, in patriarchal and feudal cultural contexts that they have become almost unserviceable for popular usage.

5. *No doctrinal decision of the past directly solves a question that was not asked at the time.*

Biblical and conciliar texts have often been abused to make them answer questions that are asked today but were not in the minds of the original authors. For example, Paul in Romans and the Council of Trent, quoting Paul, assert that Adam was a single individual and that he is the source of original sin. Modern science has raised the question whether the human race might not be descended from more than one original couple. Some theologians have invoked the authority of Paul and Trent to refute polygenism. But to this it may legitimately be objected that neither of these texts was dealing formally with the question of the origins of the human race, and further that the question of monogenism versus polygenism had not even arisen at the time. They spoke in passing of Adam as a single individual because this seemed to them to be the obvious interpretation of Genesis, but it may be doubted whether they wished to settle authoritatively a question which could scarcely have entered their minds.[9] For us today, the matter is not so simple. For one thing, the teaching of Genesis on the point is far from clear. In some passages the term "Adam" must be interpreted as a collective noun, signifying mankind (both male and female). More importantly, the man of today would scarcely go to the Creation narrative in Genesis to solve a scientific question such as the origins of man. If Paul and the fathers at Trent did so, it was because the historicity of Genesis was something they took for granted. Precisely because they took it for granted, they were never forced to reflect on the matter, and hence they could not have settled any subsequent disputes that might have arisen about the historicity of the early chapters in Genesis.

This general principle—that nobody can decisively answer a question that has not come up at the time[10]—has very wide application in dogmatic theology. For example, Christian tradition for at least fifteen hundred years was virtually unanimous in accepting the physical universality of the Flood. Yet we cannot draw up a valid proof from a morally unanimous consensus on the question. A significant consensus would have to follow from a reflective weighing of the pros and cons such as could scarcely have taken place until more information had been gathered about the literary forms of Genesis and the data of paleontology. Today almost nobody imagines that the universality of the Flood can be proved from the naïve statements of Scripture or church tradition.

A more difficult question occurs where the magisterium attempts to settle a question and it later turns out that the decision was based on inadequate information. This occurred many times with decisions of the Biblical Commission in the first two decades of the twentieth century. Anxious to head off new ideas that might undermine the faith of Catholics, the Biblical Commission took very conservative positions, which later proved impossible to defend. In 1955 officials of the Commission acknowledged that previous decrees on critical or historical questions, insofar as these were based on the state of the evidence at the time, were subject to revision.[11]

Extending this principle we can perhaps say that whenever the state of the evidence on any question materially changes, you have a new question that cannot be fully answered by appealing to old authorities.[12] If this were admitted, some very interesting discussions could arise with regard to decisions made at Trent and even Vatican I. Some of the scriptural and historical arguments on which the fathers relied would not stand up very well in view of what is known today about the formation of the New Testament. Perhaps new arguments can be fashioned that prove the same conclusions; but perhaps also the conclusions might be said to admit of some modification since they were not, and could not have been, based on evidence that would today be convincing. To return to an example already used in Chapter 10, I doubt whether any well-informed theologian, if he were speaking for the first time on the subject, would think of saying, as did Vatican I, that Christ made Peter "prince of all the apostles and visible head of the entire Church militant" and gave him "primacy of true and proper jurisdiction."[13] The phraseology, at least, is bound up with the political experience of Western Europe in a certain historical era. If the question were coming up for new decision today, we would doubtless look for other ways of talking about the Petrine office in conformity with current New Testament scholarship and contemporary political forms.

6. *In Holy Scripture and in authoritative doctrinal*

statements, one should be alert for signs of social pathology and ideology.

The Church, since New Testament times (inclusively), has been an organization of weak and sinful men. At no time in history have Christians been free from fear, anxiety, resentment. Those in authority are naturally inclined to govern in a way that increases the docility of the faithful, even if this means suppressing certain facts that might raise embarrassing questions. Often the faithful themselves like to attribute magical powers to their leaders, partly in order to stimulate their corporate pride in the organization and partly to relieve themselves of responsibility for their own religious positions. These ideological factors go far to explain the peculiarities of curial rhetoric on which I have already commented. Charles Davis, after expressing the desire that a literary expert should study ecclesiastical language, remarks quite correctly: "Hyperbole in support of the established order and accepted doctrines or in fear-provoking condemnation of vaguely adumbrated errors is greatly encouraged."[14] Davis adds: "Above all, there is never an admission of past error or a frank avowal that present statements contradict past teaching."[15]

Gregory Baum, in his reply to Davis,[16] points out that what Davis is criticizing is a type of social pathology to which the Church as a religious institution is particularly subject. He shows how in the New Testament community itself sociopathological forces were at work, causing the early Christians to project their inadequacies and failures upon the Jews who had not accepted Christianity. Much of the defensiveness and fanaticism in the Church, especially in the post-Tridentine period, can be sociologically explained. When the traditional claims of the Church were contested by the Protestants, Catholics reacted by insisting exorbitantly on the divine powers and infallibility of the Church. Only in Vatican II do we see a change for the better. Here the Church frankly recognizes that it, as an institution, is affected by sin and must constantly pursue the path of repentance and reform. In *Gaudium et spes* the Council admits that the Church has no answer to many of the troublesome questions of our time, and that it must humbly listen to what competent specialists have to say.[17]

For anyone reading the older church documents, it is important to make allowance for sociological factors that may have led to narrowness (some interpretations of the axiom *extra Ecclesiam nulla salus!*), exorbitant claims (the bull *Unam sanctam!*), harshness toward adversaries, and the like. The divine truth is not taught by the Church in divine form, but in a human form, and thus it is always difficult to draw the line between what is a matter of Christian faith and what is to be set aside as a human perversion. The more precious the truth, and the more esteemed it is in the community, the more the heirs of the tradition are tempted to indulge in pride, fanaticism, and calumny.

At the beginning of this chapter I called attention to the doctrinal crisis in the Church today. The question arose, why are so many doctrines, which were apparently in peaceful possession for many centuries, suddenly being questioned from within the Church? If my argument has been sound, we are now in a position to give a partial answer. After a long period of resistance, historical relativity has broken through into Catholic theology. Any sophisticated theologian today knows that he has to reckon with the historical conditioning of all ecclesiastical statements. Every pronouncement has to be critically analyzed in terms of sociocultural factors. What was the historical *Sitz im Leben* out of which it arose? What literary conventions and figures of speech were employed in its formulation? What general picture of the world was simply taken for granted by the authors? What philosophical categories did they presuppose as the framework for their concepts? What was the full connotation of the terms to the men who first used them to express the mysteries of revelation? What precise question was in the minds of the authors, and how does it differ from the question that confronts us today? What effects of human weakness and sinfulness can be noted in the formulation of the doctrine itself?

Some may feel that the emphasis of this chapter has been excessively negative, but my intention is to clear the way for a more positive appreciation of the tradition. Many people reject ecclesiastical authority because they think it prevents them from criticizing the defects of past presentations of the Christian message. In my opinion it is only when we have been able to recognize and, so to speak, "siphon off" the human limitations and distortions that we are able to discover in and behind the faulty words of men the divine truth that is coming to expression through, and partly in spite of, its human witnesses. Once revelation is rightly understood as a divine action, it is obvious that there can be no absolute equation between the word of God and the words of men. But there can be a paradoxical or dialectical identity between the two. Consciousness of the historical relativity of all human utterances, far from negating the word of God, enables us to situate the human coefficient and thus to perceive more clearly the truth that is divine.

To acknowledge the relativity of historical formulations, then, is not to fall prey to relativism, but rather to escape imprisonment within the historical limitations of any one cultural period.[18] The present helps us to liberate ourselves from the tyranny of the past, and the past, to escape the idolatry of the present. The truth of revelation, in a mysterious way, preserves its dynamic identity amid the changing formulations. Each of the formulations must justify itself as an authentic articulation of the one gospel to which Christians are committed in faith. The truth of the gospel must come to us through human formulas, for otherwise it could not reach us where we are. It does not come to us in any eternally valid representations, because man's concepts are necessarily drawn from the fluctuating world in which he finds himself.

As we face the task of restating the Christian message for the twentieth century, we must of course beware of prematurely jettisoning formulas that are still meaningful and that serve to link us with the past. It would be a tragedy if the current confessional formulas failed to manifest the unity of our faith with that of the apostles and if they no longer pointed back to the experience of the first Christians. We certainly do not want a diluted version of the gospel—one that would sacrifice anything of the revelation given, once and for all, in Christ. Christianity must always retain its solid anchorage in the unrepeatable events of the first century.

It is important likewise for the Church to maintain a vital link with the earlier stages of its own tradition. If all doctrinal formulations are inadequate, it stands to reason that traditional statements, no longer in the current idiom, may often have something to offer as correctives to more current expressions. History, after all, is not all progress.

Biblical anthropology, had it been taken more seriously in
the seventeenth century, would have offered a healthy cor-
rective to Cartesian dualism. The biblical notion of God,
had it been taken more seriously, would have prevented
theologians from presenting God as an impassive and self-
enclosed Being. Profiting from the mistakes of our predecessors we avoid hastily dismissing formulations that do
not fit in with our preconceived opinions. For example the
term "transubstantiation," even though it may be unassimilable into modern metaphysics, remains valid as a testimony to the ancient faith of the Church. Doctrinal statements that are inconsistent with our world view may be
susceptible of a "retrieve" (in the Heideggerian sense) and
thus deserve to be retained in dynamic tension with more
recent conceptualizations.[19]

To prevent the gospel from losing its impact, however,
we must not shirk the task of modernization. It is not
enough to repeat the verbal formulations of an earlier time
or even to translate them, one by one, into a new idiom.
We live in an age that differs radically from anything that
went before. Mankind has been projected, as it were, over-
night into the computer age. As a result, the Christian
message as a whole must be refocused in a way that speaks
immediately and directly to the deepest concerns of the
present. Such a creative refocusing cannot be achieved by
simply finding new equivalents for old terms and formulas.
Vatican II recognized that dogmas are not isolated statements, but are articulations of a single vision, some closer
to, and some more distant from, the heart of the Christian
mystery.[20] In restating the Christian message for our day
we need a system of dogmas that develops organically out
of what our faith has to say most urgently to contemporary
man. Some dogmas that were very functional and important for systems based on a different perspective will perhaps have less prominence, although they will not be
directly contradicted, in new, dynamic restatement of the
faith.

If new questions demand new answers, the function of
tradition cannot be simply to transmit materially what
has been said in the past. Rather tradition must provide
effective guidelines for achieving Christian answers to current questions. It is not enough to repeat what our predecessors have said; we must imitate their courage and leadership. There is no reason why the Church today should

not offer men a richer fare of truth, inspiration, and guidance than ever before. Our contemporaries need what the Church ought to be able to say. They are no less bewildered, victimized, and dejected than the people of Palestine in the first century. They are still like sheep without a shepherd. We cannot nourish them with the stale fragments of a meal prepared for believers of the fourth or the thirteenth or the sixteenth century. A theology adapted to the times must be based on a fully modern understanding of man and the world. It may be as different from the medieval systems as the computer is from the abacus. Thinkers of the stature of Paul Tillich and Teilhard de Chardin have pointed the way. From such a creative theology new doctrinal insights will emerge and they, in turn, may crystallize into new dogmas.

These new dogmas, like their predecessors, will be vital for a time. But eventually, when the perspectives of man's consciousness shift again, they too will lose their actuality. They will serve their purpose if they orient the men of their own time to Christ, who is the same yesterday, today, and forever (Heb. 13:8), and if they help to relay the Christian message to ages yet to come.

The "Irreformability" of Dogma

In speaking of the mutability of dogma, as I have done in several previous chapters, I am conscious of having raised the specters of Modernist subjectivism and historical relativism. To prevent misunderstanding and to refine what has thus far been stated in rather global terms, I should like to add a closing chapter, somewhat technical in nature, examining at greater depth the problem of stability and flexibility in dogma. This problem has enormous consequences for the self-understanding and proclamation of the Church, especially in contemporary Roman Catholicism. Nothing has been more deeply impressed on the minds of the Catholic faithful in the first half of the twentieth century than the imperative necessity that no particle of revealed truth should be allowed to perish. It has been taken for granted that dogmas, once defined, must stand forever. Can a faithful Christian today hold otherwise?

The Catholic Church, being committed to the view that Christ made provision for a permanent living magisterium to herald in an authoritative manner the revelation communicated in apostolic times, has throughout its history had to defend its position against two sets of adversaries. On the one flank are the archaists, who maintain that the apostolic faith, as set forth in the Bible, admits of no further doctrinal evolution. According to this view, the Bible would be self-interpreting, at least to those who have the Spirit of Christ, and no authoritative magisterium would be required. On the other flank are the evolutionistic Rationalists and Modernists, who contend that the native power of the human intelligence to achieve progress in all fields demands that the Church should not commit itself to any past revelation as permanently normative for the present and the future.

In the time of Pius IX the Roman magisterium, seeking to address itself to both these sets of objections, adopted the idea that dogma can develop homogeneously. In several authoritative documents the Holy See quoted the phrase of Vincent of Lerins to the effect that the Church's teaching evolves "in the same doctrine, in the same understanding, and in the same opinion."[1] This formula, like the Chalcedonian definition regarding the two natures of Christ, is not so much a solution as an effort to fend off simplistic solutions that would be achieved by suppressing one aspect or other of the problem. Further probing is necessary in order to discern how dogma can remain self-identical while evolving. Is there some legitimate sense in which the later teaching may be said to have been implicit in the earlier?

The term "irreformability," which appears in the title of this chapter, has been familiar to all students of Catholic theology since Vatican Council I. In its Constitution on the Church, *Pastor aeternus*, the Council declared that the definitions of the Roman pontiff are irreformable, not by reason of the consent of the Church, but "by their very nature."[2] In the context, the point of the definition is evidently not to affirm the fact of irreformability, but rather to identify its source—namely, the infallibility of the pope. Read against the background of the Gallican "Four Articles" of 1682, from which the term comes, "irreformable" may be taken to mean "not subject to review by any higher authority."

In the Modernist crisis at the end of the nineteenth century the question of irreformability became differently focused. Alfred Loisy took the position that all truth is perpetually in flux as man and the world progressively evolve. Revelation and dogma, he held, are mutable because truth as such is mutable. This tenet was explicitly condemned by the Holy Office in 1907, though Loisy was not named as the adversary.[3] The anti-Modernist oath of 1910 repudiates the view that dogmas evolve by passing from one meaning to another, different from that which the Church previously accepted.[4]

Driven underground but not solved by the condemna-

tion of Modernism, the problem of dogmatic change sur-
faced again in the *nouvelle théologie* of the 1940s. In the
conclusion of his celebrated study on the Thomistic doctrine of grace, the French Jesuit Henri Bouillard attempted to do justice to the necessarily conditioned character of all human discourse and at the same time to avoid
the pitfalls of relativism. He declared:

> Christian truth never subsists in a pure state. By this
> we do not mean that it must inevitably be presented
> mingled with error, but that it is always imbedded in
> contingent notions and schemes which determine its ra-
> tional structure. It cannot be isolated from these. It can
> be liberated from one system of notions only by passing
> into another. . . . Thus the divine truth is never acces-
> sible prior to all contingent notions. Such is the law of
> incarnation.
>
> History does not, however, lead to relativism. It ena-
> bles one to grasp, in the heart of the theological evolu-
> tion, an absolute. Not indeed an absolute of representa-
> tion, but an absolute of affirmation. If the notions,
> methods, and systems change with time, the affirma-
> tions which they contain remain, even though they are
> expressed in different categories. Yet more, it is the
> affirmations themselves which, to retain their meaning
> in a new intellectual universe, determine new notions,
> methods, and systems in correspondence with this uni-
> verse.[5]

Although Bouillard in this study was primarily concerned with theological systems (Augustinianism and Tho-
mism), he applied his conclusions also to conciliar definitions.[6] Councils, he asserted, have often used contingent
technical notions in their declarations, but they have not
intended to consecrate these terms as linked with the philosophical system from which they are taken. Since truth
resides not in the concept but in the judgment, Bouillard
contended, the councils do not sanction notions, but propositions.[7]

How did Bouillard safeguard the immutable truth of
the affirmation while allowing for the contingency of the
notions? Every notion, he argued, has its meaning in the
context of other notions. When an old truth is inserted
into a new system, it cannot be affirmed by means of the

old concept, but must be conceived in a new way proportioned to the new system. "When the mind evolves, an immutable truth maintains itself only thanks to a simultaneous and correlative evolution of all the notions, maintaining an identical relationship among them. A theology which was not up to date [*actuelle*] would be a false theology."[8]

As is well known, the proposals of Bouillard were unfavorably received in conservative Scholastic circles. M.-J. Garrigou-Lagrange and others accused Bouillard and his cohorts of falling into relativism, of compromising the irreformable teachings of the magisterium, and of reviving the errors of Modernism. Among Bouillard's opponents, M.-M. Labourdette and M.-J. Nicolas contended that the God who had revealed himself in human language has likewise guaranteed the relationship between the concepts of faith and the salvific realities to which they refer. They held therefore that the concepts and even the terminology of the conciliar definitions are irreplaceable.[9]

In response to this controversy, the magisterium once more intervened. Pius XII's encyclical *Humani generis* (1950), without singling out any particular theologians for condemnation, rejected the view of those who "contend that the mysteries of faith can never be signified by adequately true notions, but only by what they call 'approximative' and always mutable notions, by which the truth is in some measure manifested but is necessarily also deformed."[10] Whatever some other theologians might have said, Bouillard had not stated that the notions inevitably deform the truth, nor had he said that all theological notions were mutable; but he would hardly have admitted that the notions used in definitions of faith are "adequately true."

In the following paragraph *Humani generis* went on to deplore the "dogmatic relativism" of those who would hold that the same divine truth may be expressed on the human side by concepts which, even though mutually opposed, signify the same divine reality. In opposition to this, *Humani generis* taught that the theological notions in the Catholic tradition are based on a true knowledge of created things and that some of these notions, moreover, have been used and even hallowed by ecumenical councils, so that it would be wrong (*nefas*) to depart from them.[11] True, the terms and concepts of the Scholastic and dog-

matic tradition could always be further perfected and pol-
ished; but to treat them with disrespect would inevitably
undermine the vigor of speculative theology.[12]

Fifteen years after *Humani generis* and just before the
close of Vatican Council II, Paul VI reiterated substantially the same doctrine, in very similar words. In his encyclical on the Eucharist,[13] he taught that the formulas
used by the Council of Trent to express the Church's eucharistic faith, "like the others which the Church uses to
propose the dogmas of the faith, express concepts which
are not tied to a certain definite form of human culture, or
to a certain stage of scientific progress, or to one theological
school or another, but exhibit that which the human mind,
in its universal and necessary experience of reality, perceives. . . . Hence they are suited to men of all times and
places." Although these formulas "can be more clearly and
evidently explained," they can and should be retained in
their original meaning.[14]

From the documents thus far cited, it would seem that
the magisterium since Vatican I has continued to insist on
the irreformability of dogma and has interpreted this as
signifying not merely that the affirmations must be retained, but that the very concepts and even the terms,
when endorsed by the highest authority, are to remain in
force. The only admissible type of development would be
a further refinement of what is in the original teaching. A
discontinuous shift into a different thought system, such
as Bouillard was describing, does not appear to be counte-
nanced.

The documents of Vatican II, however, seem to take
a more liberal approach. This is notably true of the Decree
on Ecumenism and the Pastoral Constitution on the
Church in the Modern World.

The Decree on Ecumenism includes a very interesting
analysis of the diversity between the styles of thought and
expression in the East and West. "The heritage handed
down by the apostles," it affirms, "was received in different forms and ways, so that from the very beginning of the
Church it has had a varied development in various places,
thanks to a similar variety of natural gifts and conditions
of life."[15] Renouncing any pretension of the West to impose its own thought-forms on the East, the Decree finds
positive value in the diversity of traditions: "It is hardly
surprising if sometimes one tradition has come nearer than

the other to an apt appreciation of certain aspects of a revealed mystery, or has expressed them in a clearer manner. As a result, these various theological formulations are often to be considered complementary rather than conflicting."[16] In these sentences the Council seems to imply that the formulas of proclamation and theology in the East and West are, at least in some instances, culturally conditioned and hence not suited to all times and places.

The temporal aspects of doctrinal adaptation are more explicitly dealt with in the Pastoral Constitution, *Gaudium et spes*. In its introductory statement this document points out the necessity of familiarizing oneself with the contemporary mentality in order to be able to speak to men's questions "in language intelligible to each generation."[17] Man, explains the Constitution, is undergoing a spiritual revolution that has vast repercussions in the religious area. In particular, "the human race has passed from a rather static concept of reality to a more dynamic, evolutionary one."[18] In subsequent paragraphs, *Gaudium et spes* encourages theologians to work out new ways of presenting the faith to men of today.[19] Here *Gaudium et spes* adds, practically quoting Pope John XXIII: "The deposit of faith or revealed truths are one thing; the manner in which they are formulated without violence to their meaning and significance is another."[20] This process of reformulation, according to the Council, is no novelty, "for from the beginning of her history she [the Church] has learned to express the message of Christ with the help of the ideas and terminology of various peoples and has tried to clarify it with the wisdom of the philosophers, too. . . . Thus each nation develops the ability to express Christ's message in its own way."[21]

Thus there seems to be, prima facie, a difference in emphasis if not in teaching between two sets of documents. Some documents, such as *Humani generis* and *Mysterium fidei*, accent the universal and timeless value of the Church's concepts and formulas. Others, such as *Unitatis redintegratio* and *Gaudium et spes*, allow for, and even encourage, a variety of formulations in accordance with the mentality and traditions of different peoples and ages.

Since Vatican Council II the question of the irreformability of dogma has become acute throughout the Church. In its effort to break out of the narrow mold of Neo-

Scholasticism, Catholic theology has been seeking to enter into fruitful contact with other traditions of thought, such as pragmatism, existentialism, and process theology. Under such circumstances new questions become urgent; many of the ancient doctrines of the Church seem to demand translation into new terms and concepts if they are to retain their intelligibility in new frameworks. In the present turmoil the guarded statements of Bouillard, which aroused such controversy twenty years ago, seem prudent and moderate.

In contemporary Catholic theology one may distinguish, at least schematically, three main positions. On the right are those who see no reason for modifying the views of Garrigou-Lagrange and the conservative Scholastics of the 1940s. On the left are theologians who maintain that doctrine is always reformable because the Church in all its declarations, is fallible. In the center are those who accept the infallibility of the teaching Church, but wish to make room for some kind of reformability in dogma, at least with regard to the formulas and concepts in which it is expressed.

The first of these three positions is frequently defended on the ground that faith is knowledge and, as such, cannot be dissociated from the propositions in which it is expressed.[22] To change the terms and formulas, it is argued, would be inevitably to change the content and hence to do away with the affirmation itself. Some adherents of this "right-wing" position concede that the words and imaginative representations accompanying the concepts may be discarded, but they demand that the concepts themselves be retained, as inseparable from the dogmas themselves.[23]

This position, however, overlooks the intrinsic connections between concepts, imaginative representations, and forms of speech; it neglects what we may call the "historicity" of concepts. Concepts are always constructed on the basis of determinate experiences, interpreted in the light of certain presuppositions and concerns. When the experiences, presuppositions, and concerns change, the old concepts become inaccessible or inappropriate, and new concepts take their place. This can be illustrated with reference to the Bible itself. Many of the biblical concepts of God are tied to agricultural, pastoral, familial, and military forms of life that do not correspond to the historical experience of modern man. To appreciate these concepts requires an effort of historical imagination and empathy. The modern Christian generally finds it hard to think of God as the "Lord of armies," even though this biblical designation has been retained in the "Sanctus" of the Roman Mass. Even the concept of God as "Father" has lost many of the rich overtones it had in ancient patriarchal society.

If the preaching of the Church is too closely tied to articulations out of phase with modern culture, the content of the faith, far from being retained intact, is inevitably impoverished and distorted. In its actual practice, the Church has always recognized this. In New Testament times, the concept "Son of Man," being excessively tied to the Jewish apocalyptic background, was gradually dropped as a designation of Jesus, and concepts such as "Lord" became more prevalent. In the early centuries, when the divinity of Jesus was questioned, the creeds began to insist that he was "consubstantial" with the Father. The term "God," rarely if ever applied to Jesus in the New Testament, because of fear that Christian monotheism might be compromised, became current when the chief danger was that Jesus might be understood as a mere creature.

So in our day, it may well be necessary to employ new concepts, not in order to reduce the content of faith, but to be able to herald the gospel with full power. Several illustrations immediately come to mind. It may no longer be adequate to divide human sinfulness into "personal sin" and "original sin," as was done in earlier times. The sinfulness accruing to man by reason of the world in which he lives was formerly attributed to a fault biologically inherited from the "first man Adam." To revitalize the notion of man's corporate sinfulness, some contemporary theologians prefer to speak of the "sin of the world." Besides being a more biblical term (cf. Jn. 1:29), this is a more existentially meaningful concept than "original sin," if the latter is interpreted in purely traditional categories. Perhaps the concept of "sin of the world" will eventually replace "original sin" as a primary theological category. The change might be a positive enrichment rather than an impoverishment of our dogmatic heritage.

To give one more example, it may be helpful at this point to refer again to the recent efforts to substitute some new term (and concept) for that of "transubstantiation" to designate the wonderful change effected in the bread and wine at the eucharistic meal. The purpose of this reconceptualization would not be to do away with what was effectively affirmed by the older formula, but rather to protect this. The concept of substance, in contemporary thought, has become so static and physical that it no longer functions effectively to convey the sacramental, personal, and dynamic presence of Christ in the Eucharist. The term "transubstantiation" is more likely to suggest a magical material transmutation than the mysterious change which the medieval Scholastics had in mind. For the majority of men today, the Scholastic concept of "substance"—although it was no doubt the most suitable category in the philosophical framework of Thomistic Aristotelianism—has become practically unavailable. Hence there are urgent pastoral reasons for seeking a new concept and a new term which will do for modern man what "transubstantiation" did for medieval man. The terms "transignification" and "transfinalization," helpful though they may be to some, are probably too ambiguous to gain universal currency in the Church as adequate enunciations of its eucharistic faith. Thus the search for a renewed conceptuality and a new terminology must be continued.

Let me turn now to the second position—that which would deny the infallibility of magisterial declarations (though not necessarily the infallibility of the Church). This position has been taken by Bishop Francis Simons[24] on the ground that the doctrine of infallibility is not sufficiently biblical and by Leslie Dewart on the quite opposite ground that it is not sufficiently progressive. Since Bishop Simons' position is not well developed theologically, I shall confine my attention to the very sophisticated position of Professor Dewart. On the basis of an evolutionary theory of knowledge, not altogether unlike those of Alfred Loisy and George Tyrrell, he argues that the notion of unconditionally binding propositions, either in Scripture or in church documents, is totally unacceptable to modern man. Rather, he asserts, God "reveals himself in and through human concepts whose truth is ever inconclusive, ever growing, ever evolving, since these concepts share in the nature of all human conscious life."[25] Unlike the Modernists, Dewart is convinced that the faith experience which gives rise to continually new concepts is brought about not by man's instinctual drives but by the free and personal response of God to human history.[26]

As will be apparent to any reader who has followed my argument thus far, I fully concur with Dewart's insistence that the concepts and propositions expressing the Church's faith should be constantly updated to keep pace with the growth of human consciousness under the impact of successive historical experiences. But his denial of doctrinal infallibility, as I understand it, flows from a conceptual agnosticism that I do not fully share. He apparently regards all concepts as merely pragmatic instruments, enabling the believer to deal effectively with successive situations and to intensify his faith experience. I should be prepared to argue, on the contrary, that some concepts, at least, have an authentically cognitive role. They enable one to achieve noetic insight into the realities to which they refer; they mediate a contemplative union between the knower and the known. To this I should add that concepts are not our only means of knowledge. They express and elaborate, to some degree, what we have already come to know, in a vital but inarticulate way, through experience. In religious knowledge man's preconceptual awareness of God is a factor of immense importance.

Dewart vigorously attacks the correspondence theory of truth. He is of course right in saying that truth is not a relationship of similarity between an idea (conceived of as a photograph) and an original. But as he develops his own position he seems to minimize excessively the content set forth in the Christian creeds and confessions. He sometimes speaks as though believers, in proclaiming that Jesus is the incarnate Word or that he rose from the dead, had no other aim than to heighten their own religious consciousness.[27] I believe, on the contrary, that it is essential for Christianity to insist on the reality of the events to which the creeds, confessions, and dogmas make reference. Occasionally Dewart, with apparent inconsistency, seems to admit this. For instance, he describes the Redemption as "having been accomplished as a concrete and discrete historical event."[28] If Dewart would agree that to acknowledge this reality (however variously it may be conceptualized and verbalized) is essential to Christianity, he would have to concede, in principle, that there might be such things as infallible statements—statements that could not be denied without loss of the substance of Christianity. Dewart's present position seems to me unsatisfactory because it does not make room for such statements.

Having rejected the first and second positions, we are left with the third—that which affirms the doctrinal infallibility of the Church while allowing for reformulation in terminology and concept. Relying upon theologians such as Edward Schillebeeckx, Karl Rahner, and Walter Kasper, I should like to set forth this position as I understand and accept it.

In human knowledge generally, there is a paradoxical combination of the absolute and the relative. As a being within the world, man knows only from a restricted point of view, on the basis of his own experiences and contacts. Further, he cannot express what he knows, even to himself, except in terms of the conceptual materials derived from his limited experience in interaction with the world about him. As spirit, however, man always transcends the objective content of his own knowledge. Reaching out toward an absolute, with which he is already mysteriously in contact, he is conscious of the relativity and conceptual poverty of his own affirmations. When I say, therefore, "the table is square," I am simultaneously aware, at least in some vaguely implicit way, of the incomplete and approximative character of my concepts of "tableness" and "squareness." What I designate as a "table," from one point of view, another knower, from a different perspective, might grasp by means of other categories. The shape of the table, moreover, is not exactly square, even in the Euclidean sense, and perhaps it could be better measured by some other geometry than Euclid's. While conceding all this, I am also confident that whatever new concepts might be devised to speak about what I am referring to as the "squareness" of the "table," they cannot validly negate what I really mean when I say, on the basis of the evidence before me, "the table is square." My realization of the circumscribed value of my own assertion is precisely what protects it from being falsified by a subsequent, more refined statement.

Man's statements concerning revelation possess a similar absoluteness within relativity. When God reveals, he manifests to man that the mystery which surrounds him is not hostile or indifferent; God discloses himself as demanding, as merciful, as forgiving. The prophets and religious founders who have most vividly apprehended the mystery of the self-revealing God have expressed this by means of concepts derived from the cultures in which they have lived. These concepts, however, have to be interpreted against the horizon of the fundamental experience of grace. Thus Rahner can correctly say: "The imparting of grace itself is always of itself the basic mode of revelation itself, because grace as the self-revelation of God, the absolute Spirit, to the spirit and freedom of man, never resides in man as a merely objective, absolutely preconscious condition."[29] And Schillebeeckx can write: "The real content of human knowing and believing is the ever present *mystery* of promise—the mystery which is not uttered, which is everywhere reaching towards expression but in itself is never thought."[30]

In view of the primacy of the preconceptual element in faith, it evidently follows that whatever formulations are devised in order to articulate the content of faith are to be understood analogously. The analogy here in question does not consist in a comparison of object with object, but rather in a comparison of the objective materials that seek to describe the divine mystery (e.g., the designation of God as "Father") with the ineffable reality experienced in grace, but not articulately known except with the help of the proclaimed word. The dogmatic statement has its theological intelligibility by reason of its ability to conjure up, in some sort, the experience of the absolute mystery that communicates itself to us in the grace of Jesus Christ.[31] Dogmatic statements are, or at least should be, both expressive and evocative. On the one hand, they must express the faith of those who utter them; they must "symbolize" in a thematic way the interior states of soul of the believer. On the other hand, they must instill or intensify faith in those to whom they are addressed. In view of the total missionary and ecumenical situation, the Church must try to speak in such a way as to arouse faith, hope, and charity both in its own members and in the world to which the Church has been sent.

It would be a mistake, however, to imagine that because dogmatic statements are expressive and evocative, they do not in some way attain the reality of that to which they refer. In their conceptual, propositional form, confessional statements intend to be something more than symbolic statements that would express and communicate the speaker's subjective attitudes. They are propositions that make definite predications about determinate realities, as is evident from an examination of a statement such as "Jesus Christ was crucified for our salvation." Whatever difficulties there may be in verifying or falsifying such a statement, there can be no doubt but what the statement contains a demanding truth claim about an event that is alleged to have transpired at a certain moment in the past, with regard to a certain individual human being. This determinate reference is conveyed by means of the conceptual content of the statement.

Having stressed the importance of the conceptual content of doctrinal statements, let me now turn to the question of revisability. Can old concepts be replaced by new concepts; or, in other words, can old terms be replaced by new terms that are not just synonyms for their predecessors?

One factor favoring an affirmative answer is the fact that, properly speaking, concepts and terms are neither true nor false, but only apt or inept. Thus when I say that "the Father is of the same substance as the Son," I am not saying anything directly about "substance"; I am using the concept "substance" in order to say something about the divine persons.

Secondly, human concepts and terms are taken from the data of experience. Since men's experiences are various, there are diversities in the terms and concepts current in different cultures and periods of history. Even man's experience of himself changes. While man in every age is bodily, social, free, intelligent, etc., man today experiences these qualities differently than his ancestors did. Because of this experiential difference, the concepts going with these terms are different. Concepts have a history inasmuch as they evolve concurrently with man's experience of himself and the world.

By reason of the conceptual ingredient in all human discourse, there is an element of provisionality in every statement, even that which asserts an "eternal truth." For example, when I say "God is good," I can do so because, and inasmuch as, my experience affords me with instances of goodness that can in some way be applied (with due respect for the Scholastic canons of affirmation, negation, and eminence) to God. In other words, I draw on the categories afforded by my experience, and my statements are meaningful and true for others insofar as their experience equips them with similar categories. Any given society will construct a characteristic conceptual-linguistic system in accordance with its own dominant forms of experience.

Jesus Christ, as a Palestinian Jew of the first century, freely took on the local and temporal characteristics of the people among whom he moved. He expressed himself in terms of the common experiences, language, and conceptual categories of his own contemporaries. Because he, being God, did not shrink from assuming the fragmentariness of human historicity, the Christian community should not be afraid to walk the path of history. For the Christian, history is no longer an oppressive law standing over man, but rather the way in which we walk in trust and faith, assured that God is with us.[32]

How, then, can this affirmation of historicity be reconciled with the infallibility of the Church?[33] Infallibility, as currently understood, means that the magisterium in its constant and universal teaching, and in the solemn utterances of its highest organs, cannot definitively commit the entire Church to error. Yet even in its infallible definitions, which are few and far between, the Church is subject to human and historical limitations. In the minds of those who formulate and interpret the definitions, the absolutely binding dogmatic teaching is accompanied by interpretations and representational elements that are not so guaranteed. In giving utterance to the divine truth, the pilgrim Church is obliged to make use of the terms and concepts at hand in a given culture and intelligible to men of that culture. Generations may be needed before theologians have succeeded in distinguishing between the dogma itself and some of the inadequate representational schemas and false interpretations by which the definition may have originally been surrounded. For this reason every dogmatic definition is, as Rahner puts it, not so much an end as a beginning.[34] The ancient dogmas of the Church always have to be reconsidered from the vantage point of new cultural situations.

One important function of dogmatic definitions is precisely to keep open the path toward future development. More often than not, the main purpose of a dogma is to condemn a one-sided answer that would prematurely close a question calling for further discussion. As Walter Kasper has said:

> The Church lives precisely through the proclamation of its own provisionality. In the interim dogmas can be stations on the way, but they cannot be the goal. They must prove themselves true inasmuch as they point beyond themselves and open up the future of the Church rather than bring it to a halt. The Church must not rigidly cut itself off and isolate itself by means of dogmas. Rather, they should serve to maintain openness and to prevent heretical constriction and induration.[35]

All these observations about dogma in general hold with regard to the dogma of infallibility. In defining its own infallibility the Church sought to maintain the mystery of the abiding presence of divine truth in the Church and in the language by which the revealed truth is proclaimed, notwithstanding the historical limitations which encompass all human conceptuality and speech. Inevitably, the definition of 1870 was expressed in the historical situation of that time, according to the literary forms and style then prevalent in Catholic conciliar discourse. If formulated for the first time today, the definition of infallibility would probably sound very different. Perhaps even the word "infallibility" would not be used; almost certainly the confusing term "irreformable" would be omitted.

Merely to parrot the words of an old definition in a new situation is a false and inauthentic form of orthodoxy. When the sociocultural context has changed, further progress is demanded in order not to lose sight of the truth conveyed by an earlier formula. In order to develop the Church's teaching as the times require, we have to take a somewhat critical stance toward the formulas handed down to us from the past. Such critical activity is necessary in order to keep the doctrine, as Anselm Atkins puts it, "dialectically alive."[36] With suitable qualifications one may apply to the development of dogma the Hegelian triad of affirmation, negation, and resolution. The defined dogma may not be directly negated in the precise sense in which it was asserted, but a qualified negation, in terms of a new sociocultural context, may lead to a further development, or resolution, on a more comprehensive level.

Before closing I should like to address myself to several common objections to the kind of reconceptualization of dogma for which I have argued. In the first place, it may be objected that if new concepts are used, new things will inevitably be said, since different concepts are not simply equivalent to each other. But to say new things would imply that not everything had previously been said and hence that the Church had not fully understood the truth of revelation. This might seem to run counter to the traditional Catholic doctrine that the Christian revelation became complete in apostolic times.

This objection, if it has any force, would seem to tell against any theory of the development of dogma. In practically all Catholic treatments of this question, it is explained that the "completeness" of God's revelation in Christ and the apostles does not signify that the revelation was exhaustively understood in the first century, but rather that the central mystery of God's salvific plan became manifest in the Christ event as viewed in the light of the Easter experiences. Unquestionably there are many implications of the original revelation that remain to be discovered by subsequent reflection. According to the theory here proposed, such reflection would be assisted by the new kinds of secular and religious experience and knowledge that become available as mankind enters new stages of its cultural evolution. This does not detract from, but rather gives full value to, the plenitude of the original revelation on which the Church is founded. The plenitude is so great that it cannot be taken in all at one time or under any single perspective.

A second objection, directed more specifically against our theory of dogmatic reformulation, is that it opens the way to the negation or contradiction of the previously received formulas. If one admits that concepts and terminology have a history and are culturally conditioned, there is no guarantee that the Church, having said at one time that the Son is "of the same substance" as the Father, may not at some later time say that the Father and the Son are different in substance. Would not this in effect erode the contents of the Church's teaching and emasculate the anathemas by which heresies have been struck down?

On the theory I have proposed, there is no difficulty in vindicating the right and duty of the magisterium to anathematize formulas that do not suitably express the revelation of Christ. But it should be added that the condemned propositions are anathematized only within a given field of discourse. As Atkins observes, theological statements are always susceptible of a variety of possible interpretations. It is therefore sufficient, for the truth of the anathema, that one of the possible meanings of the condemned proposition should be false.[37] To discern which of the possible meanings is unacceptable one may have to ponder the original anathema in the light of the total religiohistorical development through which the Church was passing. From the standpoint of a later stage one may be able to retrieve a true meaning within the anathematized proposition. Thus a Catholic of the sixteenth century, giving a certain understanding to the term "faith," might deny that man was saved by faith alone. Today, with a wider understanding of the same term, he might affirm the proposition then denied. The two statements would not be really contradictory, for the meaning of one of the terms would have been changed.

The reformulation of dogma, as I have already explained, can never be a simple negation of that which was previously held. But the development can be jagged and discontinuous rather than logically homogeneous. When the gospel is transposed into a new linguistic-cultural framework, new things must be said in order that the full gospel may be heard and in order that distortions be avoided. As noted above, to say the old things in a new cultural situation might well result in a deformation of the revelation.

A third objection calls attention to the danger that the past will be dismissed as irrelevant and that the work of the Church in previous centuries will be cavalierly set aside. If this were to happen, however, it would not be as a result of adopting the positions for which I have been arguing. I do not maintain that formulations arrived at in a framework other than our own are meaningless or that they may properly be dismissed from memory. As embodiments of an authentically Christian concern in a previous situation, they stand as valuable witnesses as to how the Church must react to the kinds of questions and threats which have occurred and continue to occur throughout the course of history. They remain binding to the extent that similar, or analogous, questions continue to arise.

Regarding the power of the mind to transcend its own sociocultural frameworks and its own conceptual schemes, I am in full agreement with W. Norris Clarke, who writes:

> . . . I do firmly believe that the human mind can transcend its own frameworks in its inner acts of insight of the living mind. For all frameworks are only the products, the instruments of the living mind in act. The latter are never identical with or tied down to its own finite products incarnated in matter. Hence by insight the mind in act, which is a kind of inexhaustible formless reservoir of power for producing endless new mental products, can leap over the bounds of its own frameworks and grasp its own universal, permanent situation of having to construct frameworks to express itself. But once it has to express even this framework-transcending insight it must fall back on some limited culture-bound framework as an instrument.[38]

Thanks to the transcendence of the human spirit, modern man can intellectually project himself into thought worlds not his own—those of Isaiah, Paul, John, Augustine, Thomas Aquinas, or the fathers of Trent. He can likewise imagine for the moment (and hopefully realize that he is imagining!) that he still lives in the cultural world of Vatican Council I. When he does so, he can discern the religious importance of controversies that took place within a context alien to our own and can appreciate why the people of God, guided by a sure instinct of the faith, accepted and rejected certain views which were then assimilable or unassimilable by the Church.

While we take guidance from these ancient statements, we are not necessarily bound to accept the conceptual-linguistic frameworks within which they were formulated. To quote Father Clarke again:

> . . . if one finds that the lived experience and frameworks of himself or his own community are so different or incommensurable with respect to those in which the original truth statements were uttered that the latter

now appear too alien or narrow-visioned to be fruitfully assimilable by oneself or one's own community, one has the right and duty, to be exercised with the respect and reverence appropriate to the subject matter, to creatively rethink and re-express them in one's own most adequate frameworks.[39]

Christianity has been a vital religion for so many centuries because Christians of successive generations have had the courage to rethink their faith in the light of the most pressing problems of their day. This was done by the biblical authors, by the Greek and Latin Fathers, and by the great Scholastics. The ancient creeds bear the impress of the life-and-death encounters between the Christian faith and the secular cultures of the past. For the revitalization of the faith, similar initiatives have to be taken in our time. The event of Jesus Christ must be seen anew in the light of our contemporary concerns for peace, for justice, for freedom, for community, for a responsible use of world resources, and for personal experience of the transcendent. New creeds, framed in the light of these concerns, might well be introduced into the liturgy. If they have the best interests of the Church at heart, Church authorities, far from repressing such doctrinal initiatives, will actively encourage them. Otherwise Christianity will inevitably lose ground to more adaptable religions or to new forms of cult—to the great detriment, I believe, of man's authentic religious development.

We should, however, be on guard against a mindless rejection of the old. For the continuing self-identity of the Church, as a world-wide community of faith that traces its origins to biblical times, it is important to keep the memory of the past alive. By a process of education not beyond the capacities of the normal lay believer, it is still possible to grasp the message of the Bible and the ancient creeds. Discreetly used, a certain archaism in practice (as opposed to the "dogmatic archaism" reprobated at the beginning of this chapter) may actually help to sharpen the contemporary believer's awareness of his personal relationship to the Jesus of history and thus to liberate him from imprisonment within the limited perspectives of his own time and culture.

The fourth, and last, objection arises from the anxiety that if new frameworks are admitted, the Church will not possess adequate guidelines for judging the validity of new formulations. Objective criteria cannot be set up except in terms of a common framework. Where two statements are made in different universes of discourse, they are not commensurable by any common conceptual rule, and hence it is difficult to judge whether they can both be expressions of the same faith. The door seems to be flung wide open to subjectivism.

The key to this objection, and to my answer, lies in the term "objective." If revelation is essentially mystery, it can never be fully objectified. The experience of grace —inarticulate though it be—enters into the ultimate judgment as to whether a given formulation is admissible. Only the man of faith—or the community of faith—can properly judge whether a new expression, interpreted in a particular sociocultural and linguistic context, is an acceptable articulation of the faith.

I do not of course deny the indispensable assistance provided by the canonical formulations handed down from the past. Scripture and tradition have taught us what it means to be a Christian, and we must ever and again return to them for the renewal of our faith. But what we have gained from these written sources is, precisely, faith —that is to say, a living apprehension that cannot adequately be reduced to anything in writing. The light of faith, sustained by the Holy Spirit, gives the Church in every age a sure instinct for discerning the true bearing of the ancient documents upon the questions currently being asked.

The total inquiry regarding the acceptability of new doctrinal positions, formulated against the horizon of new presuppositions and new concerns, must unfold under the aegis of the Holy Spirit, who is given to the Church for the sake of adequate discernment in all times (cf. Jn. 16:13). To demand totally determinative objective norms, and to look exclusively to the letter of past magisterial pronouncements, would be to minimize unduly the role of the Holy Spirit. Overanxious traditionalists sometimes cling to a slavish literalism from which the gospel should have set them free. While avoiding arbitrary subjectivity, we should also be on guard against doctrinal legalism. The right path will be found if we are faithful to the tradition as the living Spirit enables the Church to understand it.

Because of the cultural revolution through which mankind is presently passing, teachers in the Church must be more than usually open to new formulations and slow to condemn views that are seriously proposed by prudent and committed Christians. Scripture itself, as we have seen in earlier chapters of this book, contains statements in logical tension with each other. Hence we must be prepared to consider the acceptability of new formulas of faith not evidently reconcilable, in pure formal logic, with others long venerated in the Church.

Finally, we should be content if it should be granted us to state the content of Christianity, in a meaningful and credible way, for men of our time. No one generation can capture the abiding content of the faith in a "chemically pure" state, so as to commit all future generations to repeat its formulations. With regard to the future we can say only that however men may see fit to reinterpret the gospel, they may not legitimately ignore or cancel out what previous generations of Christians have seen and, in a culturally conditioned manner, proclaimed. Because the gospel of Jesus Christ remains, throughout all conceptual and verbal changes, the faith may be said to perdure.

A tall skyscraper could not stand against the wind unless it were built so that it could sway. An ocean liner, if it could not bend with the waves, would be broken by them. Flexibility is not the antithesis of structure, but the condition of preserving it in a changing world. Quite evidently, then, the Church of Christ, precisely because it has a mission to every time and culture, must be able to adapt its message and its structures. If dogma were inflexible it would be brittle; but because dogma has an inbuilt elasticity it can and will survive.

NOTES

Abbreviations in Notes

AAS—   *Acta Apostolicae Sedis* (Rome, 1909–).
ASS—   *Acta Sanctae Sedis* (Rome, 1865–1908).
CSEL—   *Corpus Scriptorum Ecclesiasticorum Latinorum* (Vienna, 1866–).
DS—   *Enchiridion Symbolorum, definitionum et declarationum de rebus fidei et morum,* ed. by H. Denzinger, rev. by A. Schönmetzer, S.J., 32nd ed. (Freiburg im Breisgau: Herder, 1963).
IDO-C—   *Information Documentation on the Conciliar Church.* A series of bulletins begun in Rome in 1962 to supply the Dutch bishops with background information for Vatican Council II, later (1965–69) made available to subscribers in several languages. The present *IDOC International* (North American Edition, New York, 1970–) is the successor to the original publication edited from Rome.
PG—   *Patrologia graeca,* ed. by J. P. Migne. 161 vols. (Paris, 1857–66).
PL—   *Patrologia latina,* ed. J. P. Migne. 217 vols.; indexes, 4 vols. (Paris, 1878–90).
Sources chrét—*Sources chrétiennes,* ed. by H. de Lubac et al. (Paris, 1941–).

Chapter 1

1. John Dillenberger, *Contours of Faith* (Nashville: Abingdon, 1960), p. 35.

2. These seven forms of faith correspond to seven of the nine prespective views of revelation summarized in my *Revelation Theology* (New York: Herder and Herder, 1969), pp. 171–75.

3. This passage is translated in the RSV: "If you will not believe, surely you shall not be established." In my translation in the text I have attempted to bring out the play on words in the original Hebrew. As the commentators commonly point out, both verbs of the couplet come from the Hebrew root '*mn*, meaning "confirm" or "establish," and, in the causative form, "believe." See, on this point, Frederick L. Moriarty's comments in *The Jerome Biblical Commentary*, ed. by R. E. Brown, J. A. Fitzmyer, and R. E. Murphy (Englewood Cliffs, N.J.: Prentice-Hall, 1968), vol. 1, p. 270, with references to further literature.

4. Gabriel Moran, *Catechesis of Revelation* (New York: Herder and Herder, 1966), p. 37.

5. *Ibid.*, p. 137.

6. Cf. Robert McAfee Brown, *The Spirit of Protestantism* (New York: Oxford, 1961), p. 61.

7. Dietrich Bonhoeffer, *Letters and Papers from Prison*, rev. ET by R. Fuller and F. Clarke (New York: Macmillan Paperback, 1967), p. 203.

8. *Loc. cit.*

9. *Ibid.*, pp. 168–69.

10. Harvey Cox, *The Secular City* (New York: Macmillan Paperback, 1965), p. 80.

11. Karl Rahner, *Belief Today*, ET by R. and R. Ockenden (New York: Sheed & Ward, 1967), p. 52.

12. Herbert Richardson, *Toward an American Theology* (New York: Harper & Row, 1967), pp. 44–45.

13. For an analysis of this mentality, see Henri de Lubac, "The New Man: the Marxist and the Christian View," *Cross Currents* 1, Fall, 1950, 67–88.

14. Richardson, *op. cit.*, p. 42.

15. *Ibid.*, p. 44.

16. See especially *Gaudium et spes*, no. 19, in W. M. Abbott, ed., *The Documents of Vatican II* (New York: Guild Press, 1966), p. 217.

Chapter 2

1. Thomas Aquinas, *Summa theol.* 1–2ae, q. 69, a. 3; 2–2ae, q. 2, a. 1; q. 4, a. 8.

2. Augustine, *Of True Religion*, ch. 25, n. 46, ET by J. H. S. Burleigh, in Library of Christian Classics, vol. 6 (Philadelphia: Westminster Press, 1953), p. 247.

3. Blaise Pascal, "Préface sur le traité du vide," in *Opuscules et lettres (choix)*, ed. by L. Lafuma (Paris: Aubier, 1955), p. 50. My translation.

4. Charles Davis, *A Question of Conscience* (New York: Harper & Row, 1967), pp. 6–8.

5. Augustine, *The Usefulness of Belief*, ch. 8, no. 20, ET by J. H. S. Burleigh, in Library of Christian Classics, vol. 6 (Philadelphia: Westminster Press, 1953), p. 307.

6. See the collection of texts on this point assembled by E. Przywara, *An Augustine Synthesis* (New York: Sheed & Ward, 1939), esp. pp. 58–73.

7. Bernard J. Lonergan, "Theology in Its New Context," in L. K. Shook, ed., *Theology of Renewal*, vol. 1 (Herder and Herder, 1968), pp. 37–38.

8. Michael Polanyi, *Personal Knowledge: Towards a Post-Critical Philosophy* (New York: Harper Torchbook, 1964), p. 207.

9. Thomas Aquinas, *Comment. in Joann.* IV, lect. 5, a. 2. Cf. the reflections of Jacques Maritain, *The Range of Reason* (New York: Scribner, 1952), p. 209.

10. Paul Tillich discusses the dialectic of autonomy, heteronomy, and theonomy in many places. See especially his *Systematic Theology* (Chicago: University of Chicago Press, 1951), vol. 1, pp. 83–86, 147–50.

11. John Henry Newman, *Essay in Aid of a Grammar of Assent*, ch. 9, §3 (Garden City: Doubleday Image Book, 1955), pp. 281–82.

12. Michael Polanyi, "Faith and Reason," *Journal of Religion*, 41 (1961), 237–47.

13. Polanyi, *Personal Knowledge*, p. 127.

14. Cf. Thomas Aquinas, *Summa theol.* 2–2ae, q. 1, a. 4, ad 3; q. 45, a. 2, c.

Chapter 3

1. Étienne Gilson, *Reason and Revelation in the Middle Ages* (New York: Scribner, 1938).

2. H. Richard Niebuhr, *Christ and Culture* (New York: Harper Torchbook, 1956).

3. Herbert W. Richardson, *Toward an American Theology* (New York: Harper & Row, 1967), ch. 2, "Five Types of Faith."

4. I have especially in mind the two essays in Wolfhart Pannenberg, *Grundfragen systematischer Theologie* (Göttingen: Vandenhoeck & Ruprecht, 1967), pp. 223–36, 237–51.

5. John Henry Newman, *Essay in Aid of a Grammar of Assent*, ch. 9, §3 (Garden City: Doubleday Image Book, 1955), pp. 296–97.

6. *Ibid.*, ch. 6, §1, p. 138–39; ch. 8, §2, p. 239.

7. Henri de Lubac, *The Discovery of God*, ET by Alexander Dru (New York: Kenedy, 1960).

8. The *Gorgias* is perhaps Plato's most impressive presentation of this doctrine, which appears also in the *Republic.*

9. Viktor E. Frankl, *Man's Search for Meaning*, ET by Ilse Lasch (New York: Washington Sq. Press, 1963). See also his *The Will to Meaning* (Cleveland: World, 1969), pp. 83–98.

10. Augustine, *On the Predestination of the Saints*, ch. 5. ET in W. J. Oates, ed., *Basic Writings of Saint Augustine*, vol. 1 (New York: Random House, 1948), p. 780.

11. "Reason leads to understanding and knowledge. But reason is not entirely absent from authority, for we have got to consider whom we have to believe, and the highest authority belongs to truth when it is clearly known." In Augustine, *Of True Religion*, ch. 24, no. 45, ET by J. H. S. Burleigh, in Library of Christian Classics, vol. 6 (Philadelphia: Westminster Press, 1953), p. 247.

Chapter 4

1. Blaise Pascal, *Pensées*, ed. by L. Brunschvicg, ET by W. F. Trotter (New York: Modern Library, 1941), pp. 60–61.

2. Immanuel Kant, *Critique of Pure Reason*, ET by N. K. Smith (New York: St. Martins, 1961), pp. 635–44. See also C. C. J. Webb, *Kant's Philosophy of Religion* (Oxford: Clarendon Press, 1926), pp. 1–2.

3. Kant, *Critique of Practical Reason*, ET by T. K. Abbott (London: Longmans, Green, 1909), p. 227.

4. Maurice Blondel, *L'Action* (Paris, 1893), p. vii.

5. Article by F. Mallet (pseudonym for Blondel) in *Annales de philosophie chrétienne*, March, 1907, 573–74.

6. Gabriel Marcel, *Homo Viator: Sketch of a Phenomenology and a Metaphysic of Hope*, ET by Emma Craufurd (Chicago: Regnery, 1951), p. 32.

7. Herbert Plügge, *Wohlbefinden und Missbefinden: Beiträge zu einer medizinischen Anthropologie* (Tübingen: Niemeyer, 1962). Josef Pieper, to whose work I am indebted for this reference, points out the particular interest of the two sections "On Suicidal Patients" and "On Hope"; see Pieper, *Hope and History*, ET by Richard and Clara Winston (New York: Herder and Herder, 1969), pp. 24–26. See also the discussion of Plügge's findings in Wolfhart Pannenberg, *Jesus: God and Man*, ET by Lewis L. Wilkins and Duane Priebe (Philadelphia: Westminster Press, 1968), p. 85, note 78.

8. Pieper, *op. cit.*, p. 26.

9. Marcel, *op. cit.*, p. 36.

10. Peter L. Berger, *A Rumor of Angels* (Garden City: Doubleday, 1970), p. 80.

11. Viktor E. Frankl, *Man's Search for Meaning*, ET by Ilse Lasch (New York: Washington Sq. Press, 1963), p. 212.

12. Viktor E. Frankl, *The Will to Meaning* (Cleveland: World, 1969), p. 156.

13. Josef Pieper, "Sur l'espérance des martyrs," in *Espoir humain et espérance chrétienne*, Semaine des Intellectuels catholiques (Paris: Pierre Horay, 1951), pp. 76–84.

14. Ernst Bloch, *Das Prinzip Hoffnung* (Frankfurt am Main: Suhrkamp, 1959), p. 1413. See also Bloch's *Man on His Own*, ET by E. B. Ashton (New York: Herder and Herder, 1970), p. 162.

15. Henri de Lubac, *The Discovery of God*, ET by Alexander Dru (New York: Kenedy, 1960), p. 179.

16. Pierre Teilhard de Chardin, *The Phenomenon of Man*, ET by Bernard Wall (New York: Harper, 1959), pp. 287–88.

17. *Ibid.*, pp. 288–89. See also his *The Future of Man*, ET by Norman Denny (New York: Harper & Row, 1964), pp. 306–8.

18. *The Future of Man*, p. 117.

19. *Ibid.*, p. 72.

20. Pieter Smulders, *The Design of Teilhard de Chardin*, ET by Arthur Gibson (Westminster, Md.: Newman, 1967), pp. 151–61.

21. Christopher F. Mooney, *Teilhard de Chardin and the Mystery of Christ* (New York: Harper & Row, 1966), p. 143; cf. p. 246, note 95, for Mooney's comment on Smulders, *op. cit.*

22. Jürgen Moltmann, *Theology of Hope*, ET by J. W. Leitch (London: S.C.M. Press, 1967), p. 182.

23. *Loc. cit.*

Chapter 5

1. "The Barmen Declaration," text in J. H. Leith, ed., *Creeds of the Churches* (Garden City: Doubleday Anchor Book, 1963), p. 520.

2. *Loc. cit.*

3. *Loc. cit.*

4. Cf. J. C. Murray, "Freedom, Authority, Community," *America*, 115 (Dec. 3, 1966), 734–41.

5. *Lumen gentium*, no. 1, in W. M. Abbott, ed., *The Documents of Vatican II* (New York: Guild Press, 1966), p. 15.

6. Ernst Käsemann, *Essays on New Testament Themes*, Studies in Biblical Theology 41 (London: S.C.M. Press, 1964), pp. 103–4.

7. "Sancta catholica apostolica Romana Ecclesia," Vatican I, Constitution *Dei Filius*, ch. 1, (DS 3001).

8. *Lumen gentium*, no. 8, in Abbott, *op. cit.*, p. 23.

9. *Ibid.*, no. 13, p. 32.

10. *Unitatis redintegratio*, nos. 16–17, in Abbott, *op. cit.*, pp. 359–60.

11. *Gaudium et spes*, no. 42, in Abbott, *op. cit.*, p. 242.

12. *Ibid.*, no. 44, p. 246.

13. *Ad gentes*, no. 4, in Abbott, *op. cit.*, p. 588.

14. *Sacrosanctum concilium*, no. 37, in Abbott, *op. cit.*, p. 151.

Chapter 6

1. Ronald Knox, *Essays in Satire* (New York: E. P. Dutton, 1930), pp. 48–49. I have modernized Knox's archaic spelling.

2. John Heenan, "The Authority of the Church," *The Tablet* (London), 222 (18 May 1968), 488.

3. Regarding the process by which the Church, driven by the need to cope with heresy and various other pressures, gradually confined the teaching office to bishops, R. B. Tollinton remarks: "So the scholar surrendered his rights to the bishop, and when the bishop was also a scholar, all went well. But when he was not, the surrender, though inevitable, had its dangerous consequences." In R. B. Tollinton, *Clement of Alexandria: A Study in Christian Liberalism*, vol. 2 (London: Williams & Norgate, 1914), p. 229; cf. R. P. C. Hanson, *Origen's Doctrine of Tradition* (London: S.P.C.K., 1954), p. 108.

4. Cf. R. A. McCormick, "Notes on Moral Theology," *Theological Studies*, 29 (1968), 714–18.

5. *Lumen gentium*, no. 31, in W. M. Abbott, ed., *The Documents of Vatican II* (New York: Guild Press, 1966), p. 57.

6. *Ibid.*, no. 37, p. 64.

7. *Gaudium et spes*, no. 54, in Abbott, *op. cit.*, p. 260.

8. *Ibid.*, no. 62, p. 270.

9. *Ibid.*, no. 43, p. 244.

10. *Ibid.*, no. 44, p. 246.

11. *Ibid.*, no. 62, p. 270.

12. *Loc. cit.*

13. This point is forcefully made by Norbert J. Rigali, "Right, Duty and Dissent," *Catholic World*, 208 (Feb. 1969), 214–17, esp. p. 217.

14. *Loc. cit.*

15. Paul VI, *Libentissimo sane animo*, Address to the International Congress on the Theology of Vatican II, Oct. 1, 1966, *AAS* 58 (1966), pp. 889–96, 892; ET in *The Pope Speaks*, 11 (1966), 348–55, esp. p. 352.

16. Francis Dvornik, *The Ecumenical Councils*, Twentieth Century Encyclopedia of Catholicism, 82 (New York: Hawthorn, 1961), pp. 9–14. Cf. his article "Councils, General, History of," *New Catholic Encyclopedia*, vol. 4 (New York, McGraw-Hill, 1966), pp. 373–77.

17. *Lumen gentium*, no. 22, in Abbott, *op. cit.*, p. 43.

18. *Loc. cit.*

19. On the distinction between the teaching powers of bishops and theologians, see especially L. Orsy, "Academic Freedom and the Teaching Church," *Thought*, 43 (1968), 485–98; R. A. Mackenzie, "The Function of Scholars in Forming the Judgment of the Church," in L. K. Shook, ed., *Theology of Renewal*, vol. 2 (New York: Herder and Herder, 1968), pp. 118–32.

20. Yves Congar, *Jalons pour une théologie du laïcat*, Unam Sanctam 23, 2nd ed. (Paris: Cerf, 1954), p. 338. ET by Donald Attwater, *Lay People in the Church* (Westminster, Md.: Newman, 1957), p. 237.

21. Ep. 14:4. Ed. by G. Hartel, *CSEL* III/2, p. 512.

22. Ep. 74:10. Ed. by G. Hartel, *CSEL* III/2, p. 807.

23. *AAS* 58 (1966), 892–93; ET in *The Pope Speaks*, 11 (1966), 352.

24. Karl Rahner, "Theology and the Magisterium," *Theology Digest*, Sesquicentennial Issue (1968), pp. 4–16, 15.

25. Cf. Léon Joseph Suenens, *Coresponsibility in the Church*, ET by Francis Martin (New York: Herder and Herder, 1968), ch. 6, "The Coresponsibility of Theologians," pp. 136–51.

26. Yves Congar, *Vraie et Fausse Réforme dans l'Église*, Unam Sanctam 20 (Paris: Cerf, 1950), p. 516.

27. *Ibid.*, p. 517.

28. Brian Tierney, *Foundations of Conciliar Theory* (Cambridge, Eng.: Cambridge University Press, 1955), p. 47.

29. J. D. Mansi, ed., *Sacrorum Conciliorum . . . Collectio* (Venice, 1784), vol. 27, col. 561. Cf. Hans Küng, *Structures of*

the Church, ET by Salvator Attanasio (New York: Nelson, 1964), p. 88.

Chapter 7

1. Richard A. McCormick, "The Teaching Role of the Magisterium and of Theologians," *Proc. Cath. Theol. Society of America*, vol. 24 (Yonkers, N.Y.: St. Joseph's Seminary, 1970), p. 251.

2. See M. M. Bourke, "Reflections on Church Order in the New Testament," *Catholic Biblical Quarterly*, 30 (1968) 493–511.

3. See Damien van den Eynde, *Les Normes de l'enseignement chrétien dans la littérature patristique des trois premiers siècles* (Paris: Gabalda, 1933), esp. pp. 171–235; Hans von Campenhausen, *Ecclesiastical Authority and Spiritual Power in the Church of the First Three Centuries*, ET by J. A. Baker (Stanford, Cal.: Stanford University Press, 1969), pp. 174–75 *et passim*.

4. See the works of Dvornik referred to in Ch. 6, note 16, above.

5. See the works of Congar, Tierney, and Küng referred to in Ch. 6, notes 26–29.

6. Encyclical *Vehementer nos* (Feb. 11, 1906), *ASS* 39 (1906-7), 8–9. Daniel C. Maguire, in "Teaching, Authority, and Authenticity," *Living Light*, 6 (1969), 12, translates this somewhat freely.

7. William James, "The Pragmatist Account of Truth and its Misunderstanders," *The Meaning of Truth* (New York: Longmans, Green, 1909), pp. 209–10.

8. *Gaudium et spes*, no. 31, in W. M. Abbott, ed., *The Documents of Vatican II* (New York: Guild Press, 1966), p. 229.

9. *Ibid.*, no. 62, p. 270.

10. *Loc. cit.*

11. Ep. 74:10. Ed. by G. Hartel, *CSEL* III/2, p. 807. See above, p. 104.

12. Richard A. McCormick, "Notes on Moral Theology," *Theological Studies*, 30 (1969), 666.

13. The nature of dogma will be more fully explored in Chapter 10 of this book.

14. In W. M. Abbott, ed., *op. cit.*, p. 715; cf. *Gaudium et spes*, no. 62, *ibid.*, pp. 268–69; also *Unitatis redintegratio*, no. 6, *ibid.*, p. 350.

15. *Lumen gentium*, no. 8, in Abbott, *op. cit.*, p. 24.

16. *Gaudium et spes*, no. 58, in Abbott, *op. cit.*, p. 264.

17. See *Gaudium et spes*, no. 62, p. 269.

18. Gregory Baum, *Faith and Doctrine* (Paramus, N.J.: Newman, 1969), p. 133.

19. Opening Speech of the Council, in Abbott, *op. cit.*, p. 715.

20. *Dei Verbum* no. 11, in Abbott, *op. cit.*, p. 119.

21. *Lumen gentium*, no. 25, in Abbott, *op. cit.*, p. 47.

22. The connection between magisterium and liturgy has been brought out by Gregory Baum in several articles; see especially "The Problem of the Magisterium Today," *IDO-C*, Doss. 67, nos. 30–31 (Oct. 5, 1967), 1–13, and nos. 32–33 (Oct. 8, 1967), 1–15. On the connection between dogma and religious experience, see Karl Rahner, "What Is a Dogmatic Statement?" *Theological Investigations*, 5, ET by K.-H. Kruger (Baltimore: Helicon Press, 1966), pp. 42–66.

23. See Maguire, *op. cit.*

24. In Abbott, *op. cit.*, p. 716.

25. *Ibid.*, p. 715.

26. *Ibid.*, pp. 712–713.

27. *Ibid.*, p. 718.

28. *Lumen gentium*, no. 5, in Abbott, *op. cit.*, p. 18.

29. *Gaudium et spes*, no. 11, in Abbott, *op. cit.*, p. 209.

30. Jürgen Moltmann, *Theology of Hope*, ET by J. W. Leitch (London: S.C.M. Press, 1967), p. 298.

Chapter 8

1. *Mystici corporis*, no. 17; *AAS* 35 (1943), 200.

2. On the New Testament prophets, one may consult G. Friedrich, art. "Prophētēs (N.T.)," in G. Kittel, ed. *Theological Dictionary of the New Testament*, vol. 6, ET by G. W. Bromiley (Grand Rapids, Mich.: Eerdmans, 1968), pp. 828–61; P. Vielhauer, "Propheten im Christentum (im N.T.)," in *Rel. in Gesch. und Gegenw.*, 3rd ed., vol. 5 (Tübingen: Mohr, 1961), pp. 633–34.

3. *Dial.*, no. 82, ET by T. B. Falls, in *The Fathers of the Church* series (New York: Christian Heritage, 1948), p. 278.

4. As quoted in Eusebius, *Hist. Eccl.* V, 17, 1. Collection *Sources chrét.*, vol. 41 (Paris: Cerf, 1955), p. 53.

5. *Ibid.*, 17, 4, p. 54. It is not clear what Pauline texts Miltiades had in mind. G. Bardy, in the *Sources chrét.* edition, suggests 1 Cor. 1:7 taken in combination with Eph. 4:11. E. Fascher, "Propheten (in der altchristlichen Kirche)," in *Rel. in Gesch. und Gegenw.*, 3rd ed., vol. 5, p. 635, accepts this suggestion. Ronald Knox, in *Enthusiasm* (New York: Oxford, 1950), pp. 43–44, refers to 1 Cor. 13 as a possible source.

6. *Adv. Haer.*, III.11.9, in *Sources chrét.*, vol. 34 (Paris: Cerf, 1952), pp. 203–5.

7. *Contra Celsum*, VII.11; *PG* 11:1456–57.

8. Thomas Aquinas, *Summa theol.*, 2–2ae q. 174, a. 6, ad 3.

9. Cf. Thomas Aquinas, *Comment. in Matth. xi.1*. For discussion of Aquinas' views, see C. Journet, *The Church of the Word Incarnate*, vol. 1, ET by A. H. C. Downes (New York: Sheed &

Ward, 1955), p. 137, note 2; L. Volken, *Visions, Revelations and the Church*, ET by Edward Gallagher (New York: Kenedy, 1963), pp. 221–25.

10. On Aquinas' view of history, as contrasted with that of Bonaventure and other contemporaries, see Yves Congar, "Le sens de l'économie salutaire dans la 'théologie' de S. Thomas d'Aquin," in E. Iserloh and P. Manns, eds., *Glaube und Geschichte*, Festgabe J. Lortz II (Baden-Baden: B. Grimm, 1958), pp. 73–122.

11. Cf. Yves Congar, *Vraie et Fausse Réforme dans l'église*, Unam Sanctam 20 (Paris: Cerf, 1950), pp. 198–200; Hans Küng, *The Council, Reform and Reunion*, ET by Cecily Hastings (New York: Sheed & Ward, 1961), p. 73.

12. Knox, *op. cit.*, p. 590. But as Knox also points out, normative Protestantism had its own conflicts with the "prophets of Zwickau" and the radical wing of the Reformation.

13. John Henry Newman, *Discourses to Mixed Congregations*, 7th ed. (London: Longmans, Green, 1886), p. 279.

14. Karl Rahner, *Visions and Prophecies*, Quaestiones Disputatae 10, ET by C. Henkey and R. Strachan (New York: Herder and Herder, 1964), p. 106.

15. Johannes Lindblom, *Prophecy in Ancient Israel* (Oxford: Blackwell, 1962), p. 106.

16. Hans Küng, *The Church*, ET by R. and R. Ockenden (New York: Sheed & Ward, 1968), p. 433.

17. George Bernard Shaw, *Saint Joan* (New York: Brentano's, 1924), Preface, p. lv.

Chapter 9

1. Charles Davis, in *A Question of Conscience* (New York: Harper & Row, 1967), pp. 65–66, ridicules this statement with his characteristic acerbity. For an explanation of the unfairness of Davis' charges, see John T. Noonan, Jr., "The Pope's Conscience," *Commonweal*, 85 (17 Feb. 1967), 559–60.

2. This Argument, found in germ in Augustine's *De beata vita* 2.7 and *Soliloquia* 2.1.1, appears in developed form in his *De vera religione* 73 and in his *De Trinitate* 10.10.14.

3. John Henry Newman, *Apologia pro vita sua*, new ed. (London: Longmans, Green, 1895), ch. 5, p. 239.

4. Karl Rahner, "On Heresy," ET by W. J. O'Hara, in *Inquiries* (New York: Herder and Herder, 1964), p. 433; cf. *ibid.*, pp. 443–44.

5. Paul Tillich, *Dynamics of Faith* (New York: Harper, 1957), p. 22.

6. For an excellent theological probing of the believer's unbelief, see J. B. Metz, "Unbelief as a Theological Problem," *Concilium*, 6 (Glen Rock, N.J.: Paulist Press, 1965), 59–77.

7. On the points here introduced I have written in greater detail in my essay "The Modern Dilemma of Faith" in Michael Mooney *et al.*, *Toward a Theology of Christian Faith*, readings in theology compiled at the Canisianum, Innsbruck (New York: P. J. Kenedy, 1968), pp. 11–32.

Chapter 10

1. Edmund Schlink, "The Structure of Dogmatic Statements as an Ecumenical Problem," in *The Coming Christ and the Coming Church*, ET by I. H. Neilson (Edinburgh: Oliver & Boyd, 1967), p. 16.

2. Samuel H. Miller and G. E. Wright, eds., *Dialogue at Harvard* (Cambridge, Mass.: Belknap, 1964), pp. 63–64.

3. For the history of the term "dogma," see the brief survey, with many references to scholarly literature, in Walter Kasper, *Dogma unter dem Wort Gottes* (Mainz: Matthias-Grünewald, 1965), pp. 28–38. Similar shifts have occurred in the meanings of the terms "faith" and "heresy," which have only recently acquired the technical significance they bear in modern Scholastic theology and modern church documents.

4. Piet Fransen, "The Authority of the Councils," in John M. Todd, ed., *Problems of Authority* (Baltimore: Helicon Press, 1962), p. 74.

5. "Quod dogma nil aliud sit, quam doctrina et veritas divinitus revelata, quae publico Ecclesiae iudicio fide divina credenda ita proponitur, ut contraria ab Ecclesia tamquam haeretica doctrina damnetur" (quoted in Kasper, *op. cit.*, p. 36).

6. ASS 4 (1868–69), 508.

7. The theological thrust behind the document *Dei Verbum* is clearly apparent in the *relatio* prepared by the Theological Commission and presented in the aula of St. Peter's by Archbishop Florit. Cf. Gregory Baum, "Vatican II's Constitution on Revelation," *Theological Studies*, 28 (1967), 58–61.

8. William J. Richardson, "Heidegger and Theology," *Theological Studies*, 26 (1965), 91; cf. R. Latourelle, *Theology of Revelation* (Staten Island: Alba House, 1966), p. 308.

9. Kasper, *op. cit.*, pp. 101–6.

10. Richardson, *op. cit.*, p. 98.

11. Cf. Thomas Aquinas, *Summa theol.* 2–2ae, q. 1, a. 6, *sed contra*.

12. Schlink, *op. cit.*

13. Wolfhart Pannenberg, "Was ist eine dogmatische Aussage?" in *Grundfragen systematischer Theologie* (Göttingen: Vandenhoeck & Ruprecht, 1967), pp. 159–80, esp. pp. 175–76.

14. Ian T. Ramsey, *Religious Language* (New York: Macmillan Paperback, 1963), p. 191.

15. *Loc. cit.*

16. Karl Rahner, "What is a Dogmatic Statement?" in *Theological Investigations*, 5, ET by K.-H. Kruger (Baltimore: Helicon Press, 1966), pp. 46–47, 58–60.

17. In this connection one is reminded of all that Paul Tillich has to say about symbol as the bearer of the power of that for which it stands; see the texts cited in C. J. Armbruster, *The Vision of Paul Tillich* (New York: Sheed & Ward, 1967), pp. 156–59, 228–30. But the expressive and evocative functions of dogmatic statements should not be pressed to the exclusion of its denotative function, brought out by Karl Rahner.

18. Hans Urs von Balthasar, "Truth and Life," *Concilium*, 21 (Glen Rock, N.J.: Paulist Press, 1967), p. 90.

19. J. N. D. Kelly, *Early Christian Doctrines* (New York: Harper, 1958), pp. 117–19.

20. Cf. Hans Küng, *Structures of the Church*, ET by Salvator Attanasio (New York: Nelson, 1964), pp. 386–87, with references.

21. See especially the affirmations of Lateran Council IV (*DS* 802), the Bull *Unam Sanctam* (*DS* 870), and the Decree *Pro Iacobitis* of the Council of Florence (*DS* 1351). For abundant literature on this question, see the references given by Boniface Willems, "Who Belongs to the Church?" *Concilium* 1 (Glen Rock, N.J.: Paulist Press, 1965), pp. 132–36.

22. Gregory Baum, "The Magisterium in a Changing Church," *Concilium* 21 (Glen Rock, N.J.: Paulist Press, 1967), p. 69.

23. So, e.g., Hans Küng, *The Church*, ET by R. and R. Ockenden (New York: Sheed & Ward, 1968), p. 318.

24. On the manner in which the Roman emperors made use of the creed as a political instrument for securing the unity of the Empire, thus terminating the previous "peaceful coexistence" of different creeds, see the article, "The Creed in the Melting Pot," by the *Concilium* General Secretariat in *Concilium*, 51, *Dogma and Pluralism*, ed. by E. Schillebeeckx (New York: Herder and Herder, 1970), pp. 131–53, esp. pp. 135–36.

25. For some of the ideas in the following several paragraphs I am indebted to G. Dejaifve, "Diversité dogmatique et unité de la révélation," *Nouvelle Revue théologique*, 89 (1967), 16–25. For the history of the debate on the procession of the Holy Spirit, see Joseph Gill, *The Council of Florence* (Cambridge, Eng.: Cambridge University Press, 1959), ch. 7.

26. Walter Kasper, "Geschichtlichkeit der Dogmen?" *Stimmen der Zeit*, 179 (1967), 401–16, esp. 410–11.

27. *Unitatis redintegratio*, nos. 14, 17, 18, in W. M. Abbott, ed., *The Documents of Vatican II* (New York: Guild Press, 1966), pp. 341–66.

28. *DS* 1601.

29. *DS* 3055.

30. Carl E. Braaten, "Reunion, Yes; Return, No," *Una Sancta,* 23 (1966), 32–33.

31. Otto H. Pesch, *Theologie der Rechtfertigung bei Martin Luther und Thomas von Aquin* (Mainz: Matthias-Grünewald, 1967), esp. pp. 935–48.

32. Otto H. Pesch, "Existentielle und sapientiale Theologie," *Theologische Literaturzeitung,* 92 (1967), 741–42.

33. Schlink, *op. cit.,* pp. 80–84.

Chapter 11

1. *Lumen gentium,* no. 25, in W. M. Abbott, ed., *The Documents of Vatican II* (New York: Guild Press, 1966), pp. 47–50.

2. Pierre Benoit, "Inspiration," in A. Robert and A. Tricot, eds., *Guide to the Bible,* vol. 1, rev. ed. (New York: Desclee, 1960), p. 44.

3. See, for example, the excursus, "De valore et censura propositionum in theologia," by I. Nicolau in *Sacrae Theologiae Summa,* 2nd ed., vol. 1 (Madrid: B.A.C., 1952), pp. 781–96.

4. Piet Schoonenberg, "Some Remarks on the Present Discussion of Original Sin," *IDO-C,* Doss. 68, no. 4 (Jan. 28, 1967), p. 10.

5. Encyclical *Divino Afflante Spiritu,* AAS 25 (1943), 309ff.; see esp. p. 315. This selection may be found in DS 3830.

6. *Dei Verbum,* no. 12, in Abbott, *op. cit.,* p. 120.

7. By "form-critical analysis" I here mean the effort to interpret the document according to those principles of form criticism that have been acknowledged as valid for biblical interpretation, as explained in my preceding two paragraphs.

8. Rudolf Bultmann, "New Testament and Mythology," in H. W. Bartsch, ed., *Kerygma and Myth* (New York: Harper Torchbook, 1961), pp. 1–44.

9. Cf. Karl Rahner, "Evolution and Original Sin," *Concilium,* 26, (Glen Rock, N.J.: Paulist Press, 1967), 62–63.

10. Schoonenberg, in the article cited in note 4 above, pp. 8–9, lays down as a hermeneutical principle: "A text does not give a direct answer to questions which were not asked at the moment of origin." Then he states the content of this principle in positive form so as to obtain a second principle: "Texts should be interpreted according to their final affirmation according to the question which they seek to answer."

11. Cf. E. F. Siegman, "The Decrees of the Pontifical Biblical Commission: A Recent Clarification," *Catholic Biblical Quarterly,* 18 (1956), 23–29.

12. Thus Hans Küng can write: "The decisions of the Council of Trent (or of other councils) cannot be regarded as binding definitions where they concern questions which are being put dif-

ferently today in the light of different problems. The Fathers of those days could not decide upon matters they did not know about. This applies particularly to new exegetical and historical problems, which arose only in recent times and need new solutions. No council is granted a fresh revelation; its solutions are tied to the capacities of the theology of its time" (*The Church*, ET by R. and R. Ockenden [New York: Sheed & Ward, 1968], p. 419).

13. Vatican I, *Pastor aeternus*, ch. 1 (*DS* 3055).

14. Charles Davis, *A Question of Conscience* (New York: Harper & Row, 1967), p. 65.

15. *Loc. cit.*

16. Gregory Baum, *The Credibility of the Church Today* (New York: Herder and Herder, 1968). Baum treats the same point compactly and incisively in his article, "The Problem of the Magisterium Today," *IDO-C*, Doss. 67, nos. 32–33 (Oct. 8, 1967), pp. 13–15.

17. *Gaudium et spes*, nos. 43–44, in Abbott, *op. cit.*, pp. 242–46.

18. For an excellent treatment of the problem of reinterpreting dogmatic formulas without falling into relativism, see Edward Schillebeeckx, *God the Future of Man*, ET by N. D. Smith (New York: Sheed & Ward, 1968), ch. 1, "Towards a Catholic Use of Hermeneutics." More will be said about this problem in the final chapter of this book.

19. Cf. William J. Richardson, *Heidegger: Through Phenomenology to Thought* (The Hague: Nijhoff, 1963), p. 93: "What appears as 'thoughtful dialogue' in the Heidegger of 1950 finds its roots in the existential analysis of re-trieve, by which the Being of There-being becomes explicitly open with regard to the past to such an extent that the full force of Being strikes There-being as if coming out of the future."

20. The Decree on Ecumenism spoke of the order of "hierarchy" in Catholic doctrines, which "vary in their relationship to the foundation of the Christian faith"; see *Unitatis redintegratio*, no. 11, in Abbott, *op. cit.*, p. 354.

Chapter 12

1. ". . . in eodem scilicet dogmate, eodem sensu, eademque sententia," Dogmatic Constitution, *Dei Filius*, ch. 4, DS 3020; cf. DS 2802, 3043.

2. "Ex sese," DS 3074.

3. "Lamentabile sane," DS 3458.

4. "Sacrorum antistites," DS 3541.

5. Henri Bouillard, *Conversion et grâce selon S. Thomas d'Aquin* (Paris: Aubier, 1944), p. 220.

6. *Ibid.*, pp. 221–22.

7. Henri Bouillard, "Notions conciliaires et analogie de la vérité," *Recherches de science religieuse*, 35 (1948), 251–71, esp. pp. 258–63.

8. Henri Bouillard, *Conversion et grâce*, p. 219.

9. The views of these authors are summarized in E. Schillebeeckx, *Revelation and Theology*, ET by N. D. Smith, vol. 2 (New York: Sheed & Ward, 1968), p. 14.

10. DS 2882.

11. DS 3883.

12. DS 3883–84.

13. *Mysterium fidei*, AAS 57 (1965), 753–74.

14. *Ibid.*, p. 758. Cf. Paulist Press translation (Glen Rock, N.J., 1966), nos. 24–25, pp. 34–35.

15. *Unitatis redintegratio*, no. 14, in W. M. Abbott, ed., *The Documents of Vatican II* (New York: Guild Press, 1966), pp. 357–58.

16. *Ibid.*, no. 17, p. 360.

17. *Gaudium et spes*, no. 4, in Abbott, *op. cit.*, p. 202.

18. *Ibid.*, no. 5, p. 204.

19. *Ibid.*, no. 62, p. 268.

20. *Ibid.*, no. 62, pp. 268–69.

21. *Ibid.*, no. 44, p. 246; cf. no. 58, p. 264.

22. Cf. J. H. Nicolas, "La Théologie et les théologies," *La Vie spirituelle*, 103 (1960), 279, and the further amplifications of Francis Canavan in his article, "Rumors of Disbelief," *Triumph*, Feb. 1970, pp. 16–18.

23. This seems to be the position held by E. Schillebeeckx in the years between *Humani generis* and Vatican II, as expressed in his article, "The Concept of Truth," reprinted in his *Revelation and Theology*, vol. 2, pp. 5–29, esp. pp. 23–29. Since Vatican II, however, Schillebeeckx seems to admit that the concepts used in dogmatic declarations are subject to change; see his essay "Towards a Catholic Use of Hermeneutics," *God the Future of Man*, ET by N. D. Smith (New York: Sheed & Ward, 1968), pp. 3–49, esp. p. 40.

24. Francis Simons, *Infallibility and the Evidence* (Springfield, Ill.: Templegate, 1968).

25. Leslie Dewart, *The Foundations of Belief* (New York: Herder and Herder, 1969), p. 464.

26. Dewart distinguishes his views from those attributed to the Modernists in *The Future of Belief* (New York: Herder and Herder, 1966), pp. 114–16, note 26.

27. See, for instance, *The Future of Belief*, p. 112.

28. *Ibid.*, pp. 115–16, note 26; cf. the criticism by I. Trethowan, "A Theological Bombshell," in Gregory Baum, ed., *The Future of Belief Debate* (New York: Herder and Herder, 1967), p. 17.

29. Karl Rahner, *Hearers of the Word*, ET by Michael Rich-

ards from the 1963 ed., rev. by J. B. Metz (New York: Herder and Herder, 1969), p. 22, note 6. This footnote, actually written by Metz, represents the thought of Rahner.

30. E. Schillebeeckx, *God the Future of Man*, p. 40.

31. Karl Rahner, "What is a Dogmatic Statement?" *Theol. Investigations*, 5, ET by K.-H. Kruger (Baltimore: Helicon Press, 1966), p. 60.

32. Cf. Walter Kasper, "Geschichtlichkeit der Dogmen?" *Stimmen der Zeit*, 179 (1967), 416.

33. My thoughts on this question follow closely those of Karl Rahner in several of his articles, particularly "The Historical Dimension in Theology," *Theology Digest*, Sesquicentennial Issue (1968), pp. 30–42.

34. Karl Rahner, "Current Problems in Christology," *Theol. Investigations*, 1, ET by Cornelius Ernst (Baltimore: Helicon Press, 1961), pp. 149–50.

35. Walter Kasper, *op. cit.*, p. 409. On dogma as a means of keeping theological questioning alive, see the interesting article of G. Vass, "On the Historical Structure of Christian Truth," *Heythrop Journal*, 11 (1968), 129–42, 274–89.

36. Anselm Atkins, "Doctrinal Development and Dialectic," *Continuum*, 6 (1968), pp. 3–23, esp. p. 18.

37. Anselm Atkins, "Religious Assertions and Doctrinal Development," *Theological Studies*, 27 (1966), pp. 523–53, esp. pp. 532–33.

38. W. Norris Clarke, "On Facing up to the Truth about Human Truth" (Presidential Address), *Proceedings of the American Catholic Philosophical Association*, 1969, pp. 1–12, esp. p. 12.

39. *Ibid.*, p. 11.

LIST OF SOURCES

1. "The Changing Forms of Faith" was first given as a talk at the Protestant Episcopal Theological Seminary, Alexandria, Virginia, January 19, 1970, and again, with some revisions, at the Graduate Theological Union, Berkeley, California, June 22, 1970. It has not been previously published.

2. "Authority and Insight in the Assent of Faith," one of the Tuohy Chair Lectures at John Carroll University, Cleveland, Ohio, delivered in January 1969, was previously published, in somewhat longer form, in *Spirit, Faith, and Church*, by Wolfhart Pannenberg and others (Philadelphia: Westminster Press, 1970).

3. "Faith, Reason, and the Logic of Discovery" is in substance a talk given under the auspices of the Omega Club, New York University, April 25, 1969. It appeared in *Thought*, December issue, 1970.

4. "Toward an Apologetics of Hope," a lecture given under the auspices of the Cardinal Bea Institute of Spirituality, Woodstock College, New York City, April 23, 1970, appeared in the biennial volume of Bea Lectures to be published in the spring of 1971 by Fordham University Press, New York.

5. "Authority and Pluralism in the Church," a paper prepared for the National Faith and Order Colloquium, June 7–11, 1970, has not been published elsewhere.

6. "Doctrinal Authority in the Church" is an address given to the College Theology Society at Chicago, Illinois, on April 8, 1969. Under the title "The Magisterium and Authority in the Church," it appeared in the Proceedings of that society, which were published under the title *Theology in Revolution* (Staten Island: Alba House, 1970).

7. "The Magisterium in a Time of Change" was delivered under the title "The Contemporary Magisterium" as the four-

teenth annual Cardinal Bellarmine Lecture at St. Louis University Divinity School, October 8, 1969, and was published in *Theology Digest*, 17/4, winter 1969, pages 299–311.

8. "The Permanence of Prophecy in the Church" is an article previously entitled "The Succession of Prophets in the Church," published in *Concilium*, volume 34, *Apostolic Succession: Rethinking a Barrier to Unity* (Paulist Press, Glen Rock, N.J., 1968).

9. "Doubt in the Modern Church," a lecture given at the University of Iowa, Iowa City, May 9, 1968, was published in the newspaper *Delmarva Dialogue* (Wilmington, Delaware) May 31, 1968.

10. "Dogma as an Ecumenical Problem," which grows out of a Stillman Lecture given at Harvard Divinity School in Cambridge, Massachusetts, in April 1968, appeared in *Theological Studies*, volume 29 (September 1968), pages 397–416.

11. "The Hermeneutics of Dogmatic Statements," a Tuohy Chair Lecture given at John Carroll University in Cleveland, Ohio, in January 1969, previously appeared under the title "Official Church Teaching an Historical Relativity," in the collection *Spirit, Faith, and Church*, mentioned above (no. 2).

12. "The 'Irreformability' of Dogma" is a development of a paper entitled "Contemporary Understanding of the Irreformability of Dogma" delivered at the Catholic Theological Society of America, 25th Annual Convention, June 16, 1970, and appears in different form in the proceedings of that meeting.

All the preceding articles and lectures have been revised for inclusion in the present volume.

INDEX

OTHER IMAGE BOOKS

OTHER IMAGE BOOKS

A HISTORY OF PHILOSOPHY: VOLUME 5 – MODERN PHILOSOPHY: The British Philosophers, Hobbes to Hume (2 Parts) – Frederick Copleston, S.J. Part I – Hobbes to Paley. Part II – Berkeley to Hume (D138a) – $1.45; (D138b) – $1.75

A HISTORY OF PHILOSOPHY: VOLUME 6 – MODERN PHILOSOPHY (2 Parts) – Frederick Copleston, S.J. Part I – The French Enlightenment to Kant (D139a, D139b) – $1.45 ea.

A HISTORY OF PHILOSOPHY: VOLUME 7 – MODERN PHILOSOPHY (2 Parts) – Frederick Copleston, S.J. Part I – Fichte to Hegel. Part II – Schopenhauer to Nietzsche (D140a, D140b) – $1.75 ea.

A HISTORY OF PHILOSOPHY: VOLUME 8 – MODERN PHILOSOPHY: Bentham to Russell (2 Parts) – Frederick Copleston, S.J. Part I – British Empiricism and the Idealist Movement in Great Britain. Part II – Idealism in America, the Pragmatist Movement, the Revolt against Idealism (D141a, D141b) – $1.45 ea.

THE SPIRITUAL EXERCISES OF ST. IGNATIUS – Translated by Anthony Mottola, Ph.D. Introduction by Robert W. Gleason, S.J. (D170) – 95¢

WE HOLD THESE TRUTHS: Catholic Reflections on the American Proposition – John Courtney Murray, S.J. (D181) – $1.25

LIFE AND HOLINESS – Thomas Merton. Exposition of the principles of the spiritual life (D183) – 85¢

AMERICAN CATHOLICISM – John Tracy Ellis. A comprehensive survey of the American Church (D190) – 95¢

THE COUNCIL, REFORM AND REUNION – with a new Introduction by Fr. Hans Kung (D198) – 95¢

WITH GOD IN RUSSIA – Walter J. Ciszek, S.J., with Daniel L. Flaherty, S.J. (D200) – $1.45

THE TWO-EDGED SWORD – John L. McKenzie, S.J. Outstanding interpretation of the Old Testament (D215) – $1.45

STRANGERS IN THE HOUSE: Catholic Youth in America – Andrew M. Greeley (D221) – 95¢

THE DIVIDING OF CHRISTENDOM – Christopher Dawson (D229) – 95¢

NO MAN IS AN ISLAND – Thomas Merton (D231) – $1.25

CONJECTURES OF A GUILTY BYSTANDER – Thomas Merton. A collection of notes, opinions, reflections (D234) – $1.45

THE NOONDAY DEVIL: Spiritual Support in Middle Age – Bernard Basset, S.J. A funny-serious book of spiritual direction (D237) – $1.25

B 72 – 2

N51